Cloud Strategy
for
Decision Makers

*A practical guide to cloud strategy using architecture
principles and best practices from the field*

Rohit Gupta

bpb

www.bpbonline.com

First Edition 2025

Copyright © BPB Publications, India

ISBN: 978-93-65899-061

To View Complete
BPB Publications Catalogue
Scan the QR Code:

Dedicated to

My mom, wife and daughter

About the Author

Rohit Gupta is currently working as an associate director at Accenture Australia and is located in Melbourne, Australia. He obtained his **Bachelor of Engineering (B.E)** from Punjab University, Chandigarh, India in 1999 and since then he has had a distinguished career spanning more than two decades across various IT consulting organisations worldwide as a solution architect/cloud architect/enterprise architect. Along with his full time job, he has continued his commitment and passion for learning by acquiring various technical certifications from Oracle, AWS, MS Azure and Google Cloud. He also holds the prestigious AWS Gold Jacket, which is a milestone for completing and holding all AWS certifications.

About the Reviewer

Vaibhav Tupe is a distinguished Engineering Leader specializing in cybersecurity, cloud, and AI-ready data center infrastructure. With over 13 years of experience, he currently serves as a technology leader at Equinix USA, where he drives high-performance cloud interconnection, enabling private, secure hybrid and multicloud connectivity to accelerate digital transformation and AI adoption.

As a trusted advisor to startups, Vaibhav provides insightful guidance on cybersecurity, cloud innovations, and emerging technologies, shaping scalable and secure enterprise solutions. A senior IEEE member, he has published research papers and organized IEEE conferences, contributing to advancements in AI, cloud, security, and digital infrastructure. He is recognized for his thought leadership, mentoring high-performing teams, and driving transformative initiatives that improve efficiency and customer success.

Beyond his professional contributions, Vaibhav is deeply committed to AI and technology literacy in rural areas. He actively develops digital curricula for rural colleges, organizes career mentorship programs, and speaks at technology conferences to promote inclusive innovation. His expertise at the intersection of cloud, security, and next-generation digital infrastructure drives his passion for building resilient, future-ready systems that advance global innovation.

Acknowledgement

I would like to express my sincere gratitude to all those who contributed to the completion of this book.

First and foremost, I extend my heartfelt appreciation to my family for their unwavering support and encouragement throughout this journey. Their love and encouragement have been a constant source of motivation.

I would like to extend my special thanks to my peers, co-workers and mentors whom I have worked with and learned from throughout my professional journey, especially the following individuals: Mahesh Aswani and Bhaskar Chaturvedi. The knowledge, traits and skills I acquired from your guidance have been instrumental in shaping the content of this book. Thank you for your invaluable mentorship. A special mention to Ezio Armando for being an exemplary leader who has always been a great support.

I am immensely grateful to BPB Publications for their guidance and expertise in bringing this book to fruition. Their support and assistance were invaluable in navigating the complexities of the publishing process.

I would also like to acknowledge the reviewers, technical experts, and editors who provided valuable feedback and contributed to the refinement of this manuscript. Their insights and suggestions have significantly enhanced the quality of the book.

Last but not least, I want to express my gratitude to the readers who have shown interest in my book. Your support and encouragement have been deeply appreciated.

Thank you to everyone who has played a part in making this book a reality.

Preface

Cloud is not a trend or buzzword anymore; it is increasingly becoming a norm and the platform of choice for business-critical applications. Moreover, most enterprises are not limiting themselves to a single cloud platform these days. The concept of multi-cloud (also known as poly cloud) has gained immense popularity. Adopting cloud has never been an easy transformation and going multi-cloud understandably adds to the complexity. One of the reasons for this complexity is that adopting cloud in any form is not a split-second decision, rather a journey that starts from understanding the business goals and executive level motivations. This book aims to take the readers of all skill levels through that journey, talk about the steps, challenges and unravel the complexities of adopting cloud and multi-cloud.

Spread across *14 chapters*, this book starts with the basics of cloud and multi-cloud environments before gradually building up on the foundation by talking about the steps for developing a cloud strategy, technical aspects and considerations for developing a cloud strategy along with a mention of gotchas that executives and technicians should be aware of when making critical decisions.

Upto *Chapter 4*, the focus is on cloud strategy with a special mention of multi-cloud adoption. *Chapter 3* provides at an enterprise view of the cloud adoption which is important to paint a holistic picture for a cloud adoption. These 4 chapters cover the entire journey of a cloud adoption for an organization before moving onto more technical aspects of cloud architecture and operations in further chapters.

From *Chapter 5*, the focus shifts to every aspect of cloud adoption, be it security, networking, resiliency or observability.

The book culminates with *Chapter 14* throwing light on some popular trends in cloud computing that should be good read for people involved in cloud strategy because planning for present can not obliviate the future.

Through practical examples and use cases, this book aims to equip readers with a solid understanding of cloud adoption. Whether you are a novice or an experienced learner, I hope this book will serve as a valuable resource by helping you use the learnngs in real world.

Chapter 1: Understanding Cloud - This chapter will start building the foundations by talking about the basics of cloud and multi-cloud setups. Then the chapter explains 3 cloud service models, i.e SaaS, Paas and IaaS along with the key players in the space. After understanding the basics, we will talk about multi-cloud and its benefits and challenges.

Chapter 2: Cloud Adoption Strategy - A well drafted cloud adoption strategy is absolutely critical to leverage the real value of cloud, especially for large enterprise businesses having diverse functions and huge legacy of on-premises presence. In this chapter, we will look at the ingredients of a good cloud strategy and how it forms the foundation for a successful cloud adoption organisation wide with a future view. Will discuss the steps to define a cloud strategy starting with understanding the business goals and motivation to do so. This leads to next level of details around the various use cases the strategy would tackle and based on that the suitable adoption approach, i.e multi-cloud, SaaS or IaaS, Migration or Greenfields etc. Finally, we will look at the business case preparation stage which is important to get a buy in from program sponsors.

Chapter 3: The Enterprise View - This chapter will talk about the importance of an enterprise view while formulating a cloud strategy and how it can be achieved. Any cloud adoption is not complete without taking an enterprise level view of the journey. Looking at workloads in isolation and then making decisions on the suitability of a cloud platform will be inefficient and most likely pile up technical debt over time. This involves lot of cross communication, formation of centralised governance boards, assessment of skills and capabilities and a long-term roadmap for cloud adoption at the organisation level.

Chapter 4: The Journey - This chapter delves into the details of the end-to-end journey when it comes to cloud adoption at any organisation. There are typically 4 phases, i.e assess, plan, execute and operate which should be very well defined and demarcated to collectively run as a well-planned project end to end. However, there could be practical challenges that can hinder the progress of any phase or the collective project. Apart from talking about these phases, the chapter also talks about some of them based on practical use cases just to give enough information to readers to prepare them for the real world.

Chapter 5: Designing for Cloud - When designing applications for cloud and multi-cloud environments, care must be taken to adhere to certain design principles and guidelines in order to reap the benefits and real value of cloud computing. In this chapter we will look at such principles and how to design a solid foundation to deploy applications onto it. The chapter also talks about a Well-Architected Framework for cloud. All cloud vendors preach similar frameworks and hence we will talk about the common pillars of a well architected framework and how the framework helps in designing applications for cloud.

Chapter 6: Multi-cloud Adoption - This chapter will talk about the multi-cloud management overheads, challenges and best approaches to tackle them. One of the biggest challenges that organizations face when planning to go to cloud or plan for more than a single cloud environment is the management and administration of the entire setup. Executives need a single pane of glass to look at the consolidated view of their entire footprint and technicians need solutions to be able to manage the entire setup together. This also includes other aspects like networking, security and data flow between multiple platform.

Chapter 7: Cloud Networking - Networking for cloud comes with its own set of challenges as compared to the traditional on-premises networking between or within data centres. In this chapter we will look at cloud networking concepts with a focus on multi-cloud networking. The chapter talks about network security before discussing some popular vendors that provide tools and solutions for cloud networking. At the end of the chapter, we will look at the most common network topologies in cloud – Full mesh and hub and spoke.

Chapter 8: Cloud Security - Security in cloud is a huge consideration. This chapter starts with a description of shared responsibility model which is crucial in getting the security right in cloud because it is important to understand what security is provided by the cloud vendor and what is customer's responsibility. Specifically for multi-cloud environments, a Zero Trust approach is recommended, and we will look at it in this chapter. We will look at application security and infrastructure security separately to cover the entire breadth of cloud security and finally there will be a summary of popular cloud security tools.

Chapter 9: Cloud Observability - When deploying workloads on cloud platforms, monitoring of workloads should be thought through and processes defined around them. Monitoring, logging, alerting and troubleshooting are key to run workloads efficiently and to achieve and maintain the required SLAs. This chapter aims to look at all these components of observability. In a multi-cloud environment, observability is even more challenging. An integrated monitoring solution that provides a cross platform visibility is required. The chapter delves with looks into the challenges of multi-cloud monitoring and strategies to mitigate them. Finally, we will look at some observability solutions.

Chapter 10: Cloud Resiliency - *Everything fails, all the time* is a famous quote from Amazon's Chief Technology Officer Werner Vogels. Hence, it is important to design resilient architectures that can handle failures of every component of the workload. In this chapter, we will start by understanding the requirements around resiliency that should be addressed when designing applications on cloud, the important ones being **Recovery Point Objective (RPO)** and **Recovery Time Objective (RTO)**. We will then look at concepts like **business continuity planning (BCP)**, **high availability (HA)** and **disaster recovery (DR)**. It is important to understand the difference between them and how to achieve them.

Chapter 11: Interoperability - In this chapter we will understand interoperability and the various aspects of interoperability. This chapter will discuss why interoperability is more prominent in a multi-cloud environment and we will also talk about strategies like open-source technologies to design interoperable workloads. There will be discussion around interoperability challenges and design strategies to overcome them. There are practical use cases and examples that will make the the concepts easily relatable and understandable.

Chapter 12: Data Management - Data is the backbone of every application regardless of the scale and criticality and hence it needs a deeper focus in a cloud environment too. In this chapter, we will also look at the compoennts of an end to end data lifecyle along with data security and governance. There will be a mention of some hot data trends like ML and AI as they are integral to a data strategy on cloud. Finally, we will look at some real life examples of data management in cloud.

Chapter 13: Application Development - In this chapter we will look at 2 common modern application development practices and how they are relevant to cloud adoption. Today the focus is on quick time to market, building **minimal viable products** (**MVP**), faster dev and feedback loops. That is where this chapter looks at concepts like CI/CD pipelines and DevOps frameworks. We then explore cloud-native architectures like microservices, containers and serverless.

Chapter 14: Associated Trends - The final chapter of this will look at some of the key trends and concepts that are closely related to cloud along with typical uses cases to solidify reader's understanding. For example, trends like AIOps, DataOps, CloudOps and FinOps have become integral from a cloud adoption perspective. They are some of the hot trens of present and indispensable elements of future cloud adoption.

Coloured Images

Please follow the link to download the
Coloured Images of the book:

https://rebrand.ly/8r4w323

We have code bundles from our rich catalogue of books and videos available at **https://github.com/bpbpublications**. Check them out!

Errata

We take immense pride in our work at BPB Publications and follow best practices to ensure the accuracy of our content to provide with an indulging reading experience to our subscribers. Our readers are our mirrors, and we use their inputs to reflect and improve upon human errors, if any, that may have occurred during the publishing processes involved. To let us maintain the quality and help us reach out to any readers who might be having difficulties due to any unforeseen errors, please write to us at :

errata@bpbonline.com

Your support, suggestions and feedbacks are highly appreciated by the BPB Publications' Family.

Did you know that BPB offers eBook versions of every book published, with PDF and ePub files available? You can upgrade to the eBook version at www.bpbonline. com and as a print book customer, you are entitled to a discount on the eBook copy. Get in touch with us at :

business@bpbonline.com for more details.

At **www.bpbonline.com**, you can also read a collection of free technical articles, sign up for a range of free newsletters, and receive exclusive discounts and offers on BPB books and eBooks.

Piracy

If you come across any illegal copies of our works in any form on the internet, we would be grateful if you would provide us with the location address or website name. Please contact us at **business@bpbonline.com** with a link to the material.

If you are interested in becoming an author

If there is a topic that you have expertise in, and you are interested in either writing or contributing to a book, please visit **www.bpbonline.com**. We have worked with thousands of developers and tech professionals, just like you, to help them share their insights with the global tech community. You can make a general application, apply for a specific hot topic that we are recruiting an author for, or submit your own idea.

Reviews

Please leave a review. Once you have read and used this book, why not leave a review on the site that you purchased it from? Potential readers can then see and use your unbiased opinion to make purchase decisions. We at BPB can understand what you think about our products, and our authors can see your feedback on their book. Thank you!

For more information about BPB, please visit **www.bpbonline.com**.

Join our book's Discord space

Join the book's Discord Workspace for Latest updates, Offers, Tech happenings around the world, New Release and Sessions with the Authors:

https://discord.bpbonline.com

Table of Contents

CHAPTER 1
Understanding Cloud

Introduction

In this chapter, we will start with some basics of cloud computing and introduce key terminologies. The intention is not to teach cloud to beginners but to lay the foundation for more specific and intense strategic and technical content discussed in later chapters. We will talk about the cloud basics required for people to understand at any level involved in the decision-making process. Since we will discuss the general concepts of cloud, even if you are a seasoned cloud practitioner, it is highly recommended to review the topics covered in this chapter before moving on to the next chapter. If you are starting your cloud journey or want to refresh some concepts, this chapter is definitely worth a good read.

Structure

This chapter covers the following topics:

- Distributed systems
- Public vs. private cloud
- Cloud service models
- Tenancy
- Cloud financials

- Licensing on the cloud
- Know the players
- Multi-cloud vs. hybrid cloud
- Challenges of a multi-cloud environment
- Reasons to use multi-cloud

Objectives

By the end of this chapter, you will be able to understand some basic concepts of cloud and get a glimpse of multi-cloud environments. Starting with the types of cloud and service models, you will learn about cloud's financial aspects and how it differs from a traditional on-premises model. You will learn about the key cloud providers. Later, you will also be able to learn the need for a multi-cloud setup, along with its challenges and benefits that make it a compelling proposition.

Distributed systems

We will start with a definition of a very commonly used architecture these days. A distributed system architecture is where the components or functions of the system are spread across multiple nodes in the network. Simply put, the work is split among multiple servers, making the system more efficient. The network is the most integral part of distributed systems as it connects the nodes within the system and ensures that the nodes work independently but collaboratively, as expected. The popularity of such architecture is increasing. Some common examples of distributed systems are mobile networks, video conferencing systems, etc.

Though distributed systems sound like a generic architecture pattern, it is very much relevant to cloud computing. Cloud computing is characterized by several regions and availability zones within the regions. Many cloud services are spread across availability zones within the region, making them naturally distributed. In addition, an availability zone is usually a combination of geographically apart data centers. This means that even if the application is deployed within a region, it is still deployed in a distributed manner.

Public vs. private cloud

As the name suggests, a **private cloud** platform is private to your company. This means that only users and applications in your company can access the resources (e.g., servers, network, storage, etc.) unless you explicitly allow an external party to access them. We will deal with this in later chapters.

This definition makes it obvious that a private cloud resides in your own (on-premises) data center or can also be co-located in a data center provided by a third party, but the infrastructural resources are internal to your organization. You will have physical servers/ hosts in the data center and virtualization technology like *VMware*, to deploy virtual machines on top of physical servers. Similarly, physical routers or virtual networks are also permissible as long as they are within the perimeters of your authority and governance, or as long as you own them.

On the contrary, a **public cloud** platform is owned by a **cloud service provider** (**CSP**), and your company would rent the virtual infrastructure sitting on top of the physical infrastructure provided by the CSP. The underlying resources are typically shared between many tenants, i.e., on the same physical host, you could have neighbors with their virtual server, but isolated and controlled by numerous restrictions and boundaries. We will talk about them in later chapters. For now, it is important to understand how a public cloud differs from the private cloud.

Let us take a closer look at some key differences between private and public cloud platforms, given in the following *Table 1.1*:

	Private cloud	Public cloud
Control	Full control within the organization at all layers of the stack.	The underlying physical infrastructure is owned and controlled by the cloud provider.
Security	Since there is no sharing of resources and everything is controlled in-house, the security posture is considered much better. Any external access breach can be avoided much more efficiently. Also, with more control comes more responsibility i.e. all security in a private cloud environment is internal responsibility.	Security in public cloud is much more mature now as compared to a few years back. Cloud providers have made the platforms much more secure and adhere to most global and regional security principles. However, since it is a public platform, there is always an increased risk of security incidents. Note that security on public cloud is a shared responsibility i.e. cloud provider is responsible for the infrastructure security whereas customer is responsible for application and data security.
Access	Since it is the internal network of the company, its access to resources is over the intranet.	Since it is a public cloud platform, the access to resources is over the internet. Note that there are network features provided by cloud providers that make this access over the internet secure and private.

	Private cloud	Public cloud
Administration	As is obvious, more control leads to more administration overhead. Managing entire stack operations is the responsibility of the company.	All the infrastructure level administration is handled by the cloud provider. In fact, depending upon the service being used, more administration overhead can be offloaded to the cloud provider. For example, a PaaS service will not require the customers to manage the software, OS etc.
Scale	Private cloud environments cater to internal users of the company at a very limited scale.	Since public cloud providers cater to hundreds and thousands of customers, they can scale almost indefinitely.
Cost	It could be costlier as the scale is limited and difficult to reach economies of scale. Also, the upfront cost of setting up the private cloud could be much higher	Public cloud providers achieve economies of scale by buying in bulk and sharing resources. The cost benefits are passed on to the customers and hence proves much more cost-efficient overall. For the customer, the pricing dynamics shift from CAPEX to an OPEX model.
Data governance	Much more control and customization are possible	Less control, but robust access control policies can be applied to your data in the cloud

Table 1.1: Public cloud vs. private cloud

Having seen the differences, it is fair to say that there are also certain similarities between both types of cloud, listed here:

- Both use virtualization to abstract underlying hardware

- Both enable centralization of resource management

- Both work on similar infrastructure principles like on-demand, API enabled, **infrastructure as code (IaC)** etc.

Cloud service models

You will come across the term cloud strategy many times in this chapter and throughout this book. An important component of a robust cloud strategy is to recommend a service model for cloud adoption. Service models are essentially a type of cloud offering. There are three well-known cloud service models adopted by companies in some form or other, they are as follows:

- **Infrastructure as a service**: This is the most basic or raw type of cloud offering, where virtual servers are rented on demand by customers and are used for deploying their applications and workloads. **Infrastructure as a service (IaaS)**, is similar to on-premises resource procurement, with the difference being that data centre and physical infrastructure are owned and managed by the cloud provider. The virtual servers are provided to the customer via APIs and management portals. As a customer, you are responsible for managing the virtual servers you provision and use along with the components of the application, like middleware, data, etc.

- **Platform as a service**: With IaaS, the most common concern is that there is a lot of administration overhead in terms of managing servers and resources. Most companies are moving away from an IaaS-based adoption of cloud, as this does not change much in the way they have been managing infrastructure on-premises. Though it is still virtualized infrastructure, it does not provide the real value of cloud, apart from not managing the physical infrastructure. That is where **platform as a service (PaaS)** takes the cloud infrastructure to the next level by providing a fully managed platform to end users. Platform here means not only the underlying physical infrastructure but also the layer above it, called the software layer. The users just need to use the ready platform by developing and running their applications on that platform.

- **Software as a service**: This service model is the next step in terms of ease of use and management. **Software as a service (SaaS)** is defined as on-demand software in the cloud available for use on a pay as you go basis i.e. subscription-based, annual or monthly payment model. The most basic example of a SaaS based application is an email service like *Gmail* or a storage solution like *Dropbox*. SaaS solutions can be accessed from any device as long as there is a browser and an internet connection. The most obvious benefits of using a SaaS solution over IaaS or PaaS based solutions are listed here:

  o Quick time to market, as all the users have to do is subscribe and configure the application.

  o Easy to scale applications as the underlying infrastructure is provisioned on demand and managed by the SaaS provider

  o No management overhead, as it is the responsibility of SaaS providers. For you as a subscriber, there is only your data to manage

Figure 1.1 shows how these service models actually differ in terms of boundaries between the responsibilities of a customer and those of a cloud provider:

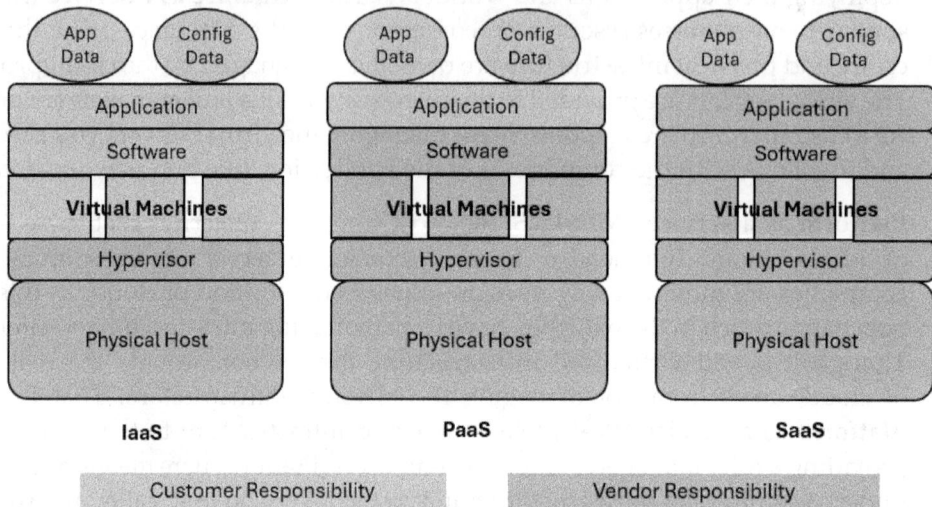

Figure 1.1: *Cloud service models*

Both IaaS and PaaS offerings are native to a cloud provider, which offers them to the customers for building and hosting their applications. For example, the basic IaaS offering on AWS is the **Elastic Compute Cloud** (**EC2**) instances, which are the same as the Azure VMs on Microsoft Azure. Similarly, a common PaaS Service on AWS is the **Relational Database Service** (**RDS**), which is akin to the Azure SQL service, as both offer the customers a relational database as a service.

An interesting thing to note about these service models is the *As a Service* aspect, which refers to the way the infrastructure is consumed by the end user. As opposed to traditional data center-based consumption, where the customer owns the assets, in a cloud *As a Service* mode, the customer is consuming the resources on a pay-as-you-go basis. This means the costing model also shifts from CAPEX to OPEX in the cloud. We will touch on the costing part in other chapters as well.

Though these service models are most commonly associated with a public cloud platform, IaaS and PaaS can be provisioned and delivered in a private cloud as well. Most organizations that use on-premises data centers for their infrastructure needs, deploy some sort of virtualization technology to create IaaS and PaaS offerings for their internal teams.

It is not a choice of one service model over another. Most companies adopt the cloud in multiple ways and combinations depending upon the workloads they want to host on the cloud. For example, a workload can consist of IaaS as well as PaaS offerings on a cloud platform and can integrate with another SaaS based workload. Hence, these service offerings should be considered complementary and used in an end-to-end architecture.

SaaS might sound like the most preferred form of cloud due to the highlighted benefits, but it has its own set of limitations that should be considered as well. Some of them include the following:

- Lack of solution customization from the SaaS vendor

- High probability of vendor lock-in

- Integration with on-premises and other cloud solutions could be complicated and limited

Apart from these three common service models that were the genesis of cloud originally, there are a couple of more cloud adoption approaches that companies are leaning towards, which are as follows:

- **Serverless**: There is no underlying infrastructure or platform to manage as far as the customer is concerned (though behind the scenes, there are still servers that the vendor manages). Its definition may sound similar to a PaaS type of service model, but there are certain important differences, like:

  o **Idle infrastructure**: Both types of offerings have underlying servers, and the customer is not responsible for managing them. However, in the case of PaaS, even if the platform is not being used, the provisioned resources remain idle and incur cost to the customer. On the contrary, in the case of serverless computing, there is no idle infrastructure waiting for execution.

  o **Costing**: A downstream impact of idle infrastructure is the unnecessary cost that is paid for a PaaS based workload even if you have over provisioned the capacity or if the application is not doing anything. This is not the case with serverless applications as you are charged only for the time when the application is running.

  o **Scalability**: A PaaS based application does not scale automatically. It either has to be configured to scale or manual intervention might be required when scaling is required. On the contrary, a serverless application scales automatically as required without any intervention from the users.

- **Container as a service**: This is a much newer offering as compared to any other discussed earlier. Containers are not new to anyone who understands application modernization and how increasingly companies are re-architecting their legacy applications to migrate to a container-based solution. However, cloud providers have taken it a step further by offering containers as a service. Just think of **the container as a service (CaaS)** similar to IaaS, but the difference is that instead of VMs, applications are hosted on containers. All major cloud providers offer a CaaS nowadays, for example, AWS **Elastic Container Service (ECS)**, GCP Docker Swarm, etc.

Tenancy

One of the most unique value propositions of a public cloud is its ability to provide a low-cost compute platform by sharing underlying physical servers with multiple customers simultaneously, making it cost efficient. Though these customers do not share the virtual servers and know nothing about their neighbors in the cloud data center, there is an obvious concern about sharing the physical servers and associated components like storage, networks, etc. This is called the default **multi-tenancy** or **shared** tenancy behavior of the public cloud.

Though it is a shared tenancy at the infrastructure level, cloud providers ensure that privacy and isolation of each customer is maintained. As per the famous *shared responsibility model*, it is the responsibility of a customer above the infrastructure layer, to ensure the security of their resources, using native cloud tools and features or any external tools.

For customers who are extra sensitive to the default shared tenancy of their computer resources, there are options that give them a dedicated tenancy of the underlying physical server and hence more control and privacy. Most cloud providers provide dedicated compute options in the form of *dedicated hosts* and *Bare Metal* instances. As the name suggests, these are the physical hosts that customers can procure for their workloads without sharing them with any other customer.

Customers spin up virtual servers on top of the dedicated hosts that are dedicated to them. This of course gives more control (at the socket level) and complete privacy for the workloads that are sensitive to sharing or fall under specific compliance guidelines. Apart from security, another common use case for a dedicated tenancy hardware is the use of certain software products that mandate core and socket-level affinity for their licensing on cloud or their cloud licensing policy, which is not cost-effective for the default shared tenancy model. A classic example is running Oracle databases on the cloud. As per their cloud licensing policy, hosting on shared tenancy virtual machines will need additional licenses as compared to hosting them in a dedicated host.

Cloud financials

The way companies operate on-premises is very different from the way they operate in the cloud, and cloud financials are a similar story. It is also very different from the way CFOs have been used to in the traditional on-premises setups. There is no pre-planned or forecasted capacity procurement anymore, no longer procurement cycles, and no over-provisioned infrastructure sitting idle to be used. Cloud is all about the *running* cost, that is, pay for what and when you use. The next section looks at fundamental differences between the traditional way of IT expenses and cloud computing.

CAPEX vs. OPEX

In the old days, companies used to plan their data center capacity months in advance and for the coming years. Thereafter, the planned infrastructure was procured and stacked in the data center, even if that meant hoarding a lot of idle resources waiting to be put to use. In terms of expenses, this meant purchasing resources upfront for coming years based on the forecasted capacity. This is called **CAPEX** i.e. **Capital Expense**. Once the infrastructure has been purchased, the operating cost would be minimal in terms of manpower required to operate it, and probably deploying some patches, updates, etc.

With the advent of cloud, a new way of paying for the infrastructure costs was introduced, called **pay-as-you-go**, it ensured that you pay only for the resources you use and not for the idle capacity that you might need six months or a year later. Cloud showed that spinning up servers is a matter of minutes, and as the demand fluctuates, scale up or down rather than purchasing the forecasted capacity upfront. This meant that you are not paying for the capital expenses, but rather for the ongoing running of those cloud resources by minutes or seconds. This is called **operating expense (OPEX)**. A completely new paradigm of budget forecasting emerged because what they were paying for the next two to three years upfront has now changed into a monthly bill of expenses like any other service you pay for.

Pricing models

The pay-as-you-go model obviously brought cost efficiencies because you pay only for and when the resources you use. This is also called the **on-demand pricing model**.

However, there are other pricing models on every public cloud that make the financials look even more lucrative, listed as follows:

- **Commitment based pricing or reserved pricing**: This type of billing is based on the notion that the more capacity you commit in advance, the more you save on your cloud bills. Reserved pricing discounts are available mostly for the computer resources on a one-year or three-year basis. Within the reserve pricing, you have options for paying all upfront, no upfront, or partial upfront. Usually, discounts are available in the range of 30% to 70%, depending on the terms of reservation and how you want to pay for those reservations. Note that reserved pricing has different features in every cloud, but the fundamentals are the same.

- **Spot pricing**: Another way of significantly saving money on compute resources is the spot pricing model. This is offered by cloud providers on a spare capacity basis and offers the best possible billing rates. However, they come with a risk of availability as they can be snapped at short notice when the spare capacity goes below a certain threshold. Hence, they are best for non-critical workloads or non-production environments where unavailability of a service for a certain duration will not prove detrimental to the business.

- **Save more by using more**: Some cloud services provide better discounts based on the volume of usage i.e. as you increase your usage of the service, the more you start saving on it. Most storage services are a great example of this type of pricing model.

Licensing on the cloud

Licensing software on cloud could be interesting and complicated at the same time. Due to their strategic partnerships with cloud providers, most software vendors have cloud-friendly or rather cloud specific licensing policies that should be considered when deciding upon a particular cloud provider. What makes it complicated are the cloud specific financial and technical clauses attached to their software policies.

Another consideration that goes hand in hand with the licensing policy of the software vendor is whether to **Bring Your Own License** (**BYOL**) or buy licenses from the cloud provider only (License included). Apart from the consideration around the licensing policy of the software cloud, the other key factors that determine if you should BYOL or use a license included, offerings from the cloud provider are as follows:

- **Existing licensing commitments**: Most companies that plan to adopt cloud and migrate their workloads to cloud have existing licensing agreements and cost commitments with the software vendors. Depending upon the cloud licensing policy of the software, these software products may or may not be portable to cloud upon migration. Hence, this could very well end up as a sunk cost.

- **Version and edition of the software product**: Specifics like version and edition play a significant part in making the decision. Large enterprises are still using legacy versions that are not supported on cloud with the license included model and hence the only option available is BYOL in that case (along with BYO support as well). Similarly, the support for required editions, i.e. enterprise, standard etc. can also be decisive.

- **Available licensing options**: Some PaaS services on cloud platforms do not offer BYOL or license-included options. For example, AWS RDS for SQL Server is a PaaS service that does not offer a BYOL option for customers.

Oracle on AWS

We will take an example of hosting Oracle on AWS to understand how licensing can play a huge role in designing a feasible solution.

To understand the Oracle licensing on the cloud, it is essential to know the following two concepts:

- **The core factor of Oracle**: Based on the vendor and processor, Oracle has defined a core factor that determines how many licenses are required to host an Oracle Database. For example, to host Oracle on most Intel based processors, the core factor of 0.5 applies.

- **The cloud licensing policy of Oracle**: When it comes to public cloud, core factor of Oracle does not apply (with some exceptions) and instead a cloud licensing policy that considers AWS, MS Azure and GCP as the *authorized cloud environments*, is applied. As per the policy, 2 vCPUs are considered equivalent to 1 oracle processor license (with multi-threading).

When it comes to AWS, there are multiple options to host Oracle Databases, namely:

- Shared EC2 instances
- Dedicated hosts
- RDS
- Bare metal instances

Out of these, the core factor of 0.5 applies only for the bare metal type instances. All other hosting options comply with the cloud licensing policy of Oracle and hence 2 vCPUs are equivalent to 1 processor license. You can use BYOL for all of these hosting options.

This was just one example of how the licensing policy of a product can make or break the deal when it comes to hosting it on cloud. A detailed discussion on licensing is not in scope for this book, but the key takeaway from the discussion is that licensing on cloud could be very different from the on-premises world and a detailed assessment should be done before finalizing the solution.

Know the players

It is time to talk about some of the key players in the public cloud domain, also known as **cloud service providers** (**CSP**) or cloud vendors or Hyperscalers.

The three most prominent market players are:

- **Amazon Web Services**: They are considered the pioneers in the public cloud space as Amazon started the cloud business with the IaaS services about two decades ago and gradually grew manyfold to offer more than two hundred services today.

- **Microsoft Azure**: Public cloud offering from Microsoft and riding high on the existing customers base who have been using MS products like Windows and SQL Server for years. However, it is fair to add that Azure has shown remarkable technological innovation over the years creating a niche.

- **Google Cloud Platform**: Public cloud offering from Google, known for its data, AI, and container management (Kubernetes) offerings.

Together, they cover more than 50% of the global public cloud market. However, the other two niche players who are growing fast and worth mentioning are:

- **Oracle Cloud Infrastructure**: Oracle came up with their public cloud offering, **Oracle Cloud Infrastructure** (**OCI**), to compete with the likes of AWS, Azure and GCP. They have been trying to tap into the market with their existing customer base for various Oracle products.

- **Alibaba Cloud**: Though not significant yet in the world arena, they are largest in Asia in terms of market share and customer base.

There are more (like IBM and Tencent Cloud) but safe to say that these five, together dominate the cloud market and make up for the majority of customers that have adopted public cloud today. In terms of market shares, we will not talk about exact numbers or percentages but at the time of writing this book, AWS is a clear leader with the largest market share worldwide but Azure is definitely catching up very fast.

There are numerous market surveys and studies that can be referred to as a more precise market dominance in terms of numbers. The Gartner magic quadrant is one of the most trusted ones.

Market share

Let us look at some of the latest market shares for each of these major cloud providers:

MARKET SHARE

▪ AWS ▪ MS Azure ▪ Google Cloud ▪ Others

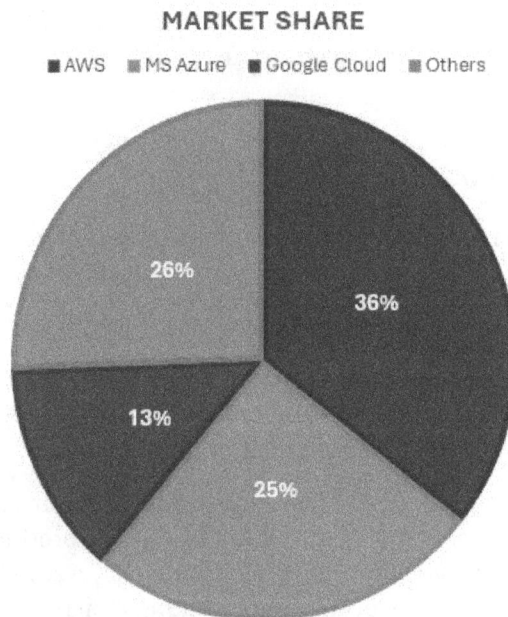

Figure 1.2: Market share of cloud providers

The others category include CSPs like *Alibaba Cloud, OCI, IBM* etc. Clearly, AWS is the market leader as of now. Competition today is fierce as you can see Azure is close on the heels of AWS.

NOTE: **These are the shares as of today but can change in future and hence, readers are requested to refer to the latest data.**

Choosing the right cloud provider

If you are starting your cloud journey, choosing the right cloud vendor could be daunting. That is one of the reasons most companies end up with more than one cloud provider, i.e., a multi-cloud environment. The choice for a particular cloud or multiple clouds is driven by many factors, such as:

- **Technical viability**: First and foremost, technical viability of the solution is must. The intended cloud platform should be able to provide services and features that enable the desired architecture and meet the requirements.

- **Cost considerations**: Of course, one of the major reasons to choose any solution is cost. Usually cloud providers compete on cost and woo the customers with offers and discounts. Assuming the technical viability of more than one cloud, it mostly comes down to the cost.

- **Cloud adoption strategy**: A well thought through strategy is decisive when it comes to choice of cloud(s) and service models as pointed out earlier. The strategy takes into account executive motivation, all workloads, TCO, business case and various other components. These are the factors that can tilt the scales in favor of one cloud over another.

- **Software licensing**: Choice of cloud could be determined by the software product you plan to deploy. The licensing policy of that product could be more conducive to a particular cloud as compared to any other cloud. For example, Oracle Databases on OCI are much more license and cost-friendly than any other cloud.

- **In-house skills**: Whatever cloud you choose, you need people to operate it. If the skills are not available in-house, you will need to train people and hire more which further adds to the cost. Hence, available skills could be an important input in cloud selection decisions.

- **Executive sponsorship**: Last but not least, cloud adoption like any other IT program needs executive level sponsorship and motivation. This also includes preferences of decision makers for a particular solution over others.

In fact, not only the cloud platform, but the million-dollar question that should be answered is what service model should be chosen. Most companies today practice the philosophy of *SaaS before PaaS before IaaS*. However, it might not be practical to adopt a SaaS solution for every workload for various technical and non-technical reasons.

In an ideal world, there is no one-size-fits-all answer for this question. The decision should be driven by the business requirements more than anything else. Of course, the other drivers mentioned above also play a key role in the decision making but if the requirements indicate a cloud provider and/or a service model best suited for the workload(s), most weightage should be given to it. This may mean different clouds and service models for different workloads, so be it.

Most companies, regardless of size and scale, do not like to lock-in with a single cloud vendor but rather opt for a multi-cloud approach nowadays. This is not only driven by the factors listed above, but there are also some strategic reasons behind a multi-cloud adoption, such as:

- Avoiding the monopoly of a single cloud provider

- Keeping the competition alive and hence best support and cost

- Leveraging the best technical features of all clouds.

Though popular and prevalent, the multi-cloud strategy has its own set of challenges that we will discuss later in this chapter.

Multi-cloud vs. hybrid cloud

We have just touched on an important concept above, multi-cloud. As the name suggests, it is an environment made up of more than one cloud platform in the mix (and in some cases, multiple service models as well). Hence, the definition is clear. Another prevailing cloud architecture and a reality for almost every organization due to their on-premises legacy is the **hybrid cloud**.

Multi-cloud and hybrid cloud are two different concepts, though both involve an element of integration between at least two geographically apart infrastructure platforms. Hybrid cloud is an environment that integrates multiple infrastructure platforms, including one or more public clouds and an on-premises data center location. Thus, by definition, there is an on-premises component in the hybrid cloud environment integrating with a public cloud, for example, on-premises VMWare hosted private cloud and AWS/Azure. In contrast, a multi-cloud environment consists of multiple public clouds, such as AWS and Azure.

Since a hybrid cloud environment can involve multiple public clouds, sometimes the terms multi-cloud and hybrid cloud are used interchangeably. As pointed above, the key difference is the presence of an on-premises component in a hybrid cloud environment whereas a pure multi-cloud environment means more than one public cloud (though some practitioners might argue that multi-cloud could comprise multiple private clouds as well).

Challenges of a multi-cloud environment

Multi-cloud strategy might sound like a good idea as it opens a world of opportunities for companies to modernize their workloads and adopt the latest technologies. However, it has its own challenges that must be considered and addressed when going for more than one cloud platform. We will touch upon them briefly in this section, but discuss them in depth in subsequent chapters. The challenges are as follows:

- **Network and integration**: Most multi-cloud environments do not have isolated cloud platforms hosting workloads independently from each other. Due to the nature of all business-critical applications, they are integrated with a surrounding ecosystem hosted locally or in a distributed multi-cloud environment. This could be used to exchange data between systems, a closely knit multi-step function spanning across multiple modules, or for any other reason. The key requirement for this integration is seamless and secure network connectivity. Networking for cloud and between clouds is always a sensitive topic because the task is not only the exchange of information, but also doing it *securely and safely*. We have a dedicated chapter on networking that will touch on many of the issues in cloud networking and plausible approaches to resolve them.

- **Security**: Security is anyway a huge concern in the cloud and it accentuates further in a multi-cloud environment, especially the consistency of security controls and policies across all clouds in use.

- **Operations and management**: Cloud operations are a lot different from the traditional on-premises operations for obvious reasons. The way resources are laid out, the way resources are accessed, the way reporting is done, and the way day-to-day operations are handled, everything is different. Add the complexity of multi-cloud to this, and it suddenly sounds close to a nightmare for the support teams managing all these tasks across multiple clouds. For example, imagine a scenario in which decision-makers need consolidated uptime reports from all clouds. A single pane of glass is required for everyone involved.

- **Financials**: A real headache for companies is managing the account books regardless of where the IT resources are located, on-premises or cloud. IT stakeholders may not deem it relevant (except for the senior executives), but managing the financials could be very difficult. Nevertheless, it is the lifeline that powers any business and runs the supporting services like IT infrastructure. As we have seen earlier in this chapter, financial considerations on cloud are hugely different from traditional on-premises setups, and it poses a real challenge for CFOs to ensure the forecasting and procurement functions are properly aligned. Similar to operations, financials across multiple clouds take it to the next level of difficulty.

We will try to tackle these issues in later chapters as much as we can and present some of the commonly used tools and approaches as well.

Reasons to use multi-cloud

Despite so many challenges, many companies nowadays prefer to move to a multi-cloud environment rather than sticking to a single cloud.

Here are some reasons why multi-cloud is gaining popularity and preference:

- **Best of all worlds**: There is a cut-throat competition between cloud providers leading to the evolution of cloud technologies very rapidly. Cloud providers are coming up with new services and features faster than companies can adopt or learn them and naturally every provider is keen to create a niche by coming up with new and revolutionary unique services. This healthy competition benefits customers, as they can now choose a cloud provider based on the best service for their needs.

Apart from new services, some services have gained popularity as the best fit for a specific use case and hence preferred by architects regardless of where their other workloads are hosted. A good example here is MS Azure AD (now known as **Entra ID**). We have seen MS Azure AD being used as a central identity and access management solution by customers who use other CSPs (like AWS) for their workloads.

- **No vendor lock-in**: No company likes to get locked into a vendor these days, whether it is cloud or any other technology. Vendor lock-in limits the growth and ability to use the best technology solutions available in the market. Therefore, going multi-cloud gives freedom to companies to experiment and use what is in their best interest.

- **Do not put all your eggs in one basket**: This is an old saying and fits quite well in this scenario as well. If there is an outage with your primary cloud platform, your critical workloads will go down leading to adversely affected internal and external customers, most likely. Thus, you can think of a secondary cloud as a backup for your primary cloud environment. An ongoing relationship with multiple cloud vendors can help draft the **Business Continuity Planning (BCP)** strategy.

- **Healthy competition**: Multi-cloud also puts you, the customer, in the driving seat. With multiple cloud vendors, there is a sense of competition. Hence, you are in a position to negotiate the terms and conditions as well. All cloud vendors try to offer best prices, discounts and freebies. For instance, you plan to host a new application or migrate certain applications to the cloud and invite tenders from multiple cloud providers. All cloud providers will vie for that piece of cake and hence, will try to put their best foot forward.

- **Support and service**: Same goes for the support and service provided by cloud providers. No cloud vendor would like to lose a customer to another vendor due to poor quality of services. Eventually, customers benefit from this healthy competitive environment.

- **Preferences change over time**: Most senior executives and decision makers have their preferred cloud vendor. It could be due to their past experiences, their professional relationships, or other reasons. More often than not, when the leadership changes, the cloud strategy of the company is re-examined, which leads to the inclusion of a new cloud service in the mix on top of the existing ones, or sometimes a complete migration from one cloud platform to another happens. Of course, there are the aforementioned challenges to deal with.

In a nutshell, multi-cloud gives you the flexibility and freedom to experiment and implement the best solutions and directly improve the customer experience. In multi-cloud or solo cloud, the decision is purely based on your requirements and strategy. There are no right or wrong answers here.

Note: We talked about distributed systems and multi-cloud environments. There is another way of looking at a distributed system on the cloud, i.e., an application stack distributed across multiple clouds. This effectively means splitting an application across more than one cloud. For example, the front end or the business layer sitting on AWS and the database layer sitting on OCI. In theory, it is possible and doable, but this type of architecture can lead to a new set of complexities and problems to deal with. Again, architecturally it is doable, and one can argue on the effectiveness of this architecture, but the most obvious problem with this architecture is added latency apart from the others, like integration, security, etc. Based on industry experience, it is advised to steer clear of such an approach and stay within the cloud for the existence of an application. Integration between applications across clouds could still be required to exchange information in a multi-cloud environment.

Conclusion

In this chapter, we looked at some key concepts and definitions of a public cloud. The cloud journey started with in-house virtualization and private clouds many years back, till about the early 2000s when public cloud came into existence and gave a completely different approach for deploying and operating your applications without any infrastructure management overhead. Private clouds are still a thing, but we have seen why public clouds have taken over swiftly. Keeping the discussions on basics, we looked at types of clouds and types of service models, which collectively form a key output of a cloud strategy. We then looked at the financials of the cloud and how they are different from those of traditional data center businesses. Public cloud providers are able to achieve economies of scale, and for the customers, the focus shifts from CAPEX to OPEX. We also learned about multi-cloud environments, their pros and cons, and why they are good choices.

In the next chapter, we will discuss cloud strategy, its components, and the key steps involved in formulating one. We will also highlight the recipe for a successful cloud strategy and examine the financial and technical considerations that help formulate it.

Points to remember

Here are some key takeaways from this chapter:

- Private cloud infrastructure is in-house managed, whereas public cloud infrastructure is provided and managed by external vendors.

- Top cloud providers are AWS, MS Azure, GCP, OCI, and Alibaba Cloud, amongst others.

- Cloud financials focus on OPEX instead of initial capital costs CAPEX.

- Multi-cloud is becoming a popular deployment model due to various benefits, like avoiding vendor lock-in, better pricing and support, leveraging the best technology of every cloud provider, and many more.

References

- **https://www.oracle.com/contracts/docs/processor-core-factor-table-070634.pdf?download=false**

- **https://www.oracle.com/assets/cloud-licensing-070579.pdf**

Join our book's Discord space

Join the book's Discord Workspace for Latest updates, Offers, Tech happenings around the world, New Release and Sessions with the Authors:

https://discord.bpbonline.com

CHAPTER 2
Cloud Adoption Strategy

Introduction

The first chapter, *Understanding Cloud,* briefly discussed cloud strategy and laid the foundation for the more comprehensive discussions we will have in this chapter. This chapter forms the crux of this book as it helps us understand what a cloud strategy is, what components make up a cloud strategy, and a step-by-step approach to developing a reasonable strategy. The following chapters in this book will focus on the details of a cloud adoption strategy with elaborate discussions on the adoption journey, as well as the technical and operational components of a cloud adoption.

Structure

This chapter includes the following topics:

- Basics of cloud strategy
- Approach to develop a cloud strategy
- Business goals and motivation
- Stakeholder involvement and expected outcomes
- Current state assessment
- Financial considerations

- Technical considerations
- Business case preparation
- Roadmap
- Cloud governance
- Guiding principles
- Decision frameworks
- Architecture frameworks

Objectives

By the end of this chapter, you will learn about the cloud adoption strategy and the steps involved in developing it. You will be able to understand the elements of a strategy, like business goal, stakeholder involvement, executive motivation, and most importantly, the financial and technical considerations. You will also understand the importance of architecture and decision frameworks in a cloud strategy.

Basics of cloud strategy

Cloud strategy acts as a roadmap for companies to migrate and build their applications in the cloud. This is a straightforward definition, but in reality, there are many parts to it. Cloud adoption poses multiple challenges to a company, which requires it to transform its existing processes and skills. The companies must be willing to adapt to changes and aware of the impact these changes will have on the operating model of the entire organization.

Strategy is all about planning and creating a roadmap that resonates with your desired business goals and outcomes. It is easy to fail and create a spaghetti of cloud solutions without a thoroughly thought-out adoption strategy, especially for large enterprises. Unless you know the answers to questions like—*Why do we need the cloud? What is the business problem we are trying to solve? What applications are best suited for the cloud? What cloud platform and service model fits the bill?*—you will end up adopting cloud in a piecemeal manner, leading to a big mess of inefficient, costly and redundant solutions which will pile up the technical debt.

Technical debt is the cost that must be incurred to rework a technical solution, which was previously deployed with a tactical view to either solve a short-term problem or to save cost without looking at the long-term strategic view of the possible solutions to the problem.

Sometimes, a technical debt is unavoidable but most of the times it can be minimized with careful planning. For example, a company has ten departments, and each has a bunch of legacy or on-premises hosted applications. There are many functions that are common across the departments, but there is a lack of collaboration amongst them, due to the scale of the company. In the absence of a cloud strategy, each department started adopting cloud for their own applications, without any centralized adoption and governance procedures in place. This decentralized approach resulted in a plethora of tactical and redundant solutions, which subsequently led to an unoptimized growth of the cloud footprint without careful planning.

Some reasons why a cloud strategy becomes necessary are:

- Collaboration across the organization

- Organization wide consistent cloud adoption

- Centralized reporting and governance

- Efficient cost management

- Investments are well aligned with business goals

- Quick time to market and hence handle growing business needs

While adopting a cloud strategy, companies should also look at minimizing the risks by undertaking the following steps:

1. Building decision frameworks to select cloud service models, providers, and appropriate services

2. Leveraging and customizing industry-standard architecture frameworks that provide a solid foundation

3. Building governance frameworks that ensure the policies, procedures, and recommendations provided in the strategy are implemented and audited

Approach to develop a cloud strategy

Let us look at the following steps and high-level approach for drafting a cloud strategy:

1. Understand the motivations and business goals.

2. Engage all stakeholders to understand the expected outcomes.

3. Assess the current state.

4. Understand the cloud financials.

5. Understand the technical considerations.

6. Draw a roadmap for adoption.

The order of these steps can be shuffled depending upon the stage of development the organization has reached and the level of cloud maturity it has attained. Also, some of these steps can be carried out simultaneously, depending on the size and availability of the team. For example, understanding the expected outcomes and assessing the current landscape usually happens parallelly, because the concerned stakeholders are different.

In the next few sections of this chapter, we will discuss these steps in detail.

Business goals and motivations

Every project should have a motivation behind it and a cloud adoption is no different. Before starting the move to cloud, it is imperative to get a good understanding of why we want to shift. This is best done by interviewing senior stakeholders from technology and business.

Most of the common motivations can be classified into the following high-level categories:

- **Upcoming critical event, for example:**
  o   Data center exit
  o   End of Support/End of Life
  o   New compliance requirements
  o   Mergers and acquisitions
- **Optimization of current landscape, for example:**
  o   Consolidation of portfolios or departments
  o   Improvement of operational processes
  o   Competitive edge
- **Innovate to scale, for example:**
  o   Expansion into new geographies
  o   Address growing demands
  o   Modernize the applications
  o   Move towards sustainable infrastructure.

There can be more than one reason behind a strategic move to cloud. For e.g., a data center exit could be the main motivation to adopt cloud, but at the same time, your CTO wants a *cloud first* policy to ensure application modernization and technical improvement as a future strategy. Hence, it is important to understand all of the motivations.

Before coming up with any kind of solution, it is important to know the motivation behind it. When architects know about the motivations behind a strategic move to the cloud, they are equipped with the necessary information to be able to provide the most appropriate solutions, in terms of cloud migration approach, hosting options, and the target architecture on the cloud. For example, if the motivation for cloud adoption is in response to a critical business event like *data center exit* or *end of life,* then you are short on time and your priority should be to make a fast move to the cloud. In such a scenario, a *lift and shift* type of migration could be the most optimal approach, and any modernization opportunities can be looked at a later stage.

Note: Lift and shift (also called rehost) is a type of cloud migration approach. With this approach, you move the current workloads as-is to the cloud without changing the underlying architecture. We will discuss more approaches at length in a later chapter.

Stakeholder involvement and expected outcomes

Stakeholder involvement is absolutely critical at the outset of this journey. In fact, this one step affects every other step of the strategy development process. Whether you are trying to understand the motivations, need to know the desired outcomes, assess the current landscape, or discuss the financial considerations, there are stakeholders who need to be involved and consulted.

Stakeholder involvement also means transparent communication and collaboration at every process stage. Lack of open communication between stakeholders is not healthy as far as an enterprise-wide cloud adoption is concerned, as this might lead to ambiguities and inefficient use of cloud technologies. This is where enterprise architects can help and governance functions like **Cloud Centre of Excellence (CCoE)** also play a significant role.

Stakeholders of varying capacities, across the organizations, need to be involved in this process, such as executive leadership, IT, finance, procurement, operations, etc. They all must have a say while developing the strategy. For example, here are the key inputs that some of these stakeholders can implement into the strategy:

- **Leadership**: Talk to them about the key business goals and the driving force behind cloud adoption. Leaders can provide input on the key objectives and outcomes that they are looking for. They would be looking at growing their market presence, meeting new customer demands, and overall business growth as some of the intended outcomes.

- **IT**: This group is probably the easiest to deal with because they understand what the cloud is and what benefits it can provide to the company. This includes the infrastructure and application **subject matter experts (SMEs)**, i.e., the technical people. They are the people who will tell you about the current state of IT in the company, what needs to be migrated to the cloud, and what technical challenges must be addressed first.

- **Procurement**: These are often overlooked but important people. They would typically manage vendor relationships and licensing for software products being used. Their inputs are important because you must know which external vendors are involved, what are the existing licensing arrangements and how they will be managed on cloud.

- **Finance**: Unsurprisingly, these are the people who make the most important decisions for any project, such as - available budget, funding approvals, forecasted expenditures and much more. As an obvious outcome, they would look at the increasing profit margins.

- **Operations**: Operations on the cloud are different from operations on-premises. The people who operate and manage your IT infrastructure need to be involved in making the cloud adoption strategy. With the popularity of frameworks like DevOps, the boundaries between development and operations teams have diminished in terms of operating procedures and required technical team skills. Therefore, you might be introducing significant changes in the team dynamics with the adoption of the cloud.

- **Human resource**: This is the set that is focused on people aspect of the company i.e. retention of existing talent and hiring of new. Based on the cloud adoption decisions, they need to be well informed on skills available and required in future.

Current state assessment

Another important consideration for completing a cloud strategy is the assessment of the current state, application, and infrastructure footprint. You can also consider it as an assessment of the overall cloud readiness of your company. Usually, when you assess the current state, you particularly look for the following:

- **IT footprint overview**: This includes all the IT infrastructure (i.e. computer, storage, networks, etc.) and the applications (i.e. internal or external applications) running on the infrastructure.

- **Use cases**: Before moving to the cloud, you need to know what use cases and technology problems you want to solve. This is also a direct outcome of workload assessment. Knowing the use case would help determine which cloud service model (IaaS, PaaS, or SaaS), single cloud or multi-cloud environment, brownfield or greenfield deployment, can be used.

- **Readiness of the organization**: Not just the state of IT, but understanding the overall readiness of your organization is important as well. This includes the assessment of leadership preparedness, financial readiness, available skills and capabilities, operational readiness etc.

The assessment is carried out through a series of focused workshops with stakeholders from all business groups of the company. You will not only understand the current state but also hear the concerns and risks that should be mitigated before adopting the cloud by interviewing the key personnel.

We will cover all the four phases of the end-to-end cloud journey in an upcoming chapter (including the *Assess* phase) in a much greater detail, along with some approaches to execute these phases.

Financial considerations

Cloud financials are very different from the way financials work in a traditional data center setup. We discussed this in *Chapter 1:, Understanding Cloud,* as well. Some key financial considerations worth noting on the cloud are:

- In the cloud, you do not plan your capacity for many years. Instead, you plan for shorter intervals and scale as required.

- Cloud uses a pay-as-you-go pricing as compared to the pay upfront for the infrastructure and licenses that the traditional on-premises financial model requires.

- In cloud, you do not pay for initial **capital expenses** (**CAPEX**), but rather pay for operating the infrastructure i.e. the ongoing **operating expenses** (**OPEX**). This is an important differentiator and was highlighted in the earlier chapter as well.

- Another financial aspect worth considering, and sometimes overlooked when budgeting for cloud, is saving the on-premises infrastructure, which is most often overestimated and over-provisioned. Firstly, you scale up only when required in cloud, ensuring that there is no wastage or idle resources. Secondly, as it is a pay-as-you-go pricing, you end up paying much less compared to the on-premises financial model.

- Lastly, cloud improves your overall efficiency from application development to operations and this directly reflects in the kind of service you provide to your customers, leading to better returns on investments. This is an indirect cost consideration, sometimes not directly perceivable.

Technical considerations

When developing the cloud strategy, you must be aware of certain technical considerations that are cloud specific and have been handled differently in the on-premises world.

Security

Security is the paramount consideration when moving to the cloud. Though cloud security services and features have matured many folds over the years, security on cloud has always been under scanner. Talking of security, every architectural component must be considered—application, infrastructure, network, and data. As per the shared responsibility model, infrastructure security on the cloud is considered the responsibility of a cloud provider (security of the cloud), and security of workloads is the responsibility of a customer (security in the cloud). Thus, as a customer, you are getting a secure infrastructure without the overhead of provisioning and maintaining it. Above the infrastructure layer, it is the responsibility of a customer to secure and comply with regulatory requirements using cloud-native or external services.

In terms of compliance, most cloud providers comply with local and global regulatory standards like **Infosec Registered Assessors Program (IRAP)**, **Health Insurance Portability and Accountability Act (HIPPA)**, **International Organization for Standardization (IOS)** etc. As most customers need their entire stack on cloud to be compliant to the prescribed regulations, the compliance of the cloud provider to these standards serves as the starting point.

Availability

All infrastructure services in cloud have pre-defined availability **service level agreements (SLAs)** i.e. the level of service expected from the vendor or promised by the vendor. As a starting point, customers need to consider these SLAs when designing their workloads on cloud. The other aspect of making the workloads highly available on cloud is how you design your target architecture. All cloud providers make use of constructs called **availability zones** and **regions**. Considering your specific availability requirements, you should design the architecture across availability zones and regions.

Scalability

Scalability and elasticity are the USPs of cloud computing. It is the ability of workload to scale up and down based on resource utilization. Due to the almost indefinite ability of cloud to scale up automatically, you can start small or with minimum resources and then let it scale based on the usage and demand. Thus, there is no overprovisioning of capacity. Similarly, when you do not need the additional capacity, you can scale down and save money. The concept of auto-scaling in cloud, i.e. to build systems that can automatically adapt to meet the demand, is the real game changer. It is explained as follows:

- **Scale out**: Scaling out refers to adding more resources in order to cater to the growth requirements. This is also known as **horizontal scaling**.

- **Scale up**: Scaling up means upgrading the existing resource to grow in size in order to handle the growth requirements. A resource can be scaled up to a limit and then you need to scale out by adding more resources. This is also known as **vertical scaling**.

Business case preparation

When planning a transformation project as a part of the larger cloud strategy, the business case is a tool that can significantly bolster your chances and help garner support from all areas of the business, especially finance. A business case is usually prepared to do the cost benefit analysis for the proposed cloud adoption. It is produced to demonstrate how the cost of moving to the cloud compares against the cost of an on-premises hosting for the next three, five, or even ten years, based on the projected growth. It is considered a very critical artefact for decision makers to review and use for further deliberation when deciding which way to go.

The key steps in a business case are listed as follows:

1. **Baselined data**: To start the business case preparation, it is important to first baseline the current data, which means the current cost of provisioning and running the data center environment.

2. **Forecasted on-premises data without cloud**: Taking the baselined data further, in this step, you would forecast the costs of running the workloads on-premises if they are not migrated to the cloud.

3. **Forecasted on-premises data with cloud**: At this step, you would do a forecasting for your residual on-premises setup, assuming you have migrated to the cloud. Thus, there will be three components to this step, they are:

    a. CAPEX cost for on-premises resources that starts at a high and decreases as the servers are migrated to the cloud.

    b. OPEX cost for the on-premises residual infrastructure which is also high initially, but decreases as more servers are decommissioned and migrated to cloud.

    c. Finally, the year-by-year cloud costs/expenses.

4. **Cost of migrating to cloud**: Now, you would calculate the forecasted cloud migration cost, also called the **migration execution cost**, over the duration of migration. For example, if the migration goes on for next three years, the migration cost should be forecasted and spread across three years as per a projected migration plan.

5. **Cost benefit report**: Finally, this is the step where you would calculate the benefits of moving to cloud. This is done using all the previously collected and calculated data. The forecasted benefits would be a difference between the on-premises costs (i.e. staying as-is) and the cloud costs (including the migration cost) over a period of time. Note that benefits should not be considered at a point in time; rather, it is the value calculated over a period of time.

Roadmap

The final part of drafting the cloud strategy is to draw a detailed roadmap and a plan for the next few years, to ensure that the desired objectives are met. The roadmap consists of proposed projects and initiatives that should be undertaken to change from the current state to a desired target state. The roadmap should not include technology-related projects only; it should also consider business, process, and people-related initiatives. A roadmap is the artefact that guides the executives in their decision-making process, for example— budgeting for key projects that will propel the adoption of cloud across the organization, or establishing a centralized identity system, which could be one of the pre-requisites for an organization with multiple business units and isolated IT systems, before moving to cloud.

The roadmap is drawn across four phases of the cloud journey—assess, plan, execute and operate i.e. all the projects and initiatives which should be carried out during these phases to successfully adopt the cloud solutions. This roadmap is created with an enterprise view and not in isolation for a particular business unit or an application. We will take it up in the next chapter, where we take an enterprise view of everything that influences or contributes to the cloud adoption at an organization.

Cloud governance

A strategy cannot be effective without having proper controls and stringent checks in place. Governance here refers to the approved processes, checks, and rules, which have been agreed upon and accepted throughout the company as standards for adopting cloud solutions. Any aberration needs to be explicitly reviewed and approved by the designated stakeholders (this is also defined in the governance framework). An effective governance has a crucial role to play throughout the process of developing a cloud adoption strategy, and even after that. Imagine, you want to have a unified cloud adoption across the company but there is no control over the multiple units operating in silos, which are using redundant cloud solutions for similar use cases. The scenario will lead to a *shadow IT* situation, unnecessary administrative overhead, and wastage of resources because of the redundancy.

Shadow IT is a term used for the use of software and/or hardware resources by a group or individuals within an organization without knowing or considering the use of IT resources by the organization as a whole.

Let us assume that the strategy has been formulated and finally endorsed, but the rules cannot be mandated across the organization unless there are checks and accountability. Also, assume there is a new requirement for modernizing an application using the cloud, and the project manager comes to the CIO for endorsement as well as funding, but there are no gates to ensure that the right solution has been identified by the team. As per the governance framework, the solution should have been reviewed and approved by the people designated to be at the review gates, before it reaches the final approval and funding stage. This way, there is a central governing body that ensures there are no redundancies, wastages, or sub-optimal solutions being deployed throughout the organization.

This is why the cloud strategy mandates formal governing processes and a framework. However, governance should enhance productivity instead of becoming an overhead for the company. This can happen in the following circumstances:

- The controls have been implemented but not monitored regularly to gauge the efficacy. Auditing the governance framework is as important as implementing it.

- Or when, in some cases, a quick solution is required without going through all the governance processes. There could be a separate decision-making process for a normal scenario as compared to the edge cases, where a quick action is required instead of going through all the gates.

Governance is usually a function of the CIO office, with multiple teams comprising stakeholders from architects of different skill sets and mostly anchored by one or more enterprise architects (depending on which governance framework has been implemented). However, there are no set rules. This framework should be customizable and should suit the requirements of the company. Rigid unmanaged policies will soon lead to frustration and lack of motivation among the employees.

Cloud governance is a vast topic that needs an enterprise lens. In the next chapter, we will discuss the details of organization wide governance procedures, framework and important groups that play a part in an effective governance function of the organization.

Guiding principles

Finally, let us look at some general and popular guiding principles for cloud enablement in an organization. The following principles are strategic in nature, help aid in cloud adoption gradually, and should be reviewed in conjunction with your motivation and objectives:

- **Reuse before buying, buy before building**: This connotes that the first preference should be to reuse an existing solution, although if reusing it is not possible and a new solution is required, then the preference should be to buy a solution available in the market. Yet, if nothing is available at all, then you need to build a solution from scratch.

- **Services over servers**: Similar to the preceding principle, give preference to services over servers, according to the following ranking:
  - ○ SaaS over COTS
  - ○ COTS overbuild
  - ○ Build using PaaS
  - ○ Build on IaaS

- **Cloud first**: As a general principle in your cloud strategy, you might want cloud as the preferred target platform for any new technical solution, to achieve agility with a DevOps mindset, foster innovation through the use of game changing cloud technologies and achieve better cost efficiency. That is why many companies have started endorsing and adopting the principle of cloud first.

- **Use of open-source components**: It advocates for interoperability, as the key benefit along with other benefit like minimization of vendor lock, which often leads to cost optimizations.

- **Reduce investment on on-premises infrastructure**: You should aim at reducing dependence and investments on the existing infrastructure. Any new investments in the data-centered technologies should be on an exception basis only.

- **Build centralized architecture and governance practices**: This is to be followed by everyone, to avoid any uncontrolled cloud deployments and purchasing.

- **Leverage enterprise architects**: These are the people who usually act as a conduit between business and technology. Architects work with the businesses to provide the right solutions which can help their move to cloud. This will also include the assessment of change management, security and integration impacts.

- **Risk assessment**: Make sure that a thorough risk assessment is carried out to support all cloud deployments, according to the risk profile of the workloads in consideration, for example, a workload with sensitive data might need much granular risk assessment as compared to an internal intranet website.

These guiding principles come in handy when coupled with decision frameworks discussed in the next section.

Decision frameworks

As part of the cloud adoption process, you will have to make a number of decisions, since new business problems appear frequently and you are tasked with finding their solutions. For example:

- Selecting a type of cloud service model—IaaS, PaaS, or SaaS

- Cloud service provider selection

- Choosing the right SaaS solution

- Choosing the right PaaS solution.

The general flow of cloud decision making resembles *Figure 2.1*. You should consider and evaluate the deployment model options and then evaluate the options for **Cloud Service Provider** (**CSPs**) based on the business and technical requirements. The following figure showcases this process:

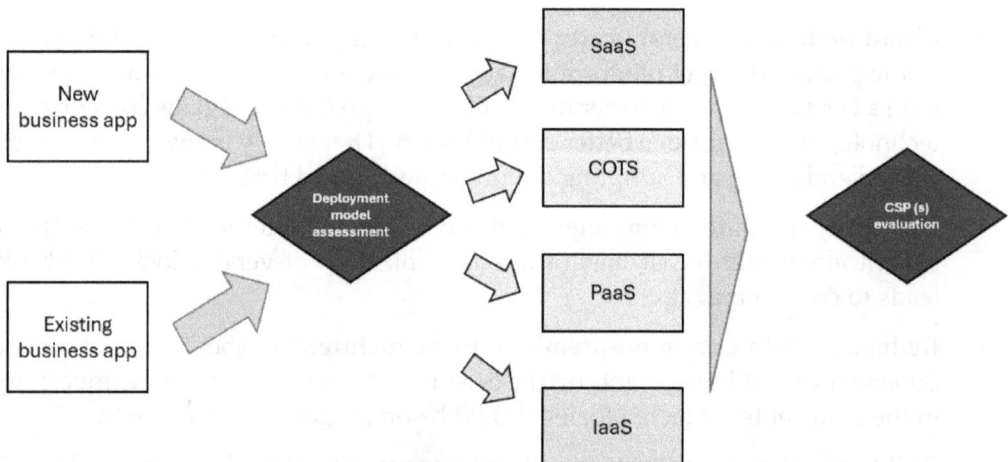

Figure 2.1: Cloud decision process

We have already seen some core principles that regulate such decisions. The decisions depend on multiple factors and are sometimes subject to popular industry trends, even if they do not align with the written rules. For example, a bank trying to adopt a cloud solution will look at similar successful case studies from other banks. The upcoming section discusses some decision points that should be considered to make a well-informed decision.

Cloud service model decision

Probably the first decision you make is to select the right cloud service model (in other words, checking the cloud suitability), i.e. SaaS, IaaS or PaaS. The choice of IaaS based solution can be taken a step further by deploying a **Commercial Off the Shelf (COTS)** product on IaaS or a bespoke solution on IaaS. You choose a service model based on factors like ease of management, level of control and flexibility, cost of solution, skills, and effort required for transformation.

This decision will also depend on the type of application for which you are seeking a cloud-based solution, for example -

- **Existing legacy applications** are a category of business applications that already run in your data center. You can plan to move them to a cloud-based solution as a part of your cloud strategy. This is when you need to make a decision on a target service model. Though a SaaS solution sounds ideal, it might not be the most suitable. Even if there are SaaS solutions available, some customers would like to migrate their existing solution to a public cloud platform using an IaaS based solution or partially transform using a PaaS based solution instead of adopting a SaaS solution as there are number of factors that go into making that change, such as time and budget available, skills required, control and access to the platform etc. Also, any sunk costs should be considered as part of the financial viability of the new solution. In summary, choosing the right service model has no set rules.

The following decision flow chart showcases an ideal case scenario for an existing application that you plan to move to the cloud. Note that the following *Figure 2.2* is a very simple representation of a complicated process, as there are many more details in the background that go into come up with a decision:

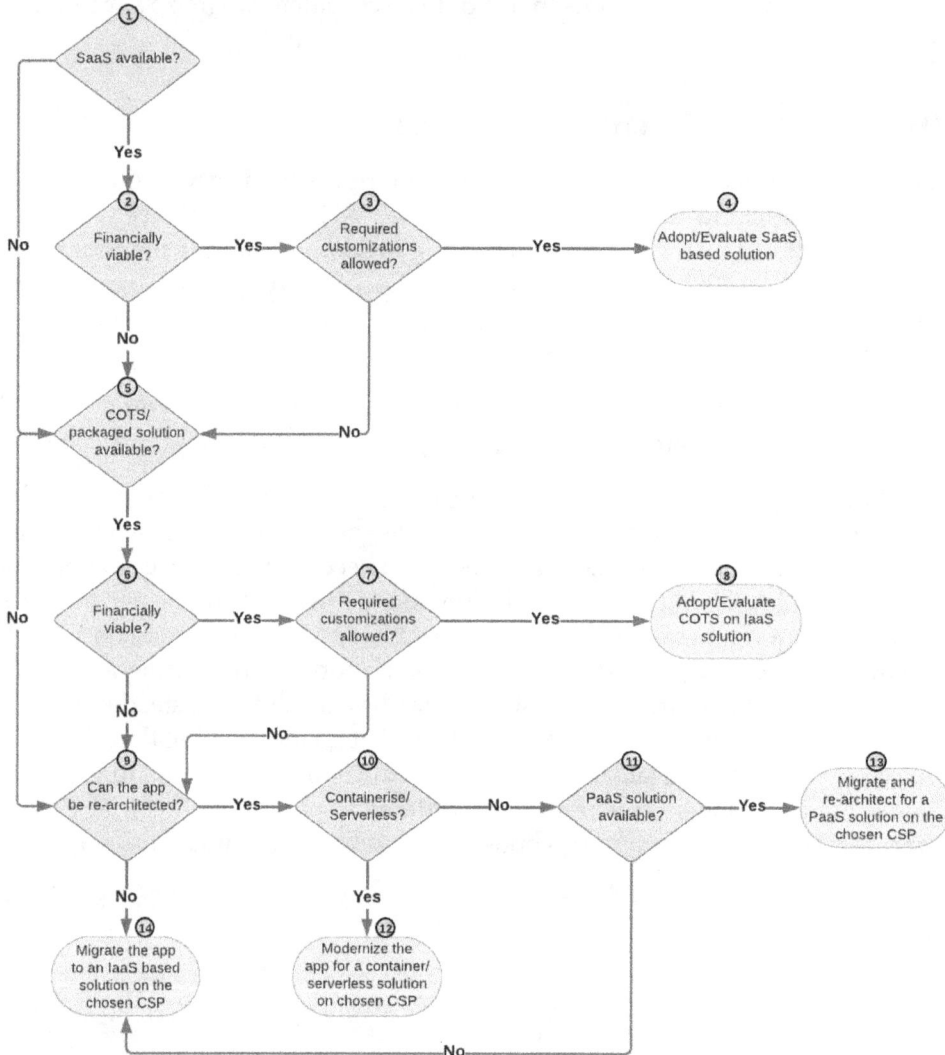

Figure 2.2: Cloud service model decision flowchart

Let us break it down and understand the flow in a bit more detail. Refer to the following table:

SaaS available? — Is there a SaaS solution available to replace this application?	
If yes	Check if the SaaS based solution is financially viable.
If no	Move directly to No.5 in the flow.
Financially viable? — Have you done a cost benefit analysis considering the factors like number of users, any required customization cost, time to replace the current app, cost to learn/hire skills etc.?	
If yes	If a financial analysis has been done and if it looks favorable, check if any customizations are allowed by the provider.
If no	Move directly to No.5 in the flow.
Required customizations allowed? — If there are no customization requirements, you should consider moving directly to No.4 in the flow. If there are customization requirements, does the SaaS provider allow them?	
If yes	SaaS based solution looks good to replace the app.
If no	Move directly to No.5 in the flow.
Adopt/Evaluate the SaaS based solution — Since the major checks have resulted in positive outcomes, you can go for the SaaS based solution.	
COTS/packaged solution available?	
If yes	Check if the packaged solution is financially viable.
If no	Move directly to No.9 in the flow.
Financially viable? — Have you done a cost-benefit analysis considering the factors like any required customization cost, time to replace the current app, cost to learn/hire skills, etc.?	
If yes	If a financial analysis has been done and if it looks favorable, check if any customizations are allowed by the provider.
If no	Move directly to No.9 in the flow.
Required customizations allowed? — If there are no customization requirements, you should consider moving directly to No.8 in the flow. If there are customization requirements, does the product vendor allow them?	
If yes	A COTS/packaged solution looks fit to replace the app.
If no	Move directly to No.9 in the flow.
Adopt/Evaluate COTS on IaaS solution — Since the major checks have resulted in positive outcomes, you can go for a solution with the COTS product on IaaS.	
Can the app be re-architected? — Since you have verified that a SaaS or packaged solution is not suitable, check if the application can be re-architected?	
If yes	Check if the application can be modernized.
If no	Move directly to No.14 in the flow.
Containerize/Serverless? — Since you have an affirmation for the possibility of re-architecting the app, check if the application can be containerized or converted into a serverless app. Note that this check means not only checking for intent but considering the factors like skills, time, and risk.	

If yes	Move directly to No.12 in the flow
If no	Check if there is a PaaS solution
PaaS solution available? — Since you indicated that a complete transformation to containers or serverless is not possible, check if there is a suitable PaaS solution to fully or partially replace the application.	
If yes	Migrate and re-architect based on the identified PaaS solution and move to No.13 in the flow
If no	Move directly to No.14 in the flow
Since a containerized or serverless solution seems suitable, consider re-architecting the app for modernization.	
Since a PaaS solution looks suitable, consider re-architecting the app to replace it fully or partially with the identified solution on the preferred cloud.	
Migrate the app to an IaaS based solution on the chosen CSP — Since all the checks for SaaS, COTS and PaaS have been exhausted and resulted in a negative outcome, you should consider moving the application as-is (lift and shift) to an IaaS based solution on the preferred cloud platform.	

Table 2.1: Cloud service model decision flowchart explanation

As apparent, if you were to opt for a SaaS based solution or pick a packaged solution from market, you need to ensure that it is financially viable and if the solution requires some customization to fit the purpose, then evaluate the ease of use. If you go for a PaaS solution like AWS Elastic Beanstalk or a **Relational Databases System** (**RDS**), your current application needs to be re-architected. If none of these are possible, an IaaS based hosting of the current application (lift & shift migration) will provide an immediate cloud solution, but that does not mark an end to your cloud journey. You can re-architect the application in the next phase and adopt a PaaS solution or a native cloud solution like serverless or containers.

Other considerations, such as the level of control required, could also exist, but the preceding decision flow highlights the most important ones.

- **New greenfield applications** is the category where you solve a business problem by introducing a new application or solution. For such scenarios, there is a general architecture principle that can be used for reference—*Reuse before buy, buy before build*. We discussed this as a part of the guiding principles in the preceding section. Ideally, if a business problem has a SaaS solution, most companies should prefer it over building the solution from scratch. Although that is not always the case. Time to market, financial viability, and customization requirements (for a SaaS solution) play an important part in making the right decision. For a new application, the decision flow could be much simpler, as there is no legacy that you need to take care of.

CSP selection decision

Once the type of service model has been decided for your workloads, the next decision is to choose preferred CSPs. Your organization must decide on target cloud platform(s) as part of finalizing or implementing the strategy. The selection of any solution depends on its fitment against your business, technical, and commercial requirements, plus the evaluation of all associated risks as depicted in the following diagram:

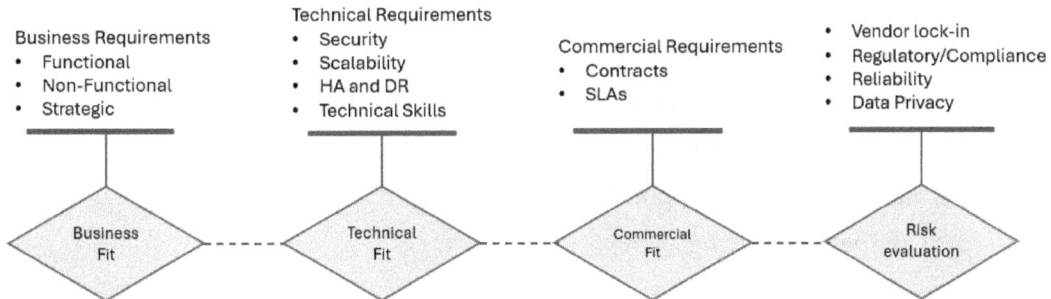

Figure 2.3: CSP selection decision-making process

In this case, it is imperative to satisfy all the conditions mentioned. All four checkpoints shown above should result in a positive outcome for the chosen cloud provider(s).

Cloud services are an extension of the operating environment and need to be properly considered against a set of evaluation criteria to ensure functional, architectural, and security alignment. Here are some of the key parameters (grouped into one of the four categories in the preceding decision tree) that you should evaluate CSPs on:

- **Security and compliance**:
  - Security of cloud infrastructure
  - Compliance with local and international certifications and standards like IRAP and more
  - Security of data in transit and at rest
  - Ability to manage identities
  - Monitoring, logging, and alerting services

- **Service and support**:
  - Available support plans and coverage for ongoing
  - Level and quality of support provided post the sale
  - Billing and accounting support

- **Technical capabilities**:
  - High availability and DR capabilities
  - Support for APIs for easy integration and access
  - Multi-cloud fitment
  - Hybrid networking capabilities
  - Use of technologies that enable interoperability

- **Commercials and contracts**:
  - Contractual terms should allow exiting and avoid lock-in conditions
  - SLAs committed by the CSP
  - Sign up and renewal policies
  - Competitive pricing

- **Overall market reputation**:
  - Existing customers and brands subscribed to the CSP
  - Business health over the years

Architecture frameworks

Another key component (or an enabler) of a cloud adoption strategy is an architecture framework. Architecture frameworks are a set of guiding principles and reference patterns for architects to refer to when describing solutions to the IT problems of their company. They provide general guidance and should be customizable based on your specific scenario. Let us look at some of the widely used frameworks with a mention of cloud-specific ones.

The Open Group Architecture Framework (TOGAF) is one of the most widely used and practiced enterprise architecture frameworks across the IT industry. It is not cloud-specific but rather a generic framework for you to design, deploy, and manage the architecture at an enterprise level by aligning business and technical resources to achieve strategic outcomes. At the core of TOGAF is the **Architecture Development Methodology (ADM)**, which broadly divides the architecture development into the following eight phases:

- Architecture vision
- Business architecture
- Information architecture
- Technology architecture
- Opportunities and solutions

- Migration planning
- Governance
- Change management

As you see, these are not specific to a domain or platform. They can be easily customized and applied to a cloud adoption as well. Try and map these phases to the previously listed components of a cloud strategy, you will see various similarities.

Aside from TOGAF, there are also some cloud-specific frameworks that should be understood and considered to effectively adopt and optimize cloud in your organization, such as:

- **Cloud Adoption Framework (CAF)**: This framework revolves around the set of principles that guide the planning and implementation of cloud in an organization. These principles define cloud adoption as a joint function of people, processes and technology. You can clearly find the similarities with a TOGAF ADM.

- **Well-Architected Framework (WAF)**: This framework provides guidance on the practices that should be adopted to optimize your cloud architecture and ensure you are getting most out of your cloud deployments in terms of performance, operations, security, reliability and cost.

In essence, these frameworks can complement the broader TOGAF framework. Since TOGAF does not mandate a set of rules, some parts of TOGAF are generally adopted along with CAF and WAF to create and implement a cloud adoption strategy. All major cloud providers have their own version of these frameworks, with minor tweaks to make them look different, but are fundamentally similar. Apart from these, there are some other frameworks that are specific to a particular domain, such as NIST for security architecture, and they can overlap with some of the design principles preached by a TOAGF or a WAF.

Note: We have used WAF as an acronym for Well-Architected Framework, but it should not be confused with another security service called web application firewall.

Conclusion

In this chapter, we looked at a cloud adoption strategy, its components, and steps to create a successful strategy. A cloud strategy starts by understanding the motivation of the business behind the move, then proceeds to an assessment of the current state, and finally aligns the learnings to a desired state by proposing the appropriate solutions. We also discussed the details of decision frameworks and architecture frameworks, which are essential to support the development and implementation of a cloud strategy. In the next chapter, we will take a look at the three dimensions of a cloud strategy and the key migration approaches to set the stage for enterprise-level aspects in the rest of the chapter. Governance, the key component of a cloud strategy, will be extensively discussed in the next chapter. Along with a governance framework, the other key aspects that deserve an enterprise level attention and will be discussed in the next chapter are the cloud adoption roadmap and capability assessment.

Points to remember

Here are some key takeaways from this chapter:

- The high-level steps for the formation of a cloud strategy are:
  - o Understand the business goals and motivations behind the move
  - o Engage the right stakeholders
  - o Assess the current state across every dimension—people, process, and technology
  - o Understand the technical and financial considerations
  - o Prepare a business case for cloud adoption
  - o Create a detailed roadmap to achieve the desired target state on the cloud
- Cloud financials are very different from the traditional on-premises IT financials. The focus on cloud shifts from CAPEX to OPEX.
- There are multiple technical considerations for a good cloud strategy, for example, security, availability, and scalability.
- A business case is a significant tool in the completion of a cloud strategy as it provides the policy makers with a view of forecasted benefits.
- Some important decision frameworks that are useful in implementing a cloud strategy are listed here:
  - o Choosing the cloud service model
  - o Choosing the cloud service provider
  - o Choosing the right SaaS solution
  - o Choosing the right PaaS solution

CHAPTER 3
The Enterprise View

Introduction

In the previous chapter, we explored cloud adoption strategy and its related components. In this chapter, we will discuss a very important aspect of developing a successful cloud strategy, i.e., the enterprise view of the strategy. It essentially means that a cloud strategy cannot be formed in isolation for certain business units or projects. You should look at all the moving parts across the organization, to ensure optimal coverage and eliminate risks of non-compliance, wastage and management overheads. We will look at the various elements of a cloud strategy that deserve an enterprise lens. This chapter will only focus on the areas that are most pertinent from a consolidated view of the organization, like setting up a governance framework or creating an end-to-end adoption roadmap.

Structure

In this chapter, we will cover the following topics:

- Dimensions of a cloud adoption journey
- Cloud adoption approaches
- Cloud governance
- Cloud centre of excellence
- Cloud onboarding toolkit

- Capability assessment
- Cloud adoption roadmap
- Importance of an enterprise view
- Cloud adoptions fail often
- Recommendations for a successful strategy

Objectives

The main objective of this chapter is to put a magnifying lens on the cloud adoption strategy discussed in the previous chapter and focus on the components that are more pertinent from an enterprise point of view, especially for large organisations. By the end of this chapter, you should have a good grasp of the elements of the cloud strategy that deserve a more holistic and detailed inspection. These are the areas where you would need enterprise architects to be involved, leading the way for the rest of the organisation, as they are equipped with the required skills and experience.

Dimensions of a cloud adoption journey

When you consider cloud adoption for the whole organization, you need to consider it from all the possible dimensions, such as

- **People**: They are the most valuable assets of any organization. The people dimension caters to the workforce that makes cloud adoption possible by learning and leveraging skills to execute the plans. It provides guidance around culture, leadership, organization structure, growth, and learning.

- **Process**: This dimension takes care of processes like business, operations, governance etc. These process side of the strategy ensures that cloud is adopted and delivered at the expected level.

- **Technology**: This dimension covers aspects like platform, security, networking, etc. Considering these aspects is essential for designing and building technically sound workloads on the cloud, including the foundations. This dimension provides guidance on the components of a secure and scalable landing zone, target state architecture, access, and authentication

Dimensions are a way of logically grouping initiatives, guiding principles, and recommendations to achieve the desired outcomes. All major cloud providers have their own adoption frameworks, which provide a different perspective on the grouping explained in this section, although the fundamentals remain the same. Whatever we are going to discuss in this chapter is relatable to one of these dimensions.

Cloud adoption approaches

When you plan an enterprise-wide cloud adoption, you cannot let every business owner run their own shadow IT and decide their own way of cloud adoption. However, at the same time, you need to provide them with some level of flexibility and a few options to pick from. Thus, it would be best to have some pre-defined patterns or approaches that can cater to most use cases.

There are multiple ways to adopt the cloud, but the famous 7R migration model is a good starting point. The model initially introduced by AWS (built on the 5Rs of Gartner) has become an industry standard now, and all large cloud providers have their own version. Let us first take a look at the 7R model:

- **Rehost**: It is probably the easiest migration approach to execute. Also referred to as *lift and shift*, this migration approach is usually adopted when there are looming deadlines, like data centre exit, as a form of motivation for cloud adoption. Hence, you cannot afford to tinker with the applications due to a lack of time. Sometimes, this approach is preferred as the first phase of cloud adoption, and then any modernization opportunities are undertaken later in the next phase once applications are stable on the cloud.

- **Refactor**: In this approach, you will aim at re-architecting the applications to adopt the latest technologies or make a move to cloud-native architecture (e.g., native PaaS services or container services, or serverless architecture). The idea is to optimize the architecture completely in order to move away from the legacy technologies on which the application has been built. This approach is certainly time-consuming. Hence, the effort and cost involved in this must be evaluated. Not all applications qualify under this category, but this approach can help achieve maximum cloud benefits.

- **Re-platform**: Using this cloud adoption approach, you can move your application to cloud by replacing one or more components of the application with a cloud-native service. Unlike re-factoring, you are not changing the architecture of the application but modernizing the application within the same architecture. E.g., consider replacing a SQL server database with a managed PaaS service like RDS for SQL server on AWS.

- **Repurchase**: This approach advocates for replacing the legacy applications with an externally managed application, that is akin to a consumption-based model (provided by SaaS application). This is also considered a quick adoption approach as you are picking a solution that is readily available in the market (though you might need some customizations).

- **Retire**: This strategy should be considered for legacy applications that are no longer required and have been replaced/superseded by another application providing similar or better functionality.

- **Retain**: This strategy is used for applications that cannot be retired or are unsuitable for any other cloud adoption approach, which would allow them to be hosted on cloud. In reality, this might not seem like a cloud adoption approach as you are retaining the application in its original form, from where it is currently hosted. Although, it is still a valid target state for applications that have been assessed for migration to cloud.

- **Relocate**: This is the newest addition to the cloud adoption approaches (and hence the 7th R). This is similar to the *rehost* approach, but the target infrastructure platform on the cloud is the same as the source platform. This ensures a lift and shift of applications, as well as servers, at the hypervisor level and, hence, is much quicker than other forms of cloud adoption. It does not change any application architecture or underlying infrastructure. The most suitable example of this approach is moving from an on-premises hosted VMware farm to an Azure-hosted VMware platform, also called **Azure VMware Solution (AVS)**. AWS also had a similar solution called **VMware on Cloud (VMC)**, and that is how the term *relocate* was coined by AWS.

When providing guidance to the stakeholders on the cloud adoption approaches as a part of the enterprise cloud strategy, you need to pick the ones that fit the technical and business use cases across the organization. Hence, it is necessary that this process is centralized and governed by people who represent every function of the organization. At the same time, the advocated approach(es) should align with the guiding principles endorsed by the leadership as part of the wider strategy (some of the key guiding principles were discussed in *Chapter 2, Cloud Adoption Strategy*). E.g., some organizations do not approve the *rehost* (lift and shift) approach of cloud adoption, unless there is a proper justification to go that route. Instead, they want the business owners to consider modern applications, open-source technologies, and cloud-native services to develop their solutions.

Some common examples of centralized cloud adoption principles used by large enterprises are as follows:

- Salesforce for all sales-related use cases, like generation of leads, centralization of sales data, customer data, opportunity management, and customer interactions.

- ServiceNow for all incident management and response, including ticketing system. Note that ServiceNow has a PaaS as well as a SaaS version.

- Cloud native technologies for greenfield applications.

- Containerized and serverless architecture patterns for applications that can be re-architected and modernized (considering factors like time, skills, and cost).

- For the public cloud platform, a single consolidated landing zone with appropriate networking and security that addresses the requirements of all workloads across the organization.

Cloud governance

In terms of cloud adoption, governance is all about helping run the cloud projects seamlessly by managing the risks at every stage. It is the strategy component that deserves enterprise-level attention because the checks and controls cannot be implemented in isolation for a part of an organization or some projects. There should be a single set of approved governance rules that are most effective when adopted for the entire organization. Going back to the discussion on dimensions, governance is a *process* that overlaps with the *people* in an organization, where we look at some of the key governance bodies that ensure the processes are well-defined, implemented, and followed.

There are some critical governance bodies, some of which can be formed or repurposed (if they already exist) as part of implementing the cloud strategy, for example:

- **Cloud centre of excellence (CCoE)**: It is a centralized cloud computing governance function that serves as the technical design authority and internal **cloud service broker (CSB)**. It acts as a consultant to central ICT, business unit IT as well as consumers of cloud services within the business. A CCoE can serve the needs of both agility-focused and efficiency-focused IT. It is a key ingredient for cloud-enabled IT transformation and is typically tasked with helping drive that transformation. There will be a detailed discussion on CCoE to follow.

- **Program management office (PMO)**: It is the owner of project management duties, including cloud projects. Usually, PMOs do not make policy-related decisions or get directly involved in most governance activities, but they should be a part of CCoE, as they are responsible for delivery.

- **Steering committee**: This is usually a group of senior leaders across the organization and has representatives from almost every part of the company. The main responsibility of this group is to review the projects and endorse/reject them based on the information provided (a lot of focus is on the financials associated with the proposed projects). These senior stakeholders are usually involved at the stage where final go/no-go decisions are required, and a decision on project funding is taken. The decision-makers in this group consist of senior leaders from technology, business, and finance. You must also have representation from the cloud to ensure that the wider organization is aware of the cloud projects and their impact on the surrounding ecosystem.

- **Architecture review board (ARB)**: This group should have representation from all departments of the organization, including those from the external vendors participating in the cloud adoption journey of the organization. It is usually anchored by the enterprise architects of the company. This is a technical forum where the technical decisions of all the projects are reviewed and endorsed or rejected.

Note that this is for general guidance only. What applies to you depends on your requirements and situation. For example, you could already have some IT governance, like ARB, in place and just wish to align it with the cloud strategy by adding relevant people, including cloud-specific agendas and policies, or changing the frequency of the meetings.

Cloud centre of excellence

One of the most impactful and useful governing bodies, which plays an integral role in successful cloud adoption at any organization, is the CCoE. It has been discussed here in greater detail, with primary focus on its structure, functions and benefits.

Composition

CCoE consists of various personas, capabilities, and skill sets, which ensures that the desired objectives of the organization are met. Some key participants of a CCoE are:

- Enterprise architects, who help coordinate the ongoing cloud adoption efforts across the organization, providing a business perspective and acting as the conduit for communication between business and technology. They are instrumental in achieving the desired target on cloud, as they have an understanding of the current state, roadmap, and capabilities required to reach the target state.

- Technical SMEs/architects who bring the perspective of cloud architecture, design patterns, engineering, and operations.

- Representatives from the finance office to review the costs associated with cloud adoption projects and guide the project teams on available funding, budgets, etc.

- Program/Project managers of the project, who help develop a leadership perspective. They are the people who can talk about the health of current projects.

Functions

Note that a CCoE focuses on brokerage and governance, not control. Some of the important activities that a CCoE contributes to are:

- Providing guidance in terms of design principles, policies, CSP selection, cloud architecture, and migration patterns.

- Reviewing and providing feedback on the proposed solution architecture for cloud projects.

- Maintaining cloud knowledge base and repository.

- Identifying internal training requirements for the staff and organize appropriate training and certification events.

Benefits

Let us look at some of the benefits that CCoE can provide:

- One of the main benefits of a CCoE is that it acts as a central governing body—it can help prevent sporadic, inconsistent, and redundant cloud adoption across the business functions in the organization. For example, multiple occurrences of the same use case across the organization should have the same solution, or rather, if multiple departments have the same use case, they should be using the same solution in a subscriber or multi-tenancy mode instead of deploying multiple instances of the same solution.

- Another big benefit of CCoE is the collaborative environment it creates by bringing in representatives from all key functions of the organization. It ensures communication between key personnels, to ensure that they are aware of all the projects and initiatives to assess, in case of any possible impact on their part.

- CCoE can help improve the efficiency of an organization by introducing optimized and automated processes.

- Inline to its key objectives, a CCoE can also ensure compliance with regulations and standards that your organization needs to adhere to.

- CCoE spreads awareness across the organization to keep up with the rapid advancements in the cloud computing space.

- Since CCoE maintains a central repository of cloud design patterns and solutions, it can help projects choose the best cloud solution for their problems.

- CCoE keeps track of staff training requirements, in line with current and new projects, to ensure that any skill gaps are being filled in time.

Cloud onboarding toolkit

It is recommended that a cloud onboarding toolkit be established to assist with cloud adoption and publish its artifacts in an easily accessible medium, e.g., the intranet. The cloud onboarding toolkit typically consists of guidelines, patterns, policies, procedures, and practices that members of the CCoE maintain for the entire community to use. Let us look at some of them:

- **Guidelines**: Information and best practices on a range of topics, e.g., DevSecOps, that can help cloud solution design teams increase the quality and lower the cost of their solutions.

- **Patterns**: Material that describes various architectural patterns endorsed by CCoE, e.g., a RESTful SaaS integration pattern, automated deployments, load balancing, scaling, security, monitoring, etc. Design teams should use one of the endorsed patterns.

- **Reference architectures**: They are a great asset to accelerate the proposed cloud implementations, simplify the maintenance and support and minimize the risk by using the proven architectures.

- **Policies**: Policy information that all solution design teams must comply with e.g. data classification, security policies etc.

- **Decision trees**: These are decision frameworks which help the business assess their requirements, constraints and determine the correct criteria-based approach for the service they wish to use. This includes a list of customer-approved CSPs that the business is encouraged to use, rather than implementing an unendorsed platform or solution.

- **Evaluation criteria**: These are the vendor and technology assessment criteria.

The toolkit is expected to be developed and enhanced over time to include additional artefacts as listed in the preceding section. A cloud onboarding toolkit is one of the CCoE's key responsibilities and deliverables.

Capability assessment

Another area where you would need your **enterprise architecture (EA)** practice to take control is the assessment of current capabilities to identify the gaps and gauge the capabilities required to reach the target state on the cloud. Capability is the competency of an organization in a particular domain, and capability assessment for cloud is the measure of the state of those competencies that would help the organization move to the cloud. Similar to governance, this assessment should be done at an enterprise level to determine if the organization is ready for cloud adoption. Capability maturity can be gauged, and subsequent gaps can be filled by hiring new skills or building new competencies internally via training.

Capabilities

Based on industry experience, the following capabilities are critical to a successful cloud adoption:

- **Cost governance and management**: Cost management, in the context of cloud computing, is the process of planning and controlling the cost of cloud service usage. Being able to analyze costs in terms of their origin, e.g., by business unit, by deployment environment (Dev, Test, Production, DR, etc.) in a granular way, is the prerequisite for effective cost management. CSPs provide constructs for logical grouping of cloud resources (e.g., Azure Resource Groups) along with cloud resource tagging strategies that enable tracking costs at the workload level. After this, cost showback can be enabled by tagging a group of resources that comprise a workload within a cost center or department.

Cost showback is the process of reporting cost information to various departments in the organization, based on their individual usage of the resources. It is a great way to enhance transparency and accountability for each department. In cloud, tagging the resources is an effective method to create usage and costing reports that are associated with each department.

In a nutshell, cloud financials are different from the traditional world of IT. We have discussed the details in other chapters of this book, but from the capability perspective, people from the finance department need to understand the differences and learn the new ways of working.

- **PMO**: Implementing the cloud strategy will generate a set of change and remediation projects, which need to be justified, prioritized, and implemented alongside other non-cloud projects. PMO is actively involved in a cloud adoption journey as they are responsible for delivering various projects that are part of the roadmap. Representatives from PMOs are also part of groups like CCoE, and they are key to the governance framework of a cloud strategy. Hence, uplifting and reskilling the PMO capability is important so that the project managers understand how a cloud project is different from a traditional project.

- **Architecture**: The cloud adoption strategy needs to be seen as part of a wider EA framework. Hence, the architecture practice should also be changed to adapt to the way in which the cloud works. The architects need to define and own the organization-wide architecture artifacts like design patterns, guiding principles, guardrails, etc. Naturally, when adopting the cloud, the whole architecture repository needs an overhaul. The architecture community is also the key participant in the governance framework of the cloud strategy. Understandably, the architectural capability requires an upliftment by reskilling and adding more cloud resources

- **Engineering**: Similar to architecture, the engineering capability needs to evolve significantly as part of a cloud adoption journey. The new deployment models, development frameworks (like agile and DevOps), automation, CI/CD capabilities, and cloud-specific tooling make it mandatory that the engineers upskill/re-skill themselves. Hence, hiring cloud engineers and cross-training people has become an immediate priority to enhance engineering capability.

- **Operations**: Unlike the traditional IT operations, **cloud operations (CloudOps)** rely more on agility and automated processes to manage cloud infrastructure. CloudOps derives a lot of its principles from the philosophy of DevOps and leverages many similar tools and services. A capability assessment exercise can correctly identify the current state of operations, team readiness, and new skills required to transform the operations team into a cloud-ready operations team.

- **Security and risk management**: Assessment of security, risk, and compliance capabilities is the top priority for most organizations planning to move to the cloud.

Awareness of cloud security principles, compliance, and regulatory requirements, and a revamped risk profile—all demand specialized skills. There are multiple specialized skills under this capability, like security of infrastructure, data, and application, identity and access management, etc.

There are many more capabilities not listed in this section, but the key takeaway is the need to acquire new skills and uplift existing skills. In general, the following considerations apply with regard to cloud capabilities upliftment:

- The focus should be on cross-skilling staff across infrastructure operations and achieving deployment acceleration by applying DevOps and DevSecOps practices.

- On-the-job training to develop skills in secure provisioning and deployment.

- Focused training on specific cloud management and monitoring tools.

Cloud adoption roadmap

A cloud adoption strategy is incomplete without a well-drawn roadmap. A roadmap, in this case, would be a detailed list of initiatives and projects that your organization must undertake to transition from its current state to the desired target state in the cloud. We discussed this very briefly in *Chapter 2, Cloud Adoption Strategy*, and deferred the detailed discussion for this chapter, because this is another area that needs the attention of an enterprise architect to come up with an enterprise-level view so that consolidation of projects and cross-business impacts can be understood.

A cloud adoption journey can be divided into four phases: assess, plan, execute, and operate. *Chapter 4, The Journey*, is a focused discussion on this topic where we will explore the details of each phase and how they are typically executed in the real world. However, the part that we are discussing here explains how an enterprise-level cloud adoption roadmap is drawn across all these phases in order to come up with a comprehensive view. The following is a brief description of the aforementioned four phases:

- **Assess**: A detailed discovery and assessment of the current state, including all three dimensions, i.e. people (skills, growth, learning etc.), processes (business, operations, service management etc) and technology (infrastructure and applications).

- **Plan**: Define and initiate projects that will enhance the organization wide readiness for cloud adoption. This is the phase where you create foundations for your future state on cloud and plan the migration with workload sequencing and high-level dates.

- **Execute**: Work on the plan you created in the previous phase by designing the target state and building your workloads on top of the foundations laid down earlier.

- **Operate**: This is the phase where you run the deployed workloads on cloud as **Business as Usual** (**BAU**) and look at opportunities to innovate and modernize the existing workloads.

Sample roadmap

A cloud adoption roadmap should cover every initiative that you must undertake in each of these phases in consultation with stakeholders across the organisation. Here is a sample roadmap that lists some important and recommended projects across each phase:

Phase	Dimension	Initiative/Project	Ideal window
Assess	Technology	Discover and assess on-premises workloads for cloud suitability and a possible migration approach	0-6 months
Assess	Technology	Review CSPs—services, platform, and technology	0-3 months
Assess	People	Assess cloud capabilities and training needs	0-3 months
Plan	Process	Define selection strategies and frameworks—CSP and Service delivery models	0-3 months
Plan	People/Process	Establish CCoE	3-6 months
Plan	People	Plan focused trainings and resourcing requirements	3-6 months
Plan	People	Raise cloud awareness	0-12 months
Plan	Process	Establish a cloud onboarding toolkit	3-12 months
Plan	Process	Establish governance frameworks for IaaS, PaaS, SaaS	0-6 months
Plan	Process	Define guiding principles for cloud adoption	3-6 months
Plan	Technology	Establish reference architectures and migration patterns	3-12 months
Plan	Technology	Define data classification based on data sensitivity and use cases	6-12 months
Plan	Technology	Create a detailed migration plan—select and sequence applications for cloud migration based on the planning workshops with the application owners	6-12 months
Plan	Technology	Design the cloud landing zone based on requirements and best practices	6-12 months
Plan	Technology	Establish an identity and access management framework	6-12 months

Phase	Dimension	Initiative/Project	Ideal window
Plan	Technology	Design and endorse the target state for applications identified for migration to cloud	6-15 months
Execute	Technology	Build the cloud landing zone as per approved design and CSP/service model decisions	12-15 months
Execute	Technology	Migrate applications as per the final migration plan	15-24 months
Execute	Technology	Post-migration testing of the migrated applications	18-27 months
Operate	Process	Auditing of migrated applications on the cloud	24-36 months
Operate	Process	Retrospection of migration approaches and documenting the lessons learned	24-30 months
Operate	Process	Track business value realization	24-36 months
Operate	Technology	Re-architect, refactor, or replace the existing applications on cloud for opportunities to further modernize	24 months—ongoing
Operate	Technology	Consolidation and rationalization of on-premises resources like servers that are not required	24 months—ongoing

Table 3.1: Sample cloud adoption roadmap

The preceding table is a sample roadmap, and not everything listed here is applicable to your particular scenario. However, this could serve as a good starting point, and you can customize the plan, as required. This list of initiatives is not ordered sequentially, as some of these steps can start sooner/later or run in parallel, depending on your current state. As you can see, a good cloud adoption roadmap should range anywhere from two-three years, depending on the size and complexity of your organization and the workload it faces.

Importance of an enterprise view

Let us understand this with a real-life example. A large government organization has multiple business units, most of which operate their shadow IT. There is no central pool of resources that manages the IT projects of the entire organization. Hence, there is a clear lack of collaboration and communication. Most business units have adopted cloud in some form or shape, be it a SaaS solution, a COTS solution on the public cloud, or an IaaS-hosted bespoke solution on the public cloud. However, due to the lack of collaboration and cohesiveness, there are certain apparent problems; such as:

- Similar business problems have multiple instances of the same solution running in silos.

- Similar business problems have different solutions, leading to inconsistencies and wastage.

- Since all business units run their own DevOps practice, there are no central code repositories.

- Inefficient and costly cloud architectures, which lack the basic principles and best practices

- Multiple cloud accounts/subscriptions create a confusing structure.

- Multiple insecure and unoptimized landing zones.

- No visibility into the consolidated cloud financials for the executive leadership of the company.

These were the most obvious and glaring problems that were taking a toll on the overall reputation of the company. In order to fix these problems, after a thorough introspection, it was decided that they should re-examine their current cloud adoption and develop a strategy for the next few years. The enterprise architect led a team to work on the strategy piece. Most of the steps taken to fix those problems have been discussed in this chapter, and the previous chapters have been dedicated to cloud strategy. In summary, the following measures were taken to fix the problems:

- Socialize the idea of a single cloud adoption across the whole organization.

- Conduct workshops with the key nominated stakeholders and understand their viewpoints (goals, objectives, desired outcomes) on a consolidated cloud adoption strategy.

- Understand the current state of cloud adoption—workloads, service delivery models, CSPs etc for all business units.

- Establish a centralized governance model with representatives from all departments/units. An ARB and a CCoE were already established.

- Relevant cloud training programs were organized for the entire staff as per their roles, skills, and competencies.

- Plan and execute projects to assess the workloads and possible migration approaches for each. This was a long process as it involved many funding requirements.

As evident, all these measures reinforce the importance of an enterprise view of the problem.

Cloud adoptions fail often

Despite following all the required steps and best practices, not all cloud adoptions go as per the plan. There can be multiple reasons for failure; some are listed here:

- **Silos across the enterprises**: As mentioned a few times, a strategy in silos will not achieve the desired results. It must be a collaborative approach with all key stakeholders involved. You need to create a collaborative environment where communication channels are open across business units, and stakeholders are aware of any projects being planned/executed.

- **Resistance to change**: This is the most obvious reason, especially in large organizations where the employees have been working and specialize in old legacy technologies. The general perception is that a new technology could impact their jobs as they do not possess the required skills.

- **Lack of awareness**: Spreading awareness about cloud, its pros and cons, is a critical activity you do as part of your cloud adoption journey. Lack of awareness is the reason why many leaders are averse to change.

- **Fear of failure**: Another reason could be the stable critical systems on legacy platforms and the risk associated with migrating them to a new platform in a new ecosystem.

- **Lack of skills and capabilities**: We have discussed this in the *people* dimension of cloud adoption. You need to gauge the skill gaps and bridge them with the right training and new hiring.

- **Uninspiring leadership**: Change always starts at the top. The leaders of the company have to feel motivated to the cloud adoption and then the message percolates down to the rest of the staff. When the leaders are motivated, they can inspire the people working under them to bring change.

Recommendations for a successful strategy

Nobody wants to fail, and certainly not when developing the cloud strategy at an enterprise level. Let us look at some practical and proven recommendations to improve the chances of success:

- Make sure that each cloud project (part of the cloud strategy) has a benefits realization process, where the anticipated benefits are identified at the outset, and can be measured and quantified. Without such a process, you will not be able to realize the full potential and benefits of the initiatives.

- The importance of communication in a cloud strategy can never be underestimated. Collaboration and communication are the backbone of this whole process as they improve involvement, enhance visibility, and reduce risks with early feedback and inputs. They are also important ingredients in knowledge sharing and spreading awareness.

- Establish a governance framework with groups like CCoE. The importance and benefits have been discussed earlier in the chapter.

- Establish a cloud onboarding toolkit with guiding principles, policies, patterns and reference architectures. The major benefit of a toolkit is that ad hoc decisions that may increase risks can be minimized.

- Establish a cloud service catalogue that provides a view of existing cloud services to businesses before deciding or exploring a new solution. For example, the organization has a full list of SaaS services currently in use.

- Establish processes to transform the organization, which means a transformation in context of all three dimensions—people, process and technology. For example, changes in the skills of people, operating model of IT, service delivery processes etc.

- Make sure a capability assessment is performed, gaps are identified, and appropriately addressed.

- Selection strategies and decision frameworks must be developed and adopted to ensure a fair and consistent selection process across the organization. We have discussed decision frameworks in the previous chapter.

- Review and uplift the cost management and governance capabilities. Most often underestimated, this is one of the key functions and reasons for a successful cloud adoption.

- Data is the basic ingredient of every workload and migration to cloud is often considered a risk for hosting workloads that are considered sensitive or confidential, like financial data or health data. It is important to have proper data classification and tagging in place.

- Establish an integrated and robust **identity and access management (IAM)** framework to ensure only the verified identities can access the resources in cloud and are authorized as per the role they play in the organization. IAM is usually a complex function in the larger security domain of cloud adoption and must be addressed well in time. Some of the key requirements of an effective IAM framework are single sign-on, role-based access control, etc.

Conclusion

The main objective of this chapter was to understand the elements and activities of the cloud journey that need a broader organization-wide view in terms of a cloud adoption strategy. For example, there are components like the governance framework and capability assessment that need an enterprise lens. We also understood the three dimensions of people, process, and technology that broadly summarize a cloud adoption journey. In the end, we learned about the roadmap and looked at a sample roadmap of 2-3 years with some key initiatives to enable a successful adoption across the four phases, namely, assess, plan, execute, and operate. In the next chapter, we are going to focus on these four phases and discuss each one of them in much greater detail. We will understand the purpose of each phase and the approaches to carrying out these phases, along with some sample deliverables produced as part of these phases.

Points to remember

Here are some key takeaways from this chapter:

- There are three dimensions of a cloud adoption strategy—people, process, and technology.

- There are seven migration approaches, also known as 7Rs of migration—rehost, refactor, re-platform, repurchase, retire, and relocate.

- The three dimensions and seven approaches are key to an enterprise-level cloud adoption strategy as they bring the required consistency.

- Cloud governance framework is vital to ensure projects envisaged as part of the strategy are run smoothly and risk free.

- CCoE is one of the most important and impactful components of the governance framework and is responsible for providing guidance and spreading awareness across the organization.

- A roadmap is the bridge between current state and the target state i.e. the steps that must be undertaken for the organization to move from the on-premises hosting to a cloud hosting. A roadmap is drawn across four stages of adoption journey—assess, plan, execute and operate.

- Without a properly planned and reviewed strategy, there are high chances of failure in adopting cloud. It is important to understand the potential reasons for failure and plan well ahead to avoid them. Consider the recommendations provided in this chapter for achieving success.

Join our book's Discord space

Join the book's Discord Workspace for Latest updates, Offers, Tech happenings around the world, New Release and Sessions with the Authors:

https://discord.bpbonline.com

CHAPTER 4

The Journey

Introduction

In the previous chapter, we discussed the details of a cloud strategy along with the steps to develop it. One of the final steps is laying out the roadmap to reach from the current state to the desired state on the cloud. To reach the desired state, your actions are grouped into four phases: assess, plan, execute, and operate. This is a standard template of an organization's cloud journey across the industry, though the exact names of these phases could differ depending on the cloud provider and the practitioners involved.

For example, both AWS and Microsoft Azure provide a **Cloud Adoption Framework (CAF)** as guidance to embark on the journey. Whereas AWS' CAF focuses on the readiness of the organization, Microsoft Azure's CAF is aligned to the entire journey, and both have some great guidance for reaching the desired target state. These phases also make up your adoption roadmap, which we discussed in the previous chapter. In this chapter, we will explore these phases in-depth and understand how they are performed, along with the inputs and outputs of each phase, some useful tools, and various approaches.

Structure

In this chapter, we will cover the following topics:

- Phases of cloud adoption
- Assess

- Plan
- Execute
- Migration Factory
- Operate

Objectives

By the end of this chapter, you should be able to understand and appreciate the end-to-end journey of cloud adoption. You should have a clear understanding of each phase, its intended outcomes, and the tools used. This will solidify your knowledge of cloud adoption strategy in terms of a practical approach to adoption. This chapter focuses more on the adoption process rather than deep technical implementation, which will be covered in later chapters.

Phases of cloud adoption

A cloud adoption journey is a lengthy process that could take years to complete or at least show some substantial results. There are multiple steps and tasks involved in this journey, which can be logically grouped into some high-level phases for ease of project planning and execution. The phases that we have referred to in this book are:

- Assess
- Plan
- Execute
- Operate

Note: There have been different names given to these phases industry-wide, but the fundamentals remain the same, i.e. meaning of each phase and what activities and outcomes are associated with each phase.

Such a grouping not only helps project managers to plan but is of immense value to everyone involved. Let us look at them in detail:

- Project progress can be tracked and reported for each phase, giving a more granular and comprehensible view.

- Funding and budgeting decisions can be made for a phase instead of the whole long journey

- Resource allocation can be based on a phase, based on the requirements of a particular phase

- An organization's cloud maturity level can be easily gauged based on these phases

In the next few sections, we will look into each phase.

Assess

Whenever you start a transformation, you have a vision and the desired target state in mind. The desired target state is always relative to the current state i.e. where you want to be after the transformation is always based on where you are now. Hence, to be able to clearly visualize the target state, knowing the current state in sufficient detail is important, and that is where an assessment kicks in. You need to know what to transform, how much to transform, what the best approach for the transformation is, and how much it might cost.

Cloud transformation is no different. An assessment of the current state must be carried out to understand what it might take for the transformation in terms of the desired target state and the cost of achieving it. Key objectives of the assessment phase are as follows:

- **What to transform**: Also known as discovery, some of the key data elements that must be gathered are:

  o Virtualization platform (VMWare, Hyper-V etc.)

  o The count and specs of servers

  o Type of storage systems i.e **Storage Area Network (SAN), Network attached Storage (NAS)**, block devices, file systems, etc, and volume of data

  o Database details (type, size, version, etc.)

  Discovery can be manual, tool-based, or a mix of both. A bit later, there will be more on the discovery approach.

- **How much to transform**: Most companies prefer a hybrid and/or multi-cloud approach instead of ultimately moving to a single cloud platform. In such architectures, you do not migrate everything to the cloud, sometimes by choice or sometimes by compulsion. By choice, when you have valid reasons not to migrate a workload to the cloud, like data sensitivity, does not allow cloud hosting. By compulsion, when there are factors that do not allow the migration even though you want to, like a legacy application with software licensing issues on the cloud.

- **Best approach for transformation**: One of the key inputs to the cost of transformation is the approach for transformation. The approach here means how you will adopt cloud or migrate to the cloud for every server and application, i.e. one of the 7Rs of migration discussed in *Chapter 3, The Enterprise View*:

  o Rehost

  o Refactor

  o Re-platform

- o Repurchase
- o Retire
- o Retain
- o Relocate

This approach will not only feed into the cost but is an important input for migration planning and decision-making. For example, the **rehost** approach is the quickest and easiest way to move to the cloud.

Depending on the urgency, management might decide to take up such workloads as a priority or just to get some early wins on the board and then learn for future migrations. On the contrary, Refactor is the most time and effort consuming approach of all but provides an opportunity to optimize and modernize your workloads. Hence, some organizations may prefer such workloads to start in parallel to the rehost ones with a completely different and dedicated team. Of course, the order of migration is a planning topic with many more parameters to consider, including application inter-dependencies, scale, complexities, etc.

- **Cost of transformation**: Total cost of transformation, also known as **total cost of ownership (TCO)**, is one of the most important inputs for decision-makers. Hence, as part of the assessment, you must provide an estimate of TCO for the next three to five years in the final report. This TCO is the key component of the business case for cloud adoption and considers various components, such as:

  - o **Migration cost**: The cost of executing the cloud migration considers the resources required and planned/proposed duration. At the time of TCO estimate, you might not know the actual duration as it is the planning phase activity. However, you can always assume the number of migration waves and the number of servers/applications per migration wave to calculate the migration cost.

  - o On-premises infrastructure ramp-down can also be referred to as the reduction in TCO due to the decommissioning of on-premises resources as the migration to the cloud progresses.

  - o Infrastructure ramp-up cost on the cloud for the duration of migration; this component should provide the cost of ramping up the cloud resources based on a percentage growth every month. The percentage is usually based on best practices, experience, and your management's appetite to migrate and available resources.

  - o Steady state cost on cloud when the migration has finished as planned, you reach the steady state where you do not grow exponentially as in the migration phase, but stay with the same resources. You can still account for a minimal growth year on year in your cloud consumption and come up with three to five years of steady-state cost.

Various tools are used to calculate the TCO. The most common one is the native pricing calculator provided by the cloud providers (every cloud provider has their own version of the pricing calculator). Some discovery tools mentioned earlier also offer suggestions for the corresponding cloud resources and an estimate of cost (for example, the **Amazon Web Services** Migration Evaluator includes recommendations for target resources on AWS and associated cost based on various pricing models). When preparing a TCO report, you usually use a combination of these tools.

Discovery approach

The approach you use for discovery is as important as what to discover because that determines the time, cost, and quality of assessment. During the discovery, the objective is to learn the application and infrastructure inventory across all on-premises locations in as much detail as possible. This discovery is usually a mix of manual and tool-based methods. Let us look at this approach in more detail:

- Manual methods include workshops and interviews with **subject matter experts (SMEs)** and any relevant documentation, such as application architecture, data centre layout/networking architecture, infrastructure details, etc. Some of the crucial workshops you should conduct are given in the following table:

Workshop	Key stakeholders	Agenda
Strategy	IT leads and enterprise architects	Walkthrough of IT strategy and goals of the proposed cloud adoption
Applications and Services	Application **subject matter experts (SME)**, product owners, Dev leads, and operations leads	High-level discovery of the applications in the landscape to understand the type, function, high-level architecture, criticality/complexity classification, development, and operations methodology, etc.
Infrastructure	Infrastructure SMEs and operations leads.	Understanding of current infrastructure footprint, like virtualization, operating systems, hardware/virtual appliances, backups, HA and DR, DC tooling etc
Databases	Database administrators, application SMEs, and solution architects	Review current database footprint, hosting infrastructure, sizes, etc
Storage	Operations leads	Review the use of SAN/NAS devices, file servers, and corporate drives
Network	Network SMEs and architects	Discover the current network architecture, including network security
Security	Security SMEs and architects	Understand security, compliance, and risk posture and architecture, future requirements.

Workshop	Key stakeholders	Agenda
Operations/ Service management	Operations/service management leads and change management SMEs	Review current operations and processes, like incident management, change management, configuration management, etc.

Table 1.1: Discovery workshops

The information in the preceding table can be used as guidance and can be prepared to be customized to your situation. Sometimes SMEs are common (for example, infrastructure and storage or applications and databases), and hence, you can plan to curtail/combine multiple workshops into a single session to make it a productive and efficient use of time.

Preparation for every workshop is as necessary as the workshop itself. Your stakeholders would not like a session just for the sake of it, and there would be no productive outcome. Hence, prior reading of all relevant documentation, along with some questionnaires, is vital to drive the discussion during the workshop.

Plenty of tools are on the market, and the choice of tools depends on your needs and the partners you are working with. Tools can be agentless or agent-based. Some of the widely used and popular discovery tools are listed in the following table:

Tool name	Discovery method	Coverage	Additional notes/features
AWS migration evaluator	Agentless	Servers, storage, SQL Server databases	AWS proprietary tool discovers physical and virtual servers, free to use
Azure Migrate: discovery and assessment tool	Lightweight appliance	Server, SQL Server databases, web apps, virtual desktops	Discovers physical and virtual servers, provides recommendations on Azure sizing, provides cost estimates, free to use
Cloudamize	Agentless, Agent-based, or Login-based	Servers, storage systems, most databases, and network devices	Can provide application and server/software process dependency, license based
Flexera cloud migration and modernization	Agentless	Servers, storage systems, databases (SQL Server, MySQL, Oracle), network devices	Discovers physical and virtual servers, can provide application and server dependency, can discover most licenses as well, subscription-based pricing

Tool name	Discovery method	Coverage	Additional notes/features
Dynatrace	Agentless, Agent-based	Servers, storage systems, databases, network devices, and containers	Discovers physical and virtual servers, can provide application and server dependency, and subscription-based pricing
AppDynamics	Agent-based	Servers, databases, containers	Discovers physical and virtual servers, can provide application and server dependency, and subscription-based pricing
Datadog	Agentless, Agent-based	Servers, storage systems, most databases, network devices, and containers	Discovers physical and virtual servers, can provide application and server dependency, and subscription-based pricing

Table 1.2: Popular discovery tools

With most of these tools, data collection worth three to four weeks is sufficient to derive some meaningful results and use them for further analysis. However, there is no thumb rule.

Overall, it assesses an organization's readiness for cloud transformation. You will use the output of the assessment phase to prepare the business case and help management decide to move ahead with the proposed cloud adoption. That is why when you have done a thorough assessment, you would better know how much your organization is ready, what the gaps/issues are identified, and what it takes (in terms of cost, effort, and time) to address them to achieve the desired cloud goals.

Plan

Once the assessment is complete and progress with the proposed cloud adoption is endorsed (based on the **assessment** phase outcome and business case presented to management), the next phase in the journey is embarked upon—the **plan** phase.

During the planning phase, as the name suggests, you develop a detailed plan and roadmap to migrate your workloads to the cloud. Some key objectives of the planning phase are as follows:

- Develop a detailed migration plan
- Identify the appropriate resources for the job

- Build the necessary cloud foundations to host and support the workloads
- Application deep dive
- Refinement of TCO

Detailed migration plan

A migration plan is not a project plan. It is a plan that depicts near accuracy (near accuracy because there is always a scope of change when you actually implement the plan due to any unforeseen reason) sequencing of workloads for migration to the cloud. Key considerations to draw a migration plan (also called a wave plan**) are as follows:

- **Duration of the project**: A migration plan must assume a certain duration for the project. Duration of migration at this stage could be more of an educated guess driven by factors like data centre exit date, holiday shutdown period like *Christmas/New Year*, etc. Based on duration, you will create migration waves that could span multiple weeks. Each wave will have a number of workloads (or part of the workload) planned for migration by a migration team.

- **Multiple migration teams**: Usually, multiple migration teams work in parallel for such cloud programs. The logic behind deploying multiple teams is simply the velocity of migration. However, employing multiple teams does not mean throwing unlimited resources will complete the migration in an unrealistic time (say in three months instead of two years). Even if you throw multiple teams at the project, the pace will depend on various other factors like the complexity of applications, interdependencies, availability of key personnel, etc. The number and composition of migration teams also vary depending on the migration approach for your workloads. For example, you might have a migration team for rehost-type workloads and a separate team focused on refactoring-type workloads.

- **Number of workloads**: As is apparent, the number of workloads must be the most essential consideration while drawing up the cloud migration plan. Based on the number of workloads and assuming a realistic load per week and month, you will be able to calculate the estimated duration of the project.

- **Complexity of workloads**: Along with the number of workloads, the other parameters to consider for the workload's complexity are the size in terms of independent and dependent components, the number of environments for each workload (prod, dev, test etc.) and whether it is a bespoke application or a **commercial off the shelf** (**COTS**) application.

- **Size of workloads**: Size here includes various parameters, like components, environments, and servers.

- **Interdependency of workloads**: The majority of workloads do not work in isolation. With data flowing between workloads, there are interdependencies that make it difficult to move workloads separately. For example, if two applications share data with each other in real-time and if one of them is moved to Cloud, the network and data latency between both workloads can be a big issue.

Note: In terms of a migration plan, a wave is a migration group of workloads or components of workloads that can be migrated together after considering all dependencies, complexities, priorities, and functionalities.

Some of the best practices for creating a migration plan are listed here:

- Start with simple and smaller apps to learn and gain experience
- Plan the lower environments of the applications in the initial waves
- Plan applications with fewer servers in the initial waves
- Large applications with multiple moving parts and a large number of servers might need to be spread across multiple waves
- Migration planning is an iterative and ongoing process. Be prepared to make changes to the migration plan on the fly because the priorities might change.

Here is a sample wave plan based on a real-life case study (take note that the app names have been concealed). Refer to the following figure:

Week	Week1	Week2	Week3	Week4	Week5	Week6	Week7	Week8	Week9	Week10	Week11	Week12	Week13	Week14	Week15	Week16	Week17	Week18	Week19	Week20	Week21	Week22	Week23	Week24	Week25	Week26
Mig Team1	Wave1					Wave4						Wave7					Wave10					Wave13				
Apps/Env	App1, App2, App3					App4 (non-prod)						App4 (Prod)					App5 (Dev/Test), App6					App5 (Prod), App7				
Servers	15					15						31					20					22				
Mig Team2		Wave2					Wave5						Wave8					Wave11					Wave14			
Apps/Env		App8, App9					App9 (Dev) + App10 (Dev/Test)						App11 (Dev/Test), App12					App9 (Test), App10 (Prod)					App9 (Test), App11 (Prod)			
Servers		25					16						24					20					25			
Mig Team3		Wave3					Wave6						Wave9					Wave12								
Apps/Env		App13 (Dev1/SIT)					App14 (Dev)						App14 (Test), App13 (UAT/Dev2)					App14 (Prod), App13 (Prod)								
Servers		14					16						29					10								

Figure 4.1: Sample wave plan

Let us break it down and understand this sample wave plan:

- This is a 26-week wave plan, with each wave spanning five weeks on average. Five weeks per wave is average, but can be customized based on the complexity of the applications. For example, Wave14 is 4 weeks, and Wave12 is six weeks because applications covered in Wave14 are less complex, and those in Wave12 are high in complexity.
- Some applications have been spread across multiple waves, such as App4, App5, App9, etc. You plan your applications in a wave based on multiple factors listed earlier.
- Some large and complex applications have been split into multiple waves based on their environments. For example, App14 seems to be highly complex and has been split into three waves.
- Every app has been kept entirely to a particular team, i.e., an app has not been split across migration teams. This is to ensure that the learnings gained from migrating

a lower environment of an app stay within the team, and hence, the migration of higher environments becomes easy.

- A number of servers have been highlighted, along with the applications in each wave. It is an important factor, but not something set in stone as a magic number per migration wave. On average, try to keep the number of servers per wave around 20-25, but as mentioned earlier, there are many other factors that influence wave formation.

Appropriate resources

Once you develop a migration plan, it is also paramount to identify the best resources to work on the project. We talked about a migration team in the previous section. Let us understand about the composition of that team here.

Some important considerations for forming migration team(s) are as follows:

- A migration team should consist of some migration specialists and some SMEs from different parts of the organization based on their technical skills.

- Based on the platform and technology stack for the workloads identified as suitable for the cloud, there might be some specific skills you will need when moving them to the cloud, for example, Oracle DBAs or a NetApp storage specialist.

- Apart from the team directly working full-time on the cloud adoption project, there are various resources attached to the project indirectly or partially. For example, there are some executive roles who are responsible for overseeing the project's day to day progress or handling any project escalations.

- If there are multiple migration teams, then some resources might be shared between teams; for example, you would not need a project manager dedicated to each team.

Here is a sample resource plan based on a real-life case study:

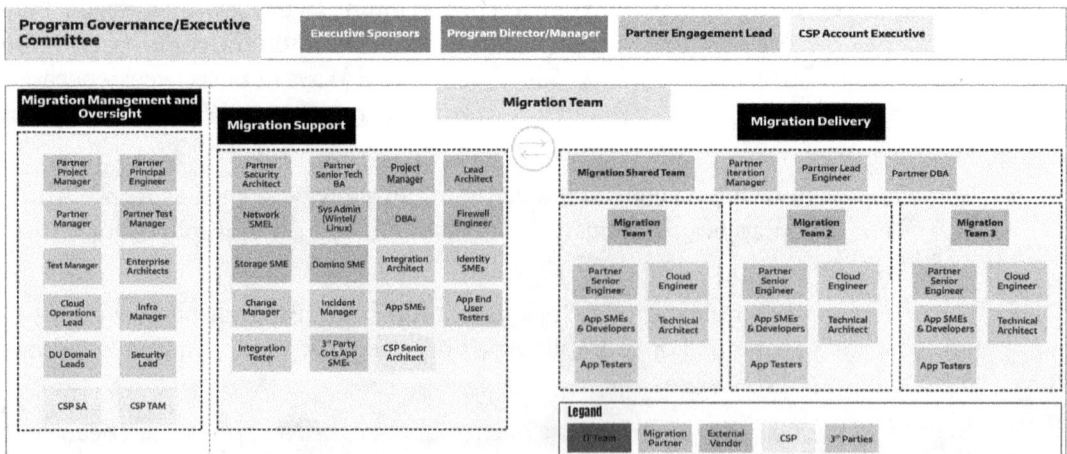

Figure 4.2: Typical migration project resource plan

Cloud foundations

While you are busy planning the migration and resources, another critical activity goes on in parallel. This is about designing and deploying the foundational elements inside your chosen cloud platform. Cloud foundations are the building blocks necessary to build a secure and scalable cloud environment for hosting workloads like security, networking, monitoring, etc.

Designing cloud foundations

The first part is the design of the cloud foundations, including a secure landing zone. A well-designed cloud foundation is key for the whole project's success and hence requires significant time, effort, and skill. You need cloud experts and the erstwhile infrastructure team working together to achieve the desired results.

A cloud landing zone is an environment in cloud consisting of multiple accounts/subscriptions built using the proven design principles and is used as the baseline to host the workloads. A landing zone is the starting point for your cloud deployment with default accounts/subscriptions and core infrastructure components.

Here is a look at some guiding design principles for a robust cloud foundation:

- Depending upon the level of security and isolation your company requires, consider an appropriate number of accounts/subscriptions in your cloud landing zone. For example, you can have accounts at an environment level (Prod, Test, Dev, etc.), or you can have an account per workload, or it could be based on business units, or a combination of any of these approaches to secure the resources at an even more granular level.

- Accounts and subscriptions are logical containers that are used to group and bill the cloud resources. They are given different names by every cloud provider, but the fundamentals are the same. For example, AWS calls them accounts, and Azure calls them subscriptions.

- Whatever approach you use for your landing zone, consider accounts or subscriptions as access boundaries (though they are a logical container only). You can then put guardrails and policies to restrict or provide access as required.

- Use guardrails to ensure the applications that will be hosted in your landing zone comply with governance policies customized to your organization. Azure provides Azure Policy, and AWS provides **service control policies** (**SCPs**) to implement this governance structure.

- The structure of the landing zone should allow future scalability without compromising on efficiency. Cost chargeback should be allowed by creating logical boundaries for application teams. With separate accounts/subscriptions based on departments or other logical boundaries, it is much easier to keep the relevant teams accountable for their cloud expenditures.

Designing for the cloud is critical and deserves much more attention. The next chapter (*Chapter 5, Designing for Cloud*) is dedicated to this, where we will look at some key design principles in the cloud and how the design of landing zones and applications in the cloud should adhere to them.

Deploying cloud foundations

Deployment is the actual implementation of the approved design that you did earlier. All cloud service providers provide tools and services to make the implementation easy and quick. For example:

- AWS provides a control tower and **Landing Zone Accelerator (LZA)**. The Control Tower provides a basic platform, and the LZA enhances the capabilities with automation. Both are used in conjunction to build a robust landing zone.

- Azure provides its own landing zone and accelerators to automate using infrastructure-as-code tools like **Azure Resource Manager (ARM)** templates.

The key takeaway is that deployment is done using the CSP's best practices, inbuilt recommended structure, and automated processes. This ensures you are all set to start hosting your workloads with the least manual effort.

Application deep dive

During the **assessment** phase, you would have gathered a list of all applications and assessed them at a high level to develop a migration approach (one out of 7Rs). When you are in the planning phase, you need to go deeper to work through the details of each application identified as suitable for the cloud. The output of this activity feeds into the migration plan that we discussed earlier and is very important for preparing application-specific playbooks (discussed in the next section).

As part of the high-level assessment during the assessment phase, you would have gathered some helpful information about the applications, like the type of application, high-level tech stack, and application owners. In this phase, you would use that information to build on it via focused workshops with application teams using detailed questionnaires. For example, some typical application-specific questions asked at this point are as follows:

App details should answer the following questions:

- How many environments are in total?

- If it is a commercial off-the-shelf application, who is the vendor, and what is the version?

- What is the technology stack, programming languages used, etc.?
- What is the type of load balancing used?
- Any hardcoded values in the application code?

Databases should answer the following questions:

- What is the associated database type and version?
- Are there any embedded SQL code or stored procedures in use?
- Any database sharing with other applications?

Security should answer the following questions:

- How is the logging/monitoring performed?
- Is there a data classification for this application?
- What are the data encryption requirements?

Testing should answer the following questions:

Do you have any existing test cases to cover unit testing, user acceptance testing, and integration tests?

Do you have any performance-related nonfunctional requirements or service level agreements that must be met after migration to the cloud?

Integrations should answer the following questions:

- List all the incoming and outgoing integrations/data flows for this application
- List all the external/internal integrations for this application.
- Are there known latency requirements for each integration?

Note: Hard-coded values are a big concern when migrating applications to the cloud, especially if there are IPs embedded in the application code. When moving to the cloud, the IPs change, and hence, you will need to make appropriate changes in the code to remediate that.

One of this detailed assessment's main objectives is to understand the application's complexity. As mentioned earlier, the complexity of the application is a major input to the migration planning process. Usually, the application owners are in the best position to determine the complexity of the application; however, here is a matrix that can be used for general guidance:

	Low	Medium	High
Criticality	Not Critical/Standard	Business Critical	Mission Critical
Integrations	0 or 1	1 to 5	6 or more
On-Prem Dependencies	None	There are but not latency sensitive	There are and latency sensitive
Data size	< 300G	upto 1 TB	> 1 TB
DB version	Latest and Supported	EOL with extended support available	EOL with no support
OS version	Latest and Supported	EOL with extended support available	EOL with no support
COTS/in-house	In-house	COTS	COTS
COTS product version	Latest and Supported	EOL with extended support	EOL and unsupported
Number of Servers	upto 3	upto 10	more than 10

Figure 4.3: Application complexity matrix

Refinement of TCO

TCO is calculated as part of the assessment phase, and it is one of the inputs for management to make decisions for future phases of the journey. However, note that in the planning phase, you have gone into the next level of application and server landscape details. It is possible to uncover unknown things at the time of initial assessment, or you would have changed the migration approach for some of the applications. Hence, during the planning phase, you should revisit the TCO and make any changes to make the numbers closer to precision.

Execute

The most hands-on phase of the journey is where the action starts, i.e., the migration of workloads to the cloud with the solid foundation built in the previous two phases. During the initial part of this phase, the team validates the outcome of prior phases and ensures everything is ready, for example, whether the landing zone is as per requirements or if all the eligible applications have been analysed. However, the main work in this phase can be grouped into two streams:

- **Preparation for migration**: As part of this stream, your team works with the application SMEs to prepare the application-specific playbooks. Your application deep dive in the planning phase is a key input to creating these playbooks.

  An application playbook (also called runbook) is a step-by-step list of activities that should be performed to migrate the application to the cloud and includes application-specific considerations. This artifact covers all environments of the application and must consist of any do's and not that the migration team should keep in mind while migrating the application.

Apart from the application migration playbooks, the other important set of activities performed in the stream is defining the governance procedures, such as the communication plan, escalation plan, and project management procedures.

- **Migration**: As the name suggests, this stream works on the actual migration of the application based on the playbook created by the other stream. As you execute migrations, you monitor and improve.

Though these are two separate streams of work, but not necessarily two different teams altogether. Resources are usually shared across both teams; for example, a cloud architect could be leading the migration stream but can participate in the process of application deep dives and playbook preparations. Usually, these two workstreams run in parallel rather than in sequence, but the preparation stream should be a few weeks ahead of the migration stream so that migration teams have everything they need to start the migration.

Migration factory

As the migration progresses, you need to make the whole process efficient and fast by creating repeatable patterns and standard procedures. Partly this is based on past experiences, and partly through a gradual evolution based on your learnings from each migration wave. You also automate a lot of procedures to make the migrations more efficient. The idea is to execute large-scale migrations in a factory manner, i.e., migrate fast based on the standard patterns rather than reinventing the wheel constantly and continuously improving. A migration factory refers to multiple teams working in parallel to execute large-scale migrations using a set of design patterns and operating procedures that evolve and improve continuously.

Tools for trade

Cloud migration and adoption is a well-explored space, and that is probably why there is no dearth of tools that help you with every phase of cloud adoption, from discovery to operations and billing. Similarly, migration is one of those phases where plenty of tools have been launched, including some from the **cloud service providers** (**CSPs**). Of course, the CSPs do it to make the move to cloud a more lucrative end-to-end package.

The choice of tool mainly depends on the cloud approach you have finalized for your application (one of the 7Rs). Most tools available in the market are meant to expedite your lift and shift type of migration (rehost), also known as block-level migration. Some of the popular ones are as follows:

- AWS Application Migration Service
- AWS Database Migration Service
- Azure Migrate
- Google Cloud Migration Centre

For the refactor and re-platform type of migration, there is no single tool that can just do the migration without any manual intervention, as in the case of most rehost type migrations. Since there is an element of re-architecture involved, most tools used for such migrations are code-based and likely part of a larger DevOps strategy. For example, AWS native tools like AWS CodePipeline, AWS CodeBuild, etc., or third-party tools like GitHub.

Note: The choice of tool depends on various factors, like the migration approach, affordable downtime, application size, etc. Hence, there may not be a one solution for every use case.

Operate

The final phase of the cloud adoption journey is when you focus on ensuring the workloads on the cloud are running smoothly and as expected. Apparently, there is a lot of focus on monitoring and troubleshooting, and the most important team here is the support team or the managed service providers (partners) who ensure normal operations. In cloud terminology, it is also called the CloudOps team. Though it sounds trivial, it is not less significant than any other phase of the journey because poor operations can spoil all the good work done during the initial phases and minimize the benefits of the cloud that you contemplated while planning the adoption.

Talking CloudOps is different from traditional information technology operations in terms of tools and procedures. In fact, it is a combination of traditional IT operations and DevOps applied to a cloud computing world. As in the traditional data-centric world, you would have operational procedures and tools to manage the infrastructure; in the cloud computing world, you have the Cloud-specific procedures and tools (jointly referred to as CloudOps) to manage the cloud infrastructure. However, unlike traditional IT operations that are manual, CloudOps aims to automate management processes as much as possible by adopting DevOps principles.

Operating in cloud is the last phase, but ideally, the operations team, i.e., the CloudOps team, should be involved in all phases of the journey so that they understand the Cloud foundation, landing zone, and workloads on them to devise or tailor specific processes that were not relevant in the legacy data centre world. For organizations that are new to the cloud adoption journey, every team struggles, including the CloudOps team. That is why, if they are brought in early, the exposure is much greater, and there is much more appreciation of how the cloud is different from the traditional data-centric world.

This phase is not only about keeping the lights on. There is another crucial part of this phase—finding opportunities to modernize your applications i.e. you continue to evolve your applications on cloud and look at adopting cloud-native services or rearchitect the applications to use modern frameworks like microservices, containers, serverless, or a combination leading into a potential second phase of cloud adoption for some applications that were just moved to cloud as-is in the initial phase.

Tools for trade

CloudOps could be a combination of various tools. There are multiple **CSP provided** native tools that can be used in combination with external tools to provide a meaningful and efficient operability of your cloud infrastructure. The tools you choose should provide capabilities such as monitoring, alerting, and comprehensive reporting/dashboards that aid in the decision-making process. Some of the popular tools are as follows:

- CSP provided native tools
  - AWS CloudWatch
  - Azure Monitor
- External tools
  - Splunk
  - Dynatrace

Conclusion

In this chapter, we explored cloud adoption divided into four phases: assess, plan, execute, and operate. we looked into the details of each phase and looked at approaches and tools to accomplish the tasks in each phase. The outcome of the assessment and discovery done in the first phase is an important trigger for the future phases as it gives a good indication of what to expect from the executive leadership regarding cloud adoption, primarily from the financial aspects.

There are also the technical aspects, like migration feasibility and complexity, that are looked at. The planning phase sets the foundation for the migration by drawing out a detailed migration plan and implementing cloud foundations in your chosen cloud platform. The first two phases are actually the backbone of the whole adoption and, if not done correctly, can lead to undesirable results in the later phases of the journey. We also looked at sample migration plans and resource plans for the migration projects. One of the important aspects of moving to the cloud is the design of cloud landing zones and the design of applications for the cloud based on certain design principles. In this chapter, we touched upon the landing zone design. We will look into the design aspect in detail in the next chapter.

Points to remember

Here are some key takeaways from this chapter:

- There are four phases of the cloud adoption journey—assess, plan, execute, and operate.

- The assess phase focuses on:
  - Discovery of current infrastructure and application footprint
  - It can be either tool-based, manual, or a combination of both approaches
  - The key outcomes are the detailed TCO and an agreed migration approach for each workload in scope

- The planning phase focuses on:
  - Developing a detailed migration plan considering factors like complexity and size of each application
  - Creating a resource plan to execute the migration. A cross-functional collaboration is required across the organization to execute the following:
  - Designing and deploying a cloud foundation (landing zone) that will be used for hosting the workloads
  - Application-specific deep dive and analysis to come up with migration playbooks for each application in scope

- The migration phase focuses on:
  - Migrating the workloads to the cloud using an appropriate approach and tools

- Operate phase focused on:
  - Operating the migrated workloads in the cloud and ensuring efficient monitoring and reporting using the appropriate tools
  - Look for potential opportunities to modernize the workloads in the cloud, i.e., microservices, containerize, etc.

Join our book's Discord space

Join the book's Discord Workspace for Latest updates, Offers, Tech happenings around the world, New Release and Sessions with the Authors:

https://discord.bpbonline.com

CHAPTER 5
Designing for Cloud

Introduction

In this chapter, we will start venturing into more technical aspects of cloud architecture. We will talk about an important concept called **Well-Architected Framework (WAF)**, along with various design principles and cloud-specific architecture best practices that differentiate application architecture on the cloud from the traditional ways of designing applications. This chapter will serve as a reference for understanding WAF across AWS, Azure, and GCP, covering key design principles, best practices, and recommendations for designing infrastructure and applications in the cloud.

Designing applications and infrastructure for the cloud is different from the way we have been doing it in the legacy on-premises world. The focus of this chapter is to understand the guiding principles and architecture best practices for designing and deploying workloads on the cloud. To make it more engaging, we will channel the discussion through a set of architectural themes, often called pillars or categories of a WAF. We will also look at WAF and its definitions, given by three major cloud providers—AWS, MS Azure, and **Google Cloud Provider (GCP)**.

Structure

In this chapter, we will cover the following topics:

- Components of a cloud architecture

- Design principles
- Cloud architecture best practices
- Operations
- Performance management
- Well- architected framework

Objectives

By the end of the chapter, readers would have learned how to make the right design choices for hosting their workloads on the cloud, along with the industry-proven best practices.

Components of a cloud architecture

Ideally, an application on cloud infrastructure should not be vastly different from the same application on an on-premises infrastructure in terms of functionality and behaviour—at least, that is the intent of business when adopting the cloud for its applications. However, the underlying architecture and the definitions of common design principles may be different because of the way cloud infrastructure is laid out and delivered to customers.

The fundamental architecture design principles, like security, scalability, high availability, etc, are applicable to an application's architecture regardless of where it is hosted – cloud or on-premises. However, the way these design principles are applied in the physical on-premises setup is very different from the way similar design principles are applied in the cloud world. These principles can be grouped under some common themes and we will focus on five such key themes in the rest of this chapter but from a cloud lens. These are the same as the categories or pillars of the WAF proposed by most cloud providers, and hence, the concepts around design principles and best practices will be much more relatable and consistent. Though WAF will also be discussed a little later in this chapter, at this point, it is important to introduce these themes of cloud architecture because they will be used as a foundation for the discussion in the rest of the chapter. These themes are as follows:

- **Security**: Security is paramount to every application and every hosting solution. It becomes even more contentious (or rather concerning) on the cloud as you move out of the comfort of your data centre to a cloud provider's data centre.

- **Operations**: Not only do you build, but you also need to operate the applications and infrastructure efficiently, making sure they run as expected, i.e., meet **service level agreements** (**SLAs**), have no unnecessary outages, do proper monitoring and alerting, etc.

- **Reliability**: All production applications have SLAs and **recovery point objective** (**RPO**)/**recovery time objective** (**RTO**) requirements that are crucial to the reliability component. The legacy approaches to improving the reliability of workloads on on-premises infrastructure were manual and constrained by the physical nature of the infrastructure. This changes completely on the cloud, with inbuilt features (like regions and zones) and various cloud-native services.

- **Cost optimization**: One of the main reasons customers are looking to adopt cloud technology is its ability to optimize costs. Though the cloud is not a magic bullet, if used carefully and intelligently, there are opportunities to make some noticeable savings.

- **Performance management**: The essential requirement for any application is to meet and maintain the expected performance. To achieve performance goals in the legacy world, you usually throw more resources at it and, most of the time, get stuck with hardware limitations. However, these limitations can be bypassed in the cloud world with features like autoscaling, automated health monitoring, better and faster infrastructure provisioning cycles, and many more.

Let us use these themes to discuss the design principles and best practices in the rest of the chapter. Hopefully, you should now have a basic premise for things to come later.

Design principles

Design principles are the guiding principles, general rules, and considerations you should follow when architecting applications. As said earlier, at a high level, the principles remain the same, but the definitions might change for the cloud. We will now explore key cloud-specific design principles aligned with each of our five architectural themes:

Security

The fundamental premise for cloud security is a Zero Trust approach. This approach means that no one should be trusted, even if they are internal to the organization, and hence, the security controls should be strong, granular, and at every layer of your network. This is contrary to the legacy mindset where internal users had open access to everything inside the network, hence posing a huge security risk by exposing all the sensitive information to even a hacker if they successfully break into the organization's network. Let us look at some of the security design principles that make up this approach:

- **Foundational design**: As the name suggests, the foundational design for security on the cloud consists of all those critical components to ensure safe and secure hosting and operations of your workloads. Foundational security consists of everything that should be done to operate your workloads on the cloud safely.

- **Identity and access management (IAM)**: Identities are the entities that need access to your resources. They include both humans and machines internal to your organization, but sometimes could be external as well, and you need a mechanism to manage them efficiently and securely in a consolidated and centralized identity system. This includes their authentication and authorization to the services and applications hosted on the cloud.

- **Detect and resolve**: This design principal advocates capturing application and infrastructure logs regularly and having a system in place to analyse and visualize the logs to proactively identify all security threats, non-compliance or unusual activities within your network. Another important aspect of early detection is configuring appropriate notifications and alerts wherever possible. Real-time monitoring can be integrated with policies and measures that allow automatic remediation of specific issues, leading to fewer downtimes.

- **Improve and evolve**: You should be on top of your game regarding security, be it cloud or on-premises. Of course, security on the cloud is much more scrutinized as imposters are coming up with new ways of intruding on your network. That is why you should regularly audit your current state and be aware of the latest trends and developments in security tooling and patching. Security is an ever-evolving space rather than a one-off activity. You need to keep improving your security posture by regularly monitoring and auditing the efficacy of controls and introducing new tools as the old ones become ineffective in dealing with the latest attacks.

- **Layered security architecture**: Your architecture typically consists of multiple layers or tiers, like the presentation layer, application layer, database layer, etc. The physical infrastructure also consists of layers like **demilitarised zone (DMZ)**, virtual LANs, firewalls, servers, etc. To face the toughest of attacks, you need to introduce security at every layer of your architecture. Multiple layers of security mean any unauthorized penetration is much more difficult.

- **Data protection**: One of the critical security principles is protecting your data throughout its lifecycle, i.e., from acquisition to visualization. The most obvious control to protect data that one can implement is the encryption of data in transit and at rest. Encryption of data also involves what keys to use and how to even secure the keys used for encryption. You also need to safeguard your data from malicious actors with a robust access and authorization system, i.e., IAM, which was discussed earlier as a separate design principle.

Operations

Operating the workloads is as important as building them. You need to ensure the workloads are supported efficiently so they deliver the right outcomes. The following design principles are focused on delivering operational excellence by introducing a cultural shift to the traditional ways of operations. Let us look at them in detail:

- **DevOps culture**: It is undoubtedly one of the most successful and embraced philosophies in recent times, aimed at bringing agility, automation, and efficiency in development and operational procedures. The idea is to encourage collaboration and communication between the development and operational teams so that they work as a single unit and, hence, attain the required efficiency and continuous improvement.

- **Observability**: Operations is about knowing your workloads, how they behave, and the **key performance indicators** (**KPIs**). Gain visibility into your workloads by deploying monitoring tools that capture logs and telemetry data consistently. Use observability data to make the right decisions, improve the performance of your workloads, and take action in real-time.

- **Automation**: The beauty of the cloud is that almost everything can be coded like any application code, i.e., the entire workload (including infrastructure and operations) can be coded. The operations associated with those workloads can then be automated because you are eventually triggering a piece of code when required or based on some events or alerts like CPU utilization going beyond a threshold. Automation is not only efficient but also helps eliminate human errors that are usually related to legacy operations.

- **Cloud managed services**: Use native cloud services as much as possible. When your architecture consists of self-hosted components on some EC2 instances, you are responsible for all the related management of the resources. However, using PaaS services (cloud-managed services), you can offload the administration part to the cloud provider. For example, the **Relational Database Service** (**RDS**) on AWS is a managed database service, and hence, AWS is responsible for various administrative tasks like backups, minor upgrades, etc.

Reliability

Reliability of a workload is the confidence you have in your workload that they will perform as expected under the worst circumstances. Failures do happen all the time, and hence, you should make the workloads reliable and resilient to failures. Resiliency is a concept we will discuss in detail in *Chapter 10, Cloud Resiliency*.

Here are some strategies to enhance the reliability of the workloads on the cloud:

- **Redundancy**: Avoid **single points of failure** (**SPOFs**). You need to have redundancy built into every component of your workload, at least the critical ones. Redundancy means copies of standby for every element so that if the primary fails, a backup node can take over the operations. Remember, introducing redundancy comes with additional cost, but that also means improved workload reliability.

- **Self-healing architecture**: Design architectures that can detect failures and recover automatically. This is called self-healing because no manual intervention results in less downtime and improved workload reliability. Essential components of the self-healing architecture are autoscaling and regular automated health checks of your resources. These are some of the core availability features on every cloud.

- **Application architecture**: Design your application architectures on the cloud to implicitly provide better reliability. For example, use cloud-native features like availability zones to spread resources and provide redundancy for better reliability.

- **Backups**: A robust backup policy is the backbone of reliability regardless of the underlying hosting platform. The backup tools and procedures might work differently on the cloud, but regular backups and snapshots are key to ensuring that the desired RPOs and RTOs are met. It is also important to consider backup storage so that timely retrieval is possible.

- **Test recovery approach**: Test your recovery strategies and procedures often to ensure they work as expected in a real scenario and minimize the risk. This includes testing the backups. On the cloud, you have the luxury of simulating the failure scenarios using various automation features and tools.

Cost optimization

Worrying about cost might seem like a non-technical area that architects need not worry about. However, cost optimization strategies should be considered when designing workloads on the cloud. Some of them are mentioned as follows:

- **Resource consumption model**: On the cloud, leverage the different types of consumption models the provider offers. Fundamentally, they all have reserved consumption models for lump sum and long-term commitments, which means higher discounts when you commit to a specific capacity for a certain duration (usually one year or three years).

- **Capacity planning**: Unlike the on-premises world of physical hardware, you do not need to plan your capacity months in advance and oversize the infrastructure. You should start at a small or optimal size and use techniques like autoscaling to scale out/in based on demand. Hence, there is no need to guess the capacity and overprovision in anticipation.

- **Monitor and optimize**: Continuously monitor your resources' usage to measure and analyze the utilization over a period. Based on the utilization analysis, you may be able to right-size your resources to avoid wastage and optimize costs. All cloud providers have native tools to monitor resource utilization; for example, AWS has a tool called cost optimizer or uses native monitoring tools like CloudWatch.

- **Accountability**: One of the most undervalued yet essential design principles is making users accountable for their spending. This is highly recommended in the cloud, where the costs can shoot sky-high if not managed by the end users. Once you make people accountable for what and where they are spending, there will automatically be a lot of control over costs. The best way to do this is to use a feature called tags. Tagging every resource based on groups or departments and then producing cost reports based on those tags can give valuable insights into the spending trends.

- **Guardrails**: To control your spending, it is also important to use guardrails along with tags. Tags alone will not do the trick, but when complemented with guardrails, you can avoid overspending and wastage. Guardrails can be implemented using policies, budgets, and spending limits using various native cloud services.

Performance management

The performance design principle is about the workload being able to deliver the desired performance and user experience under any load and demand. With an increase in load, the user experience should not be compromised. Here are some tips to improve your performance:

- **Realistic performance goals**: Always set realistic and achievable goals based on the historical data collected. Setting high standards without any evidence will lead to frustration and repeated failures. Use cloud resources efficiently to meet the agreed performance targets.

- **Take data closer to the end users**: Go global and deploy your resources across multiple cloud zones and regions to cater to global users. Services like **content delivery network (CDN)** greatly improve the request/response time by caching the data closer to users. The idea is to bring data and its processing closer to the end users and to provide a better user experience.

- **Performance testing**: The Cloud is evolving continuously with rapid innovations, new features, and services. Use them generously and regularly test your workloads' performance with varied types of resources on the cloud. Testing is also important to ensure the performance is not degrading for any reason. Using **infrastructure as code (IaC)** and automated procedures, conducting tests is quick and repetitive.

- **Monitor and optimize**: As with other architecture themes, monitoring is important for performance as well. Make sure you have enough monitoring and logging tools to collect data that can be used to continuously fine-tune the performance of your workloads.

- **Choose appropriate cloud services**: Understand your application and consumption patterns to choose the cloud services judiciously. Most cloud providers provide services and variations of those services that align with different consumption patterns. If not chosen wisely, this will not only hurt your performance but can hurt your purse as well.

Cloud architecture best practices

While design principles provide generic guidance in each area of architecture, best practices are more specific. They can go a level deeper than the principles (or consider them an extension of the principles). With the previously discussed architecture components and design principles as a base, we will look at some industry best practices pertinent to the cloud.

Security

Security is all about protecting everything that makes up your workloads: data, compute, networks, and everything else that constitutes the architecture. The prescribed best practices here will focus on all things cloud security, and we will highlight wherever they relate to any of the design principles discussed in the previous section. These best practices are essential for protecting applications, data and ensuring compliance with various regulatory requirements like GDPR, HIPAA, PCI DSS etc. All of these regulations have specific requirements around security controls and standards. This is where the security best practices play a vital role in meeting the mandatory requirements i.e. the how to achieve the regulatory compliance.

Here are some of the security best practices:

- **Landing zone that has separation of workloads**: Use multi-account/multi-subscription structure. There can be separate accounts for each workload or environment or a combination of both. All cloud providers offer native services to help you design/plan the structure. The benefits of this practice are:

  o Isolation between workloads and hence reduced blast radius if any account/ subscription gets hacked

  o Policies can be implemented at workload level

- **Harden the development practices**: Use a multi-account/multi-subscription structure. There can be separate accounts for each workload or environment or a combination of both. All cloud providers offer native services to help you design/ plan the structure. The benefits are listed here:

  o A secured application, free of vulnerabilities

  o A proactive approach to risk management

- **Stay vigilant about the new security threats and vulnerabilities**: Use cloud-native or external services to stay up to date and make sure the required patches/fixes are applied proactively. For example, services like Amazon Inspector maintain a database of **common vulnerabilities and exposures (CVEs)**. The benefit of this practice is the reduced risk of attacks if the latest patches have been applied.

- **Classify your data**: Label your data according to its sensitivity classification. Some workloads are more sensitive than others and require different design considerations like encryption, storage, etc. Use tags wherever possible. The main benefit of classification is that you can have design strategies and patterns based on the data classification

- **Reduce your scope of security**: Evaluate and use the managed services provided by cloud providers. This will reduce the scope and let you use the built-in security of the cloud provider. There are multiple benefits such as:

- o   Most heavy lifting is done by the cloud provider

- o   Better and optimized use of resources

- **Role based access control (RBAC)**: RBAC and the principle of least privileges are the fundamental concepts in the IAM space. To implement RBAC, every cloud provider has the concept of users, groups, and roles. Always start with granting the least privileges required to perform the duties based on their job requirements. Grant permission to groups based on roles instead of individual users. The main benefits are:

  - o   Protect sensitive data from unauthorized access

  - o   Compliance and regulatory purpose

  - o   Operational efficiency

- **Safeguard the identities**: Use strong password policy and **multi-factor authentication (MFA)** to protect your identities. Also, store your passwords securely using native services or external vaults. For example, you can use AWS Secrets Manager to store and rotate passwords. The main benefits are:

  - o   MFA provides additional security on top of usual passwords

  - o   Protect against unauthorized access to your systems

  - o   Secure storage for identities

- **Centralised identity system**: This is especially true for large enterprises; having multiple identity systems scattered across various departments or groups leads to confusion and inconsistency. Create a single source of truth by adopting something like an Azure Entra ID or any other proven **identity and access management (IDAM)** solution. The main benefits of having a centralised identity systems are:

  - o   A central identity system is easier to manage

  - o   Single and consistent view of every user accessing the systems

- **Layered security architecture**: Use cloud-native or third-party tools to provide security at every architecture layer. For example, in AWS, use security groups at the server level, use **network access control lists (NACLs)** at the subnet level, use a network firewall to protect all infrastructure traffic and all application traffic, and use a **web application firewall (WAF)**.

  Only have the public-facing tier of the application in a public subnet; all other tiers should be in a private subnet with no exposure to the internet. A layered security architecture provides multiple levels of security for your cloud infrastructure and workloads

- **Data encryption**: Enforce https instead of http for all your internet traffic to ensure all data is encrypted in transmission. Encrypt all the storage services to ensure data at rest is also encrypted. Most cloud providers offer encryption by default for most of their services. You can use your keys or the CSP-provided keys. Secure the keys used for encryption. The main benefits are:

- o Data in transit and data at rest are encrypted instead of plain text

- o No unauthorized access to data if keys are secured

• Detect, investigate, and resolve—make sure logging is configured at the application and infrastructure level. Alerts and notifications should be configured. Automate remediation of security alerts wherever possible. The main benefits are:

- o Sufficient logging ensures proper **root cause analysis** (**RCA**)

- o Automated remediation ensures quick response to security incidents

Operations

The operational efficiency in architecture ensures that appropriate support during the development process is provided and the cloud's post-development maintenance and running of workloads is smooth. To achieve this, people and teams should be organized to support business functions. The operational processes should be efficient enough to provide granular insights that can help further improve and evolve the processes. The following are some of the recommended practices that should be adopted to deliver the desired business value:

• **Develop a cloud operating model**: Assess the capabilities and organize internal teams accordingly. Encourage cross-team collaboration. For example, involve the operations team in the development process and vice versa. Keep evolving and improving the operating model. A cloud operating model should span people, processes, and technology. Internal teams must be well-organized to build a successful cloud operating model.

• **Align teams with organizational priorities**: Understand internal and external customer requirements and adjust the teams' focus accordingly. Encourage architecture governance by defining and mandating the organization's design and development standards and policies. For example, coding standards, specific server types, or specific roles and permissions. Understanding organization's priorities helps in many ways, such as:

- o Customer requirements and deliverables should be well understood and shared by all teams so that everyone is involved and accountable.

- o Architecture governance ensures workloads are compliant with internal policies and industry best practices.

• **Implement observability**: Enable logging and tracing at the application and infrastructure level. Add alerts and notifications for critical events. Store and analyse all collected data regularly to gain actionable insights. The main benefits of a robust observability framework are listed here:

o You can be proactive and prevent issues rather than reacting to them with the recommended measures.

o Improved user experience.

- **Streamline the change and release management processes**: Have a rollback plan for unsuccessful deployments. Have clear ownership of all components and processes in a central register that should be used for all change management procedures. Reduce production defects with subsequent releases by adopting approaches like using version control, testing every change, and automating the delivery, build, and deployment procedures. Make frequent and small releases instead of fewer large ones to make the cycle smaller and the process manageable. Here are some clear benefits:

   o A rollback plan indicates you are ready for failed deployments or bugs in production.

   o Ownership of components makes the change and release management processes smooth, as you know who the point of contact is in case of issues.

   o Optimizing the release management helps reduce the defects gradually.

Frequent and smaller releases are more manageable and quicker with fewer moving parts.

- **Operational readiness of workloads**: Assess if your workloads are ready to be operationalized with a checklist of must-haves. Assess if the skills required to support the workload are available in the team. Prepare a list of known issues, if any, for your workloads. The main benefits of being ready are:

   o Poor operational readiness leads to team frictions, longer outages, and eventually a poor user experience. Hence, a workload ready to be operationalised has much larger downstream gains.

   o Ready workload means the team is ready as well and not caught unaware.

- **Improve operational procedures**: Define a process to review past incidents and their resolutions. Maintain knowledge repositories of incidents and defects for future reference. Continuous improvement and evolution can be achieved if there is a process in place to learn from previous incidents. Repeating the same mistakes is detrimental to the overall reputation, efficiency, and performance of the team.

- **Automate operational procedures**: Automate deployments using native or external **continuous integration/continuous deployment (CI/CD)** tools. Along with applications, it also automates the deployment of infrastructure. Also, procedures like server startup and shutdown can be easily automated using event-driven architecture. With automation in place, SMEs can be freed up from mundane operational tasks.

Reliability

Reliability is the trust your users have in your workload to deliver the expected output whenever required in a consistent manner. The following is a list of industry-proven best practices to design and build reliable workloads:

- **Multi-region and multi-zone architecture**: Create active-active or active-passive architectures across multiple zones and multiple regions (if there are no compliance concerns). Use cloud resources that can be spread across multiple zones or regions, for example—AWS EC2 or AWS RDS. Include constructs like a load balancer to distribute traffic. The main benefits of such an architecture are:

  o Multi-zone and multi-region architectures provide enhanced availability.

  o Multi-region architectures provide better performance for global users.

- **Build reliable networks**: Build redundancy for your network connections, for ex-redundant network links from the on-premises network to cloud. Use cloud-managed services that provide highly available endpoints. An increased reliability and resiliency of the underlying network also improves the accessibility and availability of your workloads.

- **Microservices-based application architecture**: Segment your application based on business functionality, build loosely coupled architectures with queuing services as an intermediate layer and use an integration mechanism to allow cross-service communication. The main benefits of these practices are:

  o Failure of a component/service does not impact the whole application because the failure is localized and not distributed to the whole application.

  o Maintenance of individual components/services can be performed without impacting the whole application.

- **Implement idempotent architectures**: Design the application to return the same results for every workflow if executed repeatedly. This can be achieved by storing the results for common workflows. Idempotency ensures that multiple requests of the same type produce the same result every time, hence improving the reliability of the system.

- **Use throttling**: Establish the maximum capacity of your workload using load testing and design so that it handles the number of requests accordingly. Also, include an error and retry logic. With a throttling strategy, the workload functions normally without failure in case the load increases because the excess requests are being throttled and not eyeing for resources simultaneously.

- **Design stateless applications**: Instead of stateful applications, store the system state in a separate data store to avoid using local storage. Also, plan on using serverless services provided by cloud providers, for example, AWS Lambda functions. The main benefit of a stateless architecture is that stateless applications can withstand failures to a component much better as the failed nodes can be replaced without impacting the application.

- **Backup strategy**: Identify the data sources and their **recovery point objective (RPO)** values. Understand the backup requirements based on data types, for example, incremental backups for transactional databases and weekly or monthly full backups for cold data. The main benefit of a robust backup strategy is that a robust backup strategy improves the availability of applications and avoids data loss. Data can be restored and recovered in case of an outage to meet the RPO requirements.

- **Automated healing**: Configure the components for restart or retries wherever possible. Use autoscaling strategies Make sure the design has sufficient nodes to bear the loss of some nodes and that the applications continue to function. With auto-healing capabilities, applications can withstand failures efficiently because new nodes will spin up automatically upon failure.

- **Include monitoring for availability and notifications**: Use cloud-native or third-party monitoring tools to check for availability periodically. Configure alerts and notifications in case of a component failure. Proactive monitoring and notifications will enable proactive actions and remediation and, hence the improved availability of applications.

- **Be aware of SLAs**: Identify your workload's RPO/RTO and design the DR strategies per the agreed RPO/RTO values. When architects are aware of the SLAs, the application components can be designed and customized accordingly instead of using standard design patterns.

Cost optimization

As a business, you always want to deliver the desired value at the lowest cost. Developing an efficient FinOps model is the key to cost governance, cost control, and optimization on the cloud with close collaboration between finance and technology. Here we will highlight some best practices that can help you develop and implement a cost-optimization strategy:

- **Manage costs using budgeting and forecasting**: Create budgets and forecasts based on historical trends. Understand the granularity of your budgets, i.e., department, project, account/subscription, etc. Regularly review and update if required. Budgets and forecasts help to set limits, track costs, and act promptly if required. They will set expectations and create a sense of accountability for the teams.

- **Monitoring and alerting**: Set budgets for regions and departments and use alerts to notify if budget thresholds are exceeded. This process should be automated for weekly, monthly, or yearly periods. Most cloud providers offer native reporting tools that provide insights into resource costing and usage and cost optimization opportunities. The main benefits are:

- o Accurate reporting is a potent tool in the cost governance framework

- o Notifications can help the stakeholders respond timely and rectify mistakes causing the cost thresholds to be breached.

- **Rate optimization**: Regularly review your cloud costs and keep a check on cloud market competition. Since there is a lot of competition in the cloud market, if you keep a check on current costs and market competition, rate optimization and negotiations can be done accordingly.

- **Data collection and reporting**: Generate regular costing and billing reports. All cloud providers have native reporting tools and dashboards. Choose an appropriate frequency and granularity for your cost and usage reports. The main benefits are:

  - o Reporting aids in better analysis and understanding of high-cost areas.

  - o Any abnormal spikes in cost can be easily tracked.

- **Enforce accountability**: Use tagging to implement showback and chargeback so that internal teams are held accountable and can be billed for their spend on cloud.

- **Right-size the resources**: Use the resource utilization data to check the trends over days and weeks (especially during peak hours). Right size (downsize) the resources if utilization data suggests oversizing and underutilization. It is a common practice to oversize the resources and incur abnormal costs on the cloud. Right-sizing is an effective approach for reducing cloud spend.

- **Choose the correct cloud consumption models**: Consider reserving capacity to get cheaper pricing than the regular on-demand pricing. Use a savings plan on compute capacity (a billing model most CSPs offer). Consider using spot instances for non-production or non-critical workloads. The main benefits of the right consumption model are:

  - o Capacity reservations or savings plans provide significant cost savings.

  - o Spot instances are much cheaper than regular instances.

- **SDLC environment optimization**: Consider downsizing non-production environments to achieve optimization. Hibernating or pausing the non-production environments during off-business hours is another good strategy. Usually, non-production environments do not need to have the same capacity or uptime as production.

- **Decommission resources**: Be aware of the lifecycle of cloud resources and remember to stop/shut down when not needed. Tagging is also a very useful strategy for tracking resources. Idle resources that are no longer needed keep lingering and add significantly to the cloud bills if they go unnoticed.

Performance management

The performance component of the architecture recommends the best practices that should be followed when designing your workloads so that you are able to make the right design decisions and select the best cloud resources that will help you meet your performance goals. The design should be able to cater to the evolving performance requirements and allow you to make changes as mentioned here:

- **Design standards, patterns, and reference architectures**: Create a repository of internal design standards, patterns, and reference architectures that can serve as guidelines for the whole organization for adherence. An existing repository or set of guidelines will help make the right architecture decisions and select the fit-for-purpose cloud services.

- **Benchmark the performance**: Make sure to benchmark the performance metrics so that your design decisions aim to achieve a realistic and proven performance. This is important because of the following reasons:

  o Benchmarking ensures you have realistic goals and KPIs.

  o The team can work towards something tangible.

- **Right size the compute resources:** Collect and use performance metrics to make accurate sizing decisions. Use the elasticity of the cloud instead of under-sizing or over-sizing your resources. Always make data-based informed decisions about sizing; otherwise, you will end up wasting resources.

- **Select the appropriate compute solution**: Each cloud provider offers a range of computing options, including virtual servers, containers, and serverless. Based on your use case, select the best option. Each compute option provides multiple features. Select the features that provide the best performance for your workload. Making the right decision for your computing requirements makes the workload resource-efficient and performance-efficient.

- **Select the appropriate storage solution**: Understand the data requirements (caching, usage patterns, flows, etc.) and choose the best storage solution for your workloads. solution for your workloads. Choose the right storage option that the cloud provider provides, i.e., object storage, block storage, file storage, or databases. Using an appropriate storage solution that is fit for the use case allows the workloads to perform at peak instead of sticking to the same data stored across the board.

- **Select the appropriate network solution**: Understand your networking requirements (latency, throughput, bandwidth, multi-location connectivity etc.) and choose the best networking solution for your landscape. Choose the right network protocols that enhance the performance, for ex-UDP over TCP. Choosing the right networking solution prevents bottlenecks, provides performance efficiency, and improves user experience.

- **Make architectural changes**: Make appropriate architectural changes to improve the performance of your applications. For example—if you are a global organization with users in multiple regions, deploy in multiple regions so that users are served faster. You may also use features like a **content delivery network** (**CDN**) to cache and serve the requests faster. It is important to understand that architecture on the cloud is way different from what it has been on-premises and what we have been used to. Hence, sometimes, making cloud-specific architectural changes can significantly improve performance.

- **Regular testing**: Regularly test your workload, most importantly, performance testing and load testing. The major benefits of a regular testing strategy are:

  o Thorough testing will ensure the application is able to handle the production-scale load.

  o Performance-related issues can be anticipated well in time and tuned accordingly if a proactive test regime is followed.

Well-architected framework

A Well-Architected Framework is a set of industry best practices and recommendations based on years of architecture and design experience from the experts, aimed at helping you make the right design decisions on the cloud. All cloud providers preach their own version of WAF, but the fundamentals and high-level categories are the same as the architecture themes we have used throughout this chapter. i.e., security, operations, reliability, cost optimization, and performance management.

The aim of a WAF is to help cloud architects and engineers make the right decisions and be able to measure the outcomes of those decisions against a set of proven principles and practices in line with what we have highlighted in this chapter. WAF is not only for doers but also for executives who need to understand what it means to design in the cloud and design for the cloud. Every cloud customer on their cloud journey follows this framework wholly or partially.

To make it more formidable, customers should also go through a process called *Well-Architected Review,* a series of workshops conducted by partners or cloud providers' architects to review the customer's architecture against the WAF principles and recommendations. The output of these workshops is a report that outlines findings and recommendations to improve the cloud landscape and architecture to align with the design principles and best practices as much as possible. Based on the outcomes of the review, businesses should be able to optimize their overall cloud footprint with improved design decisions regarding every architectural theme.

For this discussion, we will consider the framework provided by the three major CSPs—**AWS, MS Azure**, and **Google Cloud Platform** (**GCP**). All three offer a similar framework with the same five pillars, though Google calls it *Google Cloud Architecture Framework* and not WAF. An aberration besides the similarities between these three frameworks is that AWS' WAF also includes a sixth pillar called *Sustainability*, which focuses on environment and energy efficiency when designing and hosting workloads on AWS. Regardless of the differences, they all serve the same purpose—helping customers design efficient cloud architectures.

Conclusion

In this chapter, we discussed what it takes to design applications for the cloud through a set of design principles and best practices. These were grouped into five architecture themes, namely security, operations, reliability, cost optimization, and performance management. Though all of these principles and practices are vital for an efficient and optimized architecture, applying everything in the real world may be challenging due to the complexity, resource, and effort requirements, as well as the cost involved. There are trade-offs when it comes to best practices and the real world. For example, sometimes it might be faster and tempting to overlook some of the best practices, as quick time to market is the priority. Hence, always weigh the priorities against principles and practices to make the right decision. In the next chapter, we will shift our focus to managing multi-cloud environments, addressing technical challenges, and related design considerations.

Points to remember

Here are some key takeaways from this chapter:

- Cloud architecture differs from traditional on-premises design due to its natural attributes like elasticity, scalability, automation, etc.

- The key architecture themes to consider when designing applications on the cloud are—security, operations, reliability, cost optimization, and performance management.

- The design principles and best practices centered around these five architecture themes should be used as guidelines and recommendations for designing and deploying workloads on the cloud.

- Always consider the challenges and trade-offs when adopting the design principles and best practices for the cloud.

- Most cloud providers offer a WAF comprising design principles and best practices. The WAF should be used by decision-makers and executors to develop well-tuned and robust cloud architectures.

Join our book's Discord space

Join the book's Discord Workspace for Latest updates, Offers, Tech happenings around the world, New Release and Sessions with the Authors:

https://discord.bpbonline.com

CHAPTER 6
Multi-cloud Adoption

Introduction

Chapter 1 introduced us to the concept of multi-cloud as we navigated through the basics of cloud computing and understood some of the challenges and benefits associated with multi-cloud computing. This chapter intends to go a level deeper into the multi-cloud landscape. Multi-cloud adoption is becoming increasingly prevalent, but it comes with challenges. We will be using architectures used as examples to make the concepts as clear as possible and start with re-iterating the benefits and challenges of multi-cloud adoption. Then, we will move on to understand the management aspects of a multi-cloud environment and how some industry-recognized tools make it easy. Finally, we will cover some popular multi-cloud scenarios

Often, multi-cloud environments are not methodically planned but developed carelessly because of unplanned cloud adoption and isolated IT shops within an organization adopting cloud solutions without a centralized cloud strategy. To solve the problems of a multi-cloud environment, thorough planning and tools are essential.

Structure

In this chapter, we will cover the following topics:

- Multi-cloud benefits

- Multi-cloud pain points
- Multi-cloud strategies
- Multi-cloud deployments across domains
- Multi-cloud examples
- Multi-cloud management
- Tools for the trade
- Solo cloud problems
- Multi-cloud scenarios

Objectives

The key objective of this chapter is to cover the width of multi-cloud adoptions without going into too much technical depth of deployments and architectures. By the end of this chapter, readers should be able to appreciate the complexity and benefits of a multi-cloud environment. The readers should be able to use the details in this chapter as a reference guide for forming their multi-cloud strategies while understanding the gotchas and pitfalls.

Multi-cloud benefits

The multi-cloud landscape is ever-growing, and everyone, including the cloud vendors, has realized that the solo cloud is soon going to be history. For example, in Australia, almost 93% of the companies have already adopted a multi-cloud strategy, as per the Flexera 2023 State of the Cloud Report. The reason multi-cloud adoption is becoming popular is due to the flexibility it provides, i.e., flexibility in choosing the right platform for your workloads, opening a plethora of options for you to explore. Flexibility in choosing the right cloud platform for your application also results in cost savings, as organizations can choose not only the platform based on technology comparison but also from a pricing point of view. The cost of similar services can vary across all cloud vendors and can even be negotiated further due to the competition. Let us re-iterate the key benefits of a multi-cloud adoption before moving ahead with a more detailed discussion:

- **Increased resiliency**: You can distribute workloads across multiple cloud computing platforms, or you can use a second cloud for purely disaster recovery purposes.
- **Performance**: You can improve performance of your workloads with global deployments, especially for the global workloads (like e-commerce websites) or you can use the secondary computing platform for scalability use cases (like high demands during a major shopping event).

- **Cost optimization**: Multiple cloud adoption provides more power to the end user in terms of leveraging the best costing models from each cloud provider and being able to negotiate better pricing.

- **Security**: Like cost, in a multi-cloud environment, you would have access to the best security features and services from each cloud provider, leading to a robust overall security posture.

- **Innovation**: Make use of the best tools and technologies available from each cloud provider. You can experiment with new services freely by creating sandbox environments in alternate clouds before making any decisions. This is an opportunity to innovate faster.

- **Flexibility**: Last but not least, as mentioned earlier, the flexibility you get with multi-cloud adoption is unmatchable.

Multi-cloud pain points

However, the diversity of cloud platforms in your IT landscape is not always favorable. The biggest challenge that comes with all these benefits is the complexity and operational burden arising from managing more than one cloud, i.e., managing varied systems and technologies, managing security across multiple cloud platforms, implementing a standard set of policies, data governance, managing costs, and keeping all systems updated at the same time. In addition, if interoperability between systems hosted across cloud platforms is a requirement, then data flow and integration pose a major headache for the business.

In the following section, we look at key strategies to adopt multiple clouds in the context of the challenges that this style of deployment poses.

Multi-cloud strategies

For organizations to be successful in multi-cloud adoption, careful planning, and thoughtful strategy are key to tackling the challenges mentioned above. Here are the most important and popular strategies if you intend to go multi-cloud:

- Be clear about the objectives and business goals for adopting more than one cloud. Just jumping on a bandwagon or following a decentralized adoption by letting shadow IT shops decide on their own cloud adoption is not healthy and will lead to failures more often than not.

- Multi-cloud means more engineering, architecture, and operations skills will be required across more than one cloud. Hence, plan for appropriate training and recruitment. Though fundamentals are the same, every cloud has its own specific constructs and services that might need a particular skill rather than generic cloud skills.

- Security concerns on the cloud are crucial, and it accentuates even further in a multi-cloud environment. Consider appropriate security controls on each cloud as having more hosting platforms in your landscape also means much more attack surface for potential cyber-attacks.

- One of the objectives of going multi-cloud is that the applications and components are transportable and not platform dependent. Hence, it is imperative that you avoid any services or features that make your application dependent or locked into the cloud platform. A good example of such services is the **platform as a service (PaaS)** or managed services provided by the cloud platforms, like the **Relational Database Service (RDS)** service provided by AWS. They have their benefits, but if the intent is to make applications agnostic of the underlying platform, then avoid such services if possible.

- Leverage the flexibility of choosing the best platform for your workloads. You should match the requirements of workloads with the strengths of different cloud providers. An incorrect assessment initially could mean a lot of effort later if you decide to move the workload.

- Invest in multi-cloud management tools that can paint a unified view of the multi-cloud landscape and build an abstraction layer for the users to interact with. You will need a central management console (cloud management platform) to create a single pane of glass or a dashboard that provides peek into everything in your multi-cloud environment. In the absence of such tools, usage and management become a nightmare. We will look at some of the widely used tools in the section titled *Tools for the trade.*

- In a multi-cloud environment, data could be flowing between systems that are deployed across different clouds. Hence, a data governance and management strategy are critical for the success of a multi-cloud deployment.

- In line with the previous consideration of data management, solid network connectivity and network security become paramount. You must prioritize network security because networking between multiple clouds will be complex, considering all the moving parts. This includes capabilities like **single sign-on (SSO)**, **multi-factor authentication (MFA)**, guest and privileged access across all clouds, and much more.

In addition, here are some of the other considerations that might affect the multi-cloud strategy but are usually ignored or less discussed:

- **Performance**: Performance across multiple cloud platforms might vary, or every cloud platform can have different performance SLAs. If you are planning to host a workload or dependent workloads across multiple cloud platforms, this could be a real consideration.

- **Data latency**: If data flow is a requirement between workloads that are spread across multiple clouds, then give a thought to the latency due to the connectivity between the clouds and whether that meets your needs or not. For distributed applications that have components across multiple cloud platforms, the latency of data could be an issue if the application's requirements and tolerance to latency are not accounted for during the design. Of course, the latency depends on the type of network connectivity between the clouds and the cloud regions being used for deployment.

- **Interoperability**: Most cloud tools and technologies are proprietary to the cloud provider, and hence, components hosted on a cloud platform may not be portable onto other cloud platforms. It is very similar to the vendor lock-in constraint, which is one of the key drivers for multi-cloud adoption.

The legacy ways of application development might not be conducive to multi-cloud environments with many more moving parts that demand interoperability and a lot of network integration. Hence, implementing a multi-cloud climate also means redefining your development methodologies and looking at modern frameworks. For example, some of the strategies that you should look at are:

- **DevOps and DevSecOps**: Practices such as continuous build, continuous integration, continuous deployment, and continuous delivery are very appropriate for any type of cloud setup, including a multi-cloud environment. These practices are an integral part of the popular DevOps and DevSecOps frameworks widely used as automation approaches for rapid software development and delivery.

- **Containerization**: this is an important software development and packaging strategy to enable consistent deployment of application components across multiple cloud platforms. The beauty of this strategy is the way the components are abstracted from the underlying infrastructure, ensuring that they can be ported from one cloud to another easily.

- **Serverless architecture:** Another important strategy that is sometimes compared to the containerization strategy is the serverless architecture. They both have their own merits and should not be seen as replacements for one another. Serverless computing enables smaller modules of code to run without worrying about the underlying infrastructure, also known as the **function as a service (FaaS)**. However, the main problem this approach suffers from is that all cloud providers have their proprietary FaaS service, which means that if you have to move the functions between cloud platforms, then there is some development effort involved to make the code work with the respective cloud platform.

- **Microservices:** This is a great strategy for workloads that can be distributed across multiple cloud platforms. The microservices-based architectures are classified as loosely coupled architectures because you can modularise your applications by splitting them into more minor services that can work independently of others, hence making it a very efficient strategy for multi-cloud setups.

Multi-cloud deployment across domains

Multi-cloud deployments have fitment for every domain as per the requirements of that domain. Let us look at some examples for key industries:

- **Education**: This domain requires specialised solutions for research courses, like high performance computing resources for labs or Artificial intelligence-based solutions for data scientists. Multi-cloud environments are good for this sector as there is flexibility in choosing the right platform for the right resources. Also consider online courses for students spread across the globe, where availability or solution close to students and network performance are key. This is also a good use case for adopting multiple clouds.

- **Banks**: Multi-cloud deployments bring numerous benefits to the banking sector. Most importantly, the high availability and disaster recovery capabilities they bring to the table. A secondary cloud can be used as a disaster recovery site in case the primary cloud completely fails and hence ensuring business continuity. In addition, the banks are too fussed about meeting security and compliance requirements, which is supported well by a multi-cloud strategy that chooses appropriate clouds and regions for workload deployments.

- **Fintech**: We will classify trading companies and the payment industry in this category. For these types of organizations, customer's trust in their online platform is the number one priority. This confidence and trust can be bolstered by a robust tech strategy that focuses on their platform's availability and security. Customers should know that even if the main hosting platform goes down or is compromised for any reason, their money and data are safe. These organizations need multi-cloud to alleviate over-dependence on a single cloud and prepare for the worst-case scenario.

- **Retail**: This sector is known for spikes and surges during festive and holiday seasons or similar growth periods. That is why they need to ensure the cloud platform is scalable and data is accessible seamlessly. In a multi-cloud environment, a secondary or an alternate cloud can be used to handle surges or just for data storage and hence provide the much-required support.

- **Logistics**: The logistics industry utilizes multi-cloud setups to optimize their supply chains and avoid disruptions to the business by using multiple cloud platforms for their DR strategies. Optimized supply chains require better visibility from every possible source of data, and that can be achieved with the help of multiple cloud-based solutions.

- **Healthcare**: The healthcare industry has a lot of focus on the privacy and safety of health data, safe access to that data for relevant people across the globe, and innovation using AI/ML. All of these make a great case for adopting multi-cloud and multi-region solutions to leverage the best security and innovative capabilities of every cloud.

- **Entertainment**: Content is the king of the entertainment industry, be it production, streaming, or on-demand. Streaming services need scalability during peak periods and the ability to reach a global audience. They also need reliable infrastructure and robust disaster recovery capabilities so that unwanted disruptions can be avoided. On-demand services need robust and cost-effective storage capabilities. All these requirements make a good case for adopting multiple clouds based on their abilities.

- **Government**: Multi-cloud adoption in government and public sector is a growing trend due to the benefits like flexibility and scalability. However, this sector has strict security and compliance requirements around data, including data residency requirements. Hence, stringent security measures and controls need to be in place. Moreover, cost could be a concern in the government sector, which needs to be managed using optimization strategies.

Multi-cloud examples

Having talked a lot about the multi-cloud strategy, its pros and cons, let us look at some of the prominent global organizations that have successfully adopted the multi-cloud strategy over the past few years.

Coca-Cola

Coca-Cola has been a prominent user of Microsoft cloud technologies like Azure, Dynamics 365, etc. They inked a strategic deal a few years back with Microsoft to use their software and cloud products, motivated mainly by the remote working arrangements brought about by the pandemic in 2019-2020. The majority of their cloud footprint is comprised of Microsoft, but at the same time, they have adopted other clouds like AWS and GCP for many of their workloads.

Netflix

Netflix has been known as an AWS shop for years, and most credit for its transformation over the years goes to AWS. Lately, Netflix has opted for Google Cloud services for data analytics and ML workloads. This is a great example of a multi-cloud environment where the best platforms and technologies are leveraged based on workload requirements rather than one solution for everything.

Multi-cloud management

Managing a multi-cloud environment is the most challenging part, which, if not carefully planned, can quickly become a nightmare. The biggest challenge is the incompatibility of the cloud platforms and a lack of a common interface. Each cloud platform has its own set of **application programming interfaces** (**APIs**) and management console, but when it comes to having a consolidated view and standardization, you need specialized tools and expertise.

The key requirements and evaluation criteria for such a tool are listed here:

- **Unified dashboard**: One of the basic requirements for any tool in a multi-cloud environment is the ability to provide a unified view of the entire landscape for everything technical (like services used) or non-technical (like billing, etc.).

- **Compatibility**: The unified view brings up another important requirement, i.e., compatibility of the tool with cloud platforms. The tool must be compatible with and support all the cloud platforms you are using or intend to use. In short, it means the tool should integrate with most cloud platforms using plugins, APIs, or other methods.

- **Automation**: Operational efficiency is another attribute of the management tools that you should look at. This can be achieved by automating repetitive tasks and workflows to avoid manual tasks. For example, automated start and shut down of servers, resizing the virtual servers, applying patches sending notifications for failed events during a workflow. Similarly, there are hundreds of such mundane tasks that can be automated, and a tool that can be used across multiple platforms is the most suitable.

- **Security**: managing security across multiple platforms could be a big headache for engineering as well as operations teams. At a minimum, the tool should provide identity and access management and security monitoring for all the clouds.

- **Cost management**: Cost management, governance, and reporting are other key aspects that a multi-cloud management tool should offer. You need a good view of billing across all cloud and optimization recommendations wherever possible. The tool should be able to help with budgeting and forecasting, setting thresholds, and set notifications for any breaches, which is a very useful approach for a FinOps practice and all involved.

- **Support**: Like any other tool or technology, the tool you want to use should have enough coverage in terms of customer service and technical support.

Tools for the trade

As evident from the abovementioned requirements, choosing the right tool is important. We will look at some of the commonly used management tools for a multi-cloud environment:

- **F5 solutions**: Provides a bunch of solutions for various standardization aspects of multi-cloud management that are popular and worth mentioning.

  o Application performance and security management using **Big IP Virtual Editions**

- ○ Centralized management of multiple cloud platforms with **Big IQ**

- ○ **F5 distributed cloud** is a suite of services encompassing security, networking, and application management. Some key capabilities of distributed cloud are as follows:

  - Multi-cloud network connect: Global fabric built on high-speed backbone that connects all clouds in your environment

  - Multi-cloud app connect: Load balancing service for applications distributed across multiple cloud platforms

  - Web app and API protection: A set of security services for the distributed apps and APIs

- **Azure Arc**: Azure Arc can manage physical and virtual servers in multiple clouds and in the on-premises corporate network. The management of servers outside Azure is similar to those in Azure, as Azure policies and tags are used. Some of the essential functions that Azure services can provide for Azure-connected servers (including those outside Azure) are:

  - ○ Auditing using Azure policy's configuration feature

  - ○ Management of security threats using Microsoft Defender

  - ○ Monitoring using VM insights

  - ○ Managing OS updates using update management feature

Here is a reference diagram depicting how Azure ARC works:

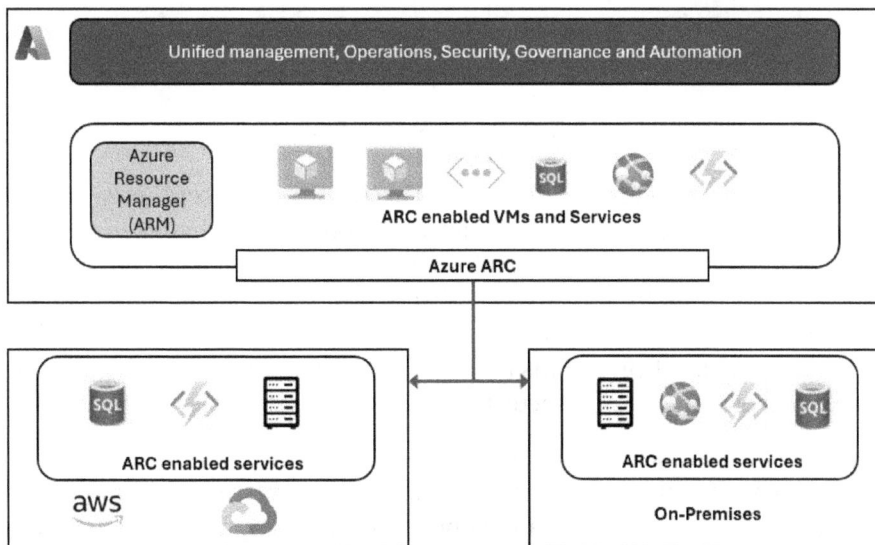

Figure 6.1: *Azure ARC architecture*

- **AWS Systems Manager**: AWS Systems Manager is a comprehensive operations service with multiple capabilities that can be used to manage servers in AWS (EC2 instances), other cloud platforms, as well as on-premises servers. Some of the key capabilities that can be used across multiple clouds are:
  - o Fleet management
  - o Sessions management
  - o Patch management
  - o Inventory management

Here is a reference diagram depicting how AWS Systems Manager works in a multi-cloud environment:

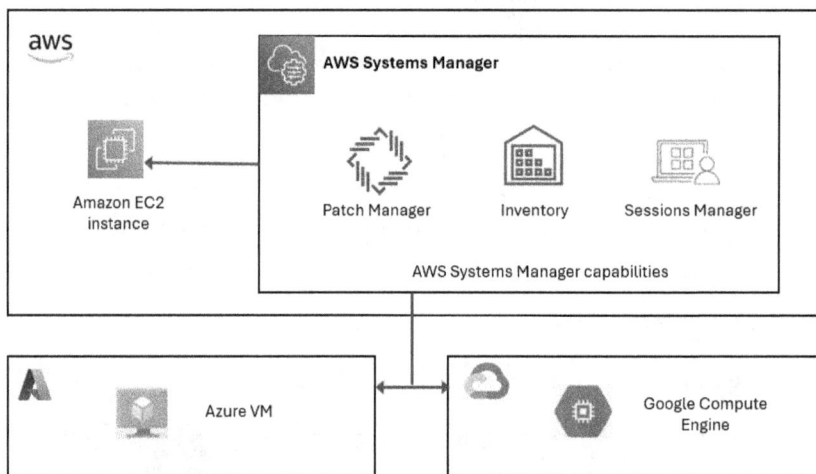

Figure 6.2: *AWS Systems Manager multi-cloud architecture*

- **Aviatrix cloud networking platform**: The Aviatrix platform is meant to provide a single pane of glass for secure network connectivity between multiple cloud platforms that have disparate native network constructs. Their cloud network platform does this by creating an abstraction layer programmatically over the cloud-native constructs to provide a consistent and unified view even though you could be using multiple clouds at the same time. In turn you can apply consistent operations procedures and security policies across the whole suite.

- **Terraform**: Terraform is another great solution for managing multi-cloud architectures. It is able to do this by abstracting the differences in the infrastructure layer of every cloud platform and hence enables deployment of consistent policies, managing networks topologies, managing dependencies and different deployment patterns.

Cloud management platform

An important tool in the armoury of cloud management and multi-cloud management is a comprehensive **cloud management platform** (**CMP**). Every cloud provider has their own console, which is usually very good and provides different types of useful dashboards and reports. However, it becomes complicated when it comes to a multi-cloud environment. We discussed some management tools earlier that help in various aspects of a multi-cloud environment management and operations, like networking, patching, deployment, etc. Let us now look at some important players in the CMP space that are popular for their management and orchestration capabilities:

- **CloudBolt**: This CMP integrates with multiple CSPs ranging from AWS, Azure, GCP and many more in the ecosystem. The highlight of the tool is the self-service interface it provides for managing and provisioning cloud resources. In addition, it also provides useful capabilities for access control, resource quota management, and visibility into costing and billing.

- **Morpheus**: This is a vendor agnostic orchestration platform that can be used for provisioning services across multiple clouds and providing self service capabilities. Owned by HPE (Hewlett Packard Enterprise), it is a product that can be deployed on cloud or on-premises.

- **CloudStack**: This is an open-source product from Apache that can be used for deploying and operating cloud infrastructure services and supports multiple public clouds and virtualization platforms like KVM, ESXi, etc.

- **Flexera**: The Flexera CMP comes with a vast set of capabilities including orchestration of operations and monitoring, self-service for end users, FinOps capabilities like cost management and planning, access control for a multi-cloud environment. You can use the CMP to discover, view, and govern multiple public and private cloud platforms.

There are many others like *Dynatrace, Datadog* etc., which are worth mentioning here. However, there is no right or wrong choice when it comes to cloud management tools. It is about the features you need and, of course, the price you want to invest in easing the management of your multi-cloud environment.

Solo cloud problems

Sticking to a single cloud has some obvious drawbacks (think opposite of multi-cloud benefits that we have already discussed), like:

- Vendor lock-in, as you are dependent on the tools and services provided by the cloud provider. This could be due to vendor-specific or proprietary technologies. To then move to a different cloud provider will entail more architecture and engineering effort.

- Vendor lock-in also leads to vendor monopoly and hence less opportunities for cost optimizations and negotiations. Obviously if there is competition then all cloud vendors will try and bid for the lowest price.

- Limiting architecture growth and innovation as you are not adopting best cloud services in the market. Every cloud has its own advantages in terms of services and features that can be leveraged if you choose the right cloud for the right workload instead of hosting everything on one cloud.

- Risk of losing business continuity in case the platform goes down, as there is no second hosting platform for a disaster scenario if the main cloud platform goes down completely. Having an alternate cloud provider for DR scenarios is a classical use case for multi-cloud deployments.

Out of these, probably the hardest hitting is the fear of losing services/app/website due to a sudden failure of the cloud platform or a misconfiguration of any of the cloud provider services. Such failures are rare but possible and there have been instances in real world that accentuate the importance of having a backup plan ready.

In May 2024, one of the big superannuation companies in Australia suffered a major outage due to a deletion of a subscription of their private cloud services on Google Cloud leading to disruption of the company's services for a prolonged period and frustration among their users. Though they had a DR plan spanning multiple geographies, but failure of their cloud platform did not leave them with any option for business continuity. Though such incidents leading to failure in all geographies involved are rare, but not impossible, and that is why having more than one hosting platform in the mix makes more and more sense. With a secondary cloud for such DR scenarios, i.e., if the primary cloud fails completely (as happened in this case), a working replica of the application could have been created much faster than the time it took to fix the problem. Of course there are other pre-requisites like full backups, network connectivity for quick access to backups etc.

We will look at a similar DR scenario involving a secondary cloud platform later in this chapter.

Multi-cloud scenarios

There are several use cases for multi-cloud deployments in the real world. Let us look at some of the most common multi-cloud architectures.

Distributed architectures

In a distributed multi-cloud architecture, an application's components are distributed or spread across multiple cloud platforms. This is a complex architecture pattern as it involves a thorough consideration of technical and operational challenges like:

- Logically dividing the application into smaller components that can be distributed

- Deciding which components should be hosted in which cloud platform based on their requirements

- Ensuring data flow between the components

- Network connectivity and security

Following is a reference diagram depicting a distributed architecture:

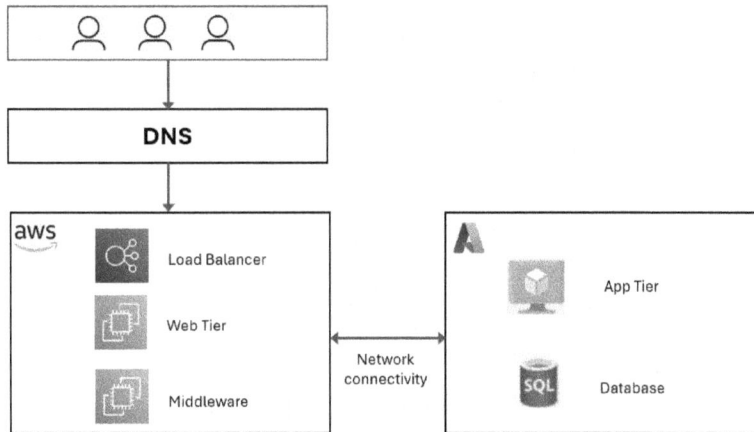

Figure 6.3: Distributed multi-cloud architecture

High availability architectures

A high-availability architecture is one of the most common and frequently deployed use cases for multi-cloud types of architecture. This is the architecture where a secondary cloud platform is used to enhance the application's availability. The application is deployed on both clouds in its entirety, but there are two variations to this architecture.

Active/Active

This is the architecture where the application is built identically on two cloud platforms (say AWS and Azure, for example), and both are active in terms of serving the production traffic from end users, i.e., at any given time, both versions of the application are serving the user requests. This kind of architecture serves various purposes, like high availability, scalability, and handling surges in user traffic.

Refer to the following figure:

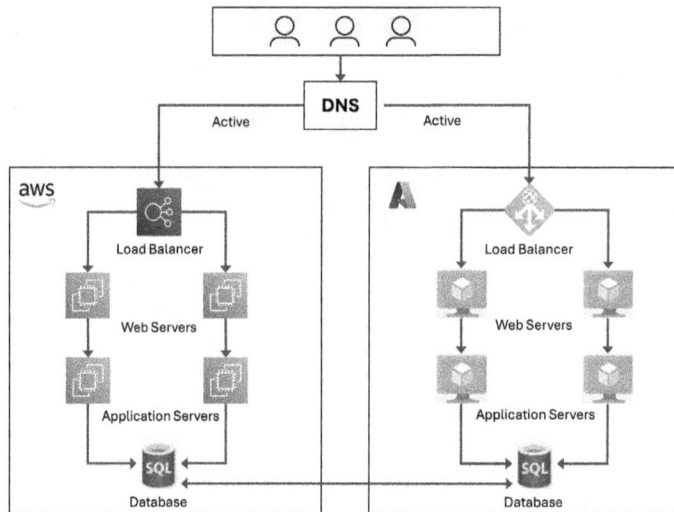

Figure 6.4: Multi-cloud Active/Active architecture

Active/Passive

This is similar to an Active/Active architecture, but the key difference here is that none of the versions/copies of the application serve the end users. Only the primary cloud platform (say AWS) serves the production traffic, and the standby copy in Azure is ready if the primary copy fails. Again, the main purpose is to provide high availability, but there could be a bit of failover time that you should account for in this type of architecture.

Refer to the following figure for a multi-cloud Active/Passive architecture:

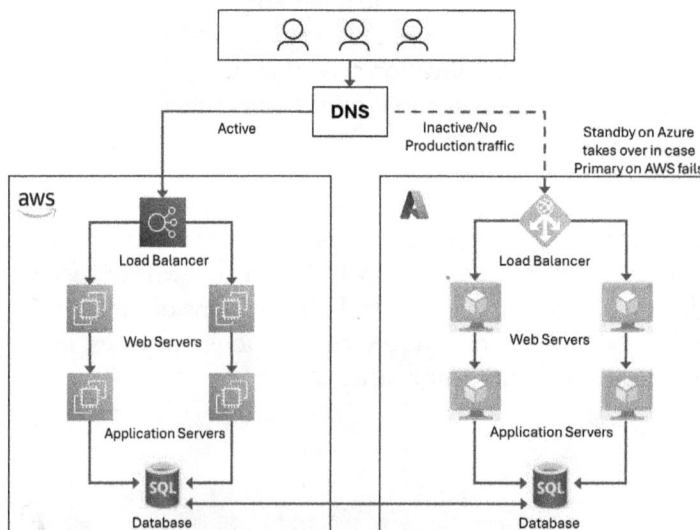

Figure 6.5: Multi-cloud Active/Passive architecture

Data analytics

This is the domain that has been growing quite rampantly over the last few years, and because there are so many organizations that are using multiple clouds to store their data, there are unique solutions now that cater to a multi-cloud environment. Analytics has two parts, computing and data storage (huge amounts of data), and both are critical for successful implementation. In a multi-cloud environment, there are two possible architectures for data analytics: centralized data storage and decentralized data storage.

Centralised data storage

More prevalent, this type of architecture requires all data stored in multiple cloud or on-premises platforms to be moved to the central cloud platform, where the data processing and computation are happening. This is kind of a hub and spoke architecture with the central cloud for all data storage and processing being the hub and all other clouds being the spokes ingesting data into the central cloud storage. Obviously, the challenging part with this type of architecture is the movement of large datasets between clouds, which is not only insecure but could prove very costly and time-consuming.

Decentralized data storage

Since data movement is a risky and costly affair, the other type of multi-cloud data analytics architecture is where data stays at its respective locations, and the processing only happens at the source. That is where specialized analytics solutions for multi-cloud setups can be very handy. One such solution is the Google Cloud's Big Query Omni. Since Big Query decouples the computing and storage layers, the Omni query engine can run SQL queries in other clouds in the region where data is stored without the need to transfer data between clouds.

Refer to the following figure:

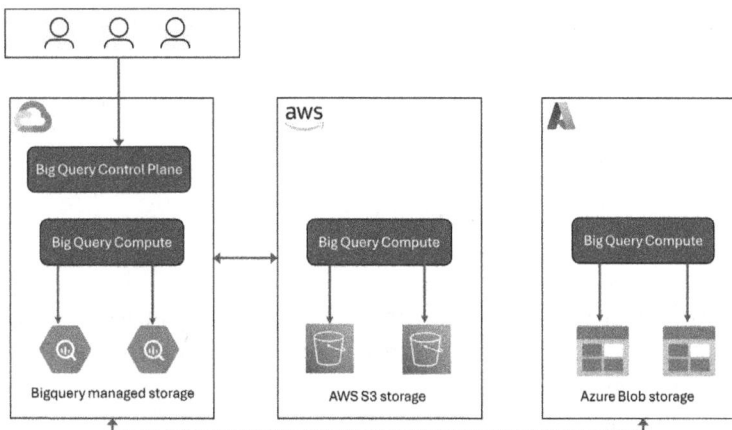

Figure 6.6: Decentralised multi-cloud data analytics with Big Query Omni

Conclusion

In this chapter, we looked at various details of a multi-cloud adoption that has recently gained popularity due to its flexibility in modernizing your IT landscape. The cloud adoption principles do not change much, but the focus was on the complexity of the multi-cloud adoption and, hence, the requirement for some specialized tools to handle such complex deployments. We looked at some industry-wide adoptions of multi-cloud strategies with real-world examples and some common architectures.

In the next chapter, we will focus on the networking aspect of cloud computing, including multi-cloud specifics. It will be a much more technical focus on networking details, along with some supporting architectures and solutions.

Points to remember

Here are some key takeaways from this chapter:

- Multi-cloud adoption has its share of problems and challenges that must be addressed as part of the planning and strategy process. To name a few:
    - Unplanned adoption
    - Complexity due to multiple hosting platforms
    - Security across the entire landscape
    - Additional skills requirements
    - Performance concerns (data latency, etc.)
- Multi-cloud strategy should consider modern development frameworks, like DevOps, DevSecOps, containerization, and microservices.
- To cater to the complexity of multi-cloud deployments, specialised tools must be adopted, to name a few (there are many more):
    - F5 suite of solutions
    - Azure ARC
    - AWS Systems Manager
    - Aviatrix cloud networking platform
    - Terraform
- Another tool that should be considered is a CMP that focusses on providing a single plan of glass and dashboard for visibility into all clouds in the environment. Some of the popular ones are (there are many more):
    - CloudBolt
    - Morpheus

- o CloudStack
- o Flexera

- Multi-cloud has applicability in almost every industry domain, for example:
  - o Retail
  - o Education
  - o Financial
  - o Entertainment
  - o Logistics
  - o Healthcare

- With the growing popularity, there are various multi-cloud architectures and scenarios possible, for example:
  - o Distributed architectures where an application is broken down into smaller components that can be spread across multiple cloud platforms.
  - o High availability architectures where an application has an identical copy deployed onto a secondary cloud that can be used in an Active/Active or Active/Passive manner.
  - o Data analytics architecture where data could be stored in multiple cloud storage, but the processing/compute is centralised in the primary cloud platform.

Join our book's Discord space

Join the book's Discord Workspace for Latest updates, Offers, Tech happenings around the world, New Release and Sessions with the Authors:

https://discord.bpbonline.com

CHAPTER 7
Cloud Networking

Introduction

When we talk about the cloud, an important facet of the whole landscape is networking, for instance, understanding how you would connect to the resources in the cloud and how you would connect various services within your cloud environment. In short, you would consider building your corporate network with cloud services in the mix, using various native cloud services and/or services provided by external vendors.

The concept of cloud networking includes connectivity between multiple clouds, between on-premises and cloud, and within the cloud. While we have touched upon the networking concept in other chapters, we will look at all these aspects of cloud networking in much greater detail in this chapter.

This chapter provides an in-depth look at the networking aspects of a cloud strategy. An important point to note here is that this is not a deep dive into the technical aspects of networking, like routers, switches, protocols, etc. Such technical discussions are out of the scope of this chapter and this book in general. The objective is to engage cloud architects and technical decision-makers enough to take the next step when developing a cloud strategy for their organization. We will look at some network scenarios grouped into inter and intra-cloud architectures. The inter-cloud networking section will also cover SD-WAN, a virtualized approach to connect multiple cloud regions and on-premises networks. Finally, we will discuss the two most common network topologies used in some form or other by most organizations, i.e., *hub and spoke* and *full mesh*.

Structure

In this chapter, we will cover the following topics:

- Cloud networking
- Network security
- Cloud networking scenarios
- Network costs
- Common cloud network topologies

Objectives

Networking in the cloud can be complex, and in the context of a cloud strategy, it is important to understand and plan how you plan to connect to the cloud environment and connect resources within it. By the end of this chapter, readers will be able to understand various elements of cloud networking and what constitutes a cloud network. Readers should also be able to grasp multiple cloud networking scenarios and topologies with the help of the provided examples and diagrams. Understanding them will help readers relate to their specific use case and plan better.

Cloud networking

In the most basic form, cloud networking is the use of technology to connect infrastructure resources in the cloud to each other, to the on-premises resources (hybrid networks across one or multiple geographies), or to other cloud platforms (multi-cloud environment). Virtualization and elasticity are the essence of the cloud, and networking is no different. Instead of using traditional physical hardware devices, cloud networking uses native cloud services or third-party virtual routers, which can scale up and down to handle traffic fluctuations efficiently and almost infinitely.

Elements of cloud networking

When it comes to cloud adoption, various networking elements and services should be considered and planned at an early stage of the journey. In this section, we will look at the most important ones based on their function in the architecture, because knowledge of these would make decision-making easier. To make these components easier to relate to and understand, we have also included the services/features offered by some of the well-known commercial cloud providers. Let us explore this in detail:

- **Zones**: A zone in the cloud is a logical deployment area within a region for infrastructure resources. A single zone could consist of one or more data centers, which is irrelevant to the users who view the zone as one consolidated entity for their architecture. Note that a zone never spans across regions.

- **Regions**: In cloud terminology, regions are geographically separate areas with multiple isolated zones. A region could be a country or isolated areas within a country, and every region has at least two (and in most cases, more than two) zones. If you design a highly available application, you should consider deploying it across multiple regional zones.

- **The isolated private section in the public cloud for launching resources**: Launching and hosting infrastructure resources in the cloud need some pre-requisites, like IP addresses (private or public, depending upon the architecture requirements), routing mechanisms, network interface, network firewalls, etc. In the cloud, these are primarily associated with an isolated section or private network dedicated to you that can be easily connected to your on-premises network, resulting in an extension of your current network to the cloud, which is protected and not accessible to anyone outside your network unless you want it to be. Every commercial cloud provider has a similar concept, though with different names. For example, AWS and Google Cloud call it a **virtual private cloud (VPC)**, and Azure has a **virtual network (VNet)**.

Remember, a virtual network can span zones within a region, and for some providers, it can span multiple areas as well (for example, a Google Cloud VPC can span various regions, whereas AWS VPC and Azure VNet are region-specific).

Note: We will use the term virtual network more generically throughout this chapter for the isolated private section on the cloud, not necessarily referring to Azure VNET (virtual network).

There are many components of a virtual network. Let us look at them in further detail:

- **Subnets**: Smaller portions carved out of your virtual networks that are used to arrange and group resources to separate them from other resources logically are called subnets. They can be private or public, depending on how you want the resources inside them to be accessible. Note that a subnet is restricted to a zone and never spans multiple zones. Another characteristic of a subnet is that once created, it can be expanded later to accommodate more IP addresses.

- **Route tables**: To guide the traffic routing from resources inside the subnets, there are route tables where you define specific routes with hops and destinations that the network packets will follow.

- **IP addresses**: You can assign private or public IP addresses to your resources inside the virtual network on the cloud. The default is a private IP address, but if you want your resources to connect to the internet and be available publicly, you can also assign a public IP address.

- **Security**: Cloud providers provide specific security controls to control and filter traffic to and from the virtual networks in the cloud. These security controls work based on inbound and outbound rules that you define. It can be implemented at the whole virtual network or subnet level, or even more granularly at the virtual machine level. For example, AWS has security groups at the server level and **access control lists** (**ACLs**) at the subnet level. Azure has **network security groups** (**NSGs**) that can be applied at the server and subnet levels. An important distinction between security groups and NACLs is that security groups are stateful, whereas NACLs are stateless. What this means is that for security groups, if you allow inbound traffic on a specific port, the corresponding outbound traffic is automatically permitted as well, without needing a separate outbound rule.

- **Connectivity between on-premises network and cloud (Hybrid connectivity)**: First and foremost, plan and design the network connectivity between your on-premises network and the proposed cloud environment. An integral part of any cloud architecture includes hybrid network connectivity to ensure that resources in your offices and private data centres can talk to the public cloud resources.

  For most commercial, public clouds, there are usually two ways of ensuring this connectivity:

  o **Virtual private network (VPN)**: This networking service connects on-premises networks to the cloud platform over the public internet. The traffic that flows over the VPN link is encrypted using the **Internet Protocol Security** (**IPSec**) protocol. The VPN connections can connect data centres to the cloud and end users who want to access resources in the cloud from remote locations. All cloud providers provide site-to-site (from office or data centre to the cloud) and point-to-site (from a user desktop to the cloud) VPN connections.

  o **Dedicated private network link**: A dedicated private link is another solution to connect on-premises data centres to the cloud. This is a solution for those organizations that need high network bandwidth and do not want their network traffic to traverse over a VPN connection due to security concerns (VPN is over the internet). It is worth noting that these dedicated network links are not encrypted, though you can use them with an IPSec VPN connection for added security. For example, the name of the dedicated network link in AWS is Direct Connect, and Azure calls it the Express route.

- **Gateways**: As part of cloud networking, traffic will either flow from cloud to cloud, or cloud to on-premises, or cloud to the internet. We have already discussed route tables to guide the traffic flow. However, to ensure that the traffic goes out to the intended destinations, another critical component is the gateways. You need a gateway for internet-bound traffic as well as one for on-premises data centre-bound traffic. Coupled with route tables, these virtual gateways ensure the traffic from/to your virtual networks reaches the correct destination. For example:

  o A NAT gateway is required for the internet-bound traffic from the private resources inside a virtual network. All cloud providers offer a NAT gateway.

o AWS offers an internet gateway for the public resources inside a VPC (virtual network in AWS). However, not every cloud provider offers this because internet access for public resources is managed in other ways.

o A VPN gateway is required to set up the VPN link between the cloud and the on-premises network. Again, all cloud providers offer a VPN gateway in some form or another.

• **Load balancing**: One of the core networking services used as part of application architectures on the cloud is load balancing. Various types of load balancers are available in each public cloud, depending on the place in the architecture where they are deployed and the type of traffic they will handle. For example:

o **External or internal**: If the load balancer is deployed in front of the web layer and handle incoming traffic from the internet, it is an external type whereas if it is deployed internally to balance the traffic from one layer of architecture to another layer within the application, it is an internal type of load balancer.

o **Layer 4 or layer 7**: As per the OSI network model, there are **seven** network communication layers. Though this book is not the right place to learn about the **Open Systems Interconnection (OSI)** model, it is essential to note that load balancers can be layer 4 or layer 7, depending on the type of traffic they can handle. Layer 4 is the network layer that handles data transmission using TCP **Transmission Control Protocol (TCP)/User Datagram Protocol (UDP)** protocols. In contrast, layer 7 is the application layer that works on http/https protocols.

For example, some of the load-balancing options offered by major cloud providers are:

• **AWS provides three types of load balancers:**
  o Network load balancers (layer 4)
  o Application load balancer (layer 7)
  o Classic load balancer (the legacy load balancer, but it is not recommended anymore)

• **Azure also provides multiple types of load balancers:**
  o Azure front door (global, layer 7)
  o Traffic manager (global, layer 4)
  o Application gateway (regional, layer 7)
  o Load balancer (regional/global, layer 4)

• **Domain Name Service**: DNS is a network service responsible for translating web names to IP addresses (just like a phone directory) that can be used for connectivity. Each cloud provider offers a DNS service that can perform multiple functions, like domain hosting, translation, health checks, load balancing, etc. For example,

AWS provides a service called Route 53, Azure has Azure DNS, and Google Cloud provides Cloud DNS.

Network security

A very crucial part of cloud networking is the security of the network. Like any other area of the cloud, networks need to be safeguarded from unauthorized access or exposure, cyberattacks, phishing, etc. Protected networks mean protected assets using those networks, including applications, data, and infrastructure resources. In the next chapter (*Chapter 8, Cloud Security*) devoted to cloud security, we will look into many tools and services dedicated to network security in detail. Some standard types of network security services are:

- Anti **distributed denial of service** (**DDoS**) services to protect applications against distributed denial of services attacks.

- **Web application firewall** (**WAF**) to protect against web attacks

- Network firewalls to protect against network attacks

A WAF and a network firewall are often confused with each other, so here is a quick differentiation

	WAF	Network firewall
Focus area	Web application security	Network level traffic
Network layer	Layer 7 (application layer)	Layer 3 (network layer)
Type of attacks prevented	SQL injection and XSS	Network intrusion

Table 7.1: WAF vs Network Firewall

Note: These are in addition to the services or features we have mentioned in the basic elements of cloud networking, like the Azure network security groups that work as a firewall at a subnet as well as the virtual machine level.

Cloud networking scenarios

Multiple use cases and scenarios involve one or more of the cloud networking elements along with some specific networking features and services. We will look at these scenarios and group them into two categories.

Intra-cloud networking

Intra-cloud networking refers to networking between components within the same cloud platform. This includes networking between layers of the architecture (virtual networks and subnets) and/or between zones or regions. Before we discuss this topic further, let us quickly understand zones and areas in the cloud world because we no longer use the term data centres as we do in the on-premises world.

An application architecture on the cloud can have multiple tiers and can span multiple zones or regions, resulting in numerous networking scenarios, such as:

- **Single zone architecture**: In this type of architecture, all components of the application are located inside a single zone in one or more virtual networks (like AWS VPCs) and one or more subnets. Several virtual networks and subnets depend on your architecture requirements, but the application is confined within a single zone. Since this architecture is not highly available, it is not recommended for critical applications. The two most common types of deployments of a single-zone architecture are:

  o **Single virtual network, multiple subnets**: Within a virtual network, there can be multiple subnets, and all subnets can communicate without any special networking arrangement.

  o **Multiple virtual networks, multiple subnets**: If the application spans numerous virtual networks and subnets, you need to peer the virtual networks to ensure network connectivity. For example, by default, two VPCs in AWS cannot talk to each other.

Note: The peering connection runs over the cloud provider's network backbone but requires additional configuration steps.

- **Multi-zonal architecture**: The applications requiring highly available and fault-tolerant architectures must span multiple zones. The fundamental concept behind improving availability and resiliency in a multi-zone architecture is that it protects against single-zone failure events. You can have different types of multi-zone architectures, like Active/Active or Active/Passive, but the idea is to avoid a single point of failure in your architecture. Most PaaS services provided by cloud providers have inbuilt multi-zonal capabilities, whereas, for IaaS services, you need to design multi-zonal architectures yourself.

  Since subnets inside a virtual network can communicate with each other, no additional steps are required for this connectivity, even if the virtual network spans multiple zones. However, communication between virtual networks follows the same concept of peering, as mentioned earlier. You would also need a load-balancing service to manage traffic distribution across zones.

- **Multi-region architecture**: Multi-region architecture is another variation of highly available and fault-tolerant architecture, such as multi-zonal architecture, but it spans multiple regions at this time. Two areas are involved in this architecture: primary and secondary configuration. A multi-region architecture is a recommended disaster recovery strategy where you use a secondary region to serve application traffic in case the primary region fails. There is more than one way to set up a multi-region architecture:

- o **Active/Passive**: In this multi-region architecture, only one of the regions is active at a given time. The other region is in a passive state and does not serve users until the primary region fails for any reason. There are a few possible configurations for this type of architecture. Let us look at them briefly:

  - **Cold standby**: This approach uses a traditional backup and restore method for disaster recovery. The primary region actively serves the application production traffic. All data is backed up to a secondary region where no application components are available under normal operations. In case of a disaster, the infrastructure is deployed, and data is restored in the secondary region using the backups and infrastructure scripts.

  - **Warm standby**: Warm standby is another approach for creating an Active/Passive multi-region architecture. In this architecture, there is a toned-down copy of the production application (including backup of live data) hosted in the primary region so that normal operation can be restored much quicker in case of disaster.

- o **Active/Active**: As the name suggests, this architecture has both primary and secondary regions in an active state and serving the application users. They are fronted by a global load balancer or a DNS service that routes the traffic based on your defined routing policy. Of course, it is one of the costliest architectures due to multiple regions with full-fledged production setups for handling traffic. In the following figure, an Active/Active architecture has been shown in which two regions host the workload, and Route 53 (AWS' DNS service) routes the traffic to the region closest to the users (assuming a latency-based routing policy has been configured):

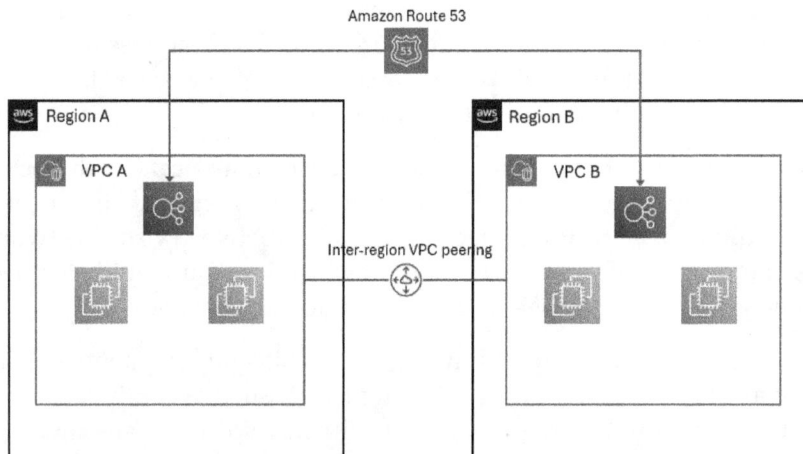

Figure 7.1: *Multi-region Active/Active architecture*

Inter-cloud networking

Next in line is an important discussion of the inter-cloud or multi-cloud networks, which have their own set of design considerations, tools, and challenges. However, the basic cloud networking concepts and constructs remain the same. However, there are specific challenges that must be addressed as part of the network architecture for multi-cloud scenarios.

Note: Though theoretically different, we will talk about hybrid cloud as part of inter-cloud networking in this section because some of the content we are presenting here applies to every scenario that involves multiple hosting platforms.

Challenges of multi-cloud networking

Here are some challenges of multi-cloud networking:

- **Separate set of controls and APIs**: As seen in the previous chapter, multi-cloud brings the complexity of dealing with a set of controls, interfaces, and APIs for each cloud provider. There is no standardization.

- **Operational scalability**: The first few connections may be simple, but adding nodes (clouds/platforms) becomes complex and additional operational overhead. If you have to connect every cloud platform, then it is an exponential increase in complexity.

- **IP addressing**: Overlapping IP addresses and number of IP addresses you have to manage.

- **Security complexity**: The more clouds in the mix, the more complex the security posture will become. Each cloud has its own security controls, which might make it challenging to deploy a standard set of policies and controls across the board.

Software-defined networking

Software defined networking (**SDN**) refers to using software applications to deploy and manage networks in data centres or across multiple data centres. Increasingly, SDN technologies are gaining popularity due to their ease of use and administrative efficiency. Now, let us understand how this is relevant to the topic at hand, i.e., cloud networking. One aspect of SDN is the **software-defined vast area network** (**SD-WAN**), the virtualized networking approach to connect multiple data centres and cloud platform(s) using native cloud or external third-party solutions. Some of the widely used SD-WAN solutions used for hybrid and multi-cloud networking are listed here:

- **Azure virtual WAN**: The SD-WAN solution from Azure that can be used to build an end-to-end WAN solution involving branch office/on-prem data centres (using Site-to-site VPNs or ExpressRoute network links) and cloud platforms (one or multiple VNets). This solution can be used to build partial SD-WAN architectures and scale gradually, i.e., connect a couple of networks to start and then add more as you evolve your architecture.

- **AWS Transit Gateway**: This is the erstwhile method of building a WAN involving multiple AWS Regions and multiple on-premises locations. Transit gateways are placed at the network edge to connect the on-premises network to the AWS networks, as shown in the following figure. However, you can also use transit gateway connect if you want to build a proper SD-WAN solution using a third-party virtual SD-WAN appliance.

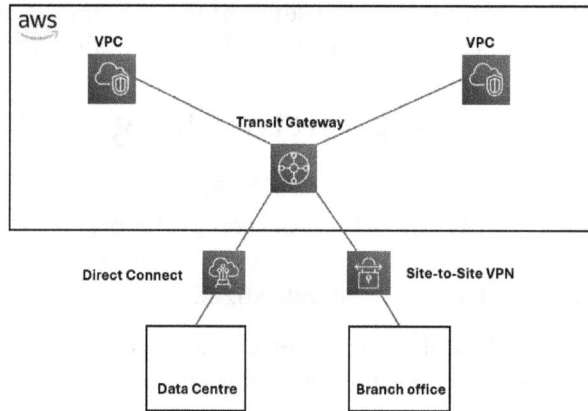

Figure 7.2: SD-WAN solution on AWS using transit gateway

- **AWS Cloud WAN**: This global WAN solution is a relatively new offering from AWS and is the recommended solution to build a virtualized WAN solution involving data centres spread across regions and multiple AWS VPCs and regions for all new customers. Customers previously using transit gateways to build WAN networks can also migrate to Cloud WAN. The following figure shows an SD-WAN solution built using AWS Cloud WAN

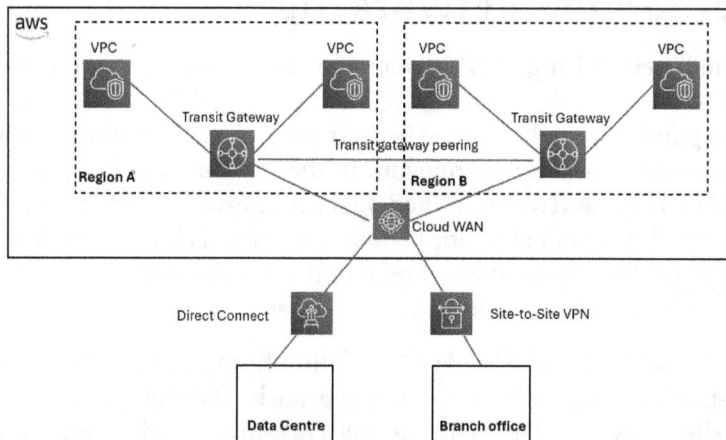

Figure 7.3: SD-WAN solution on AWS using Cloud WAN

- **Palo Alto Prisma SD-WAN**: This is one of the most sophisticated third-party solutions in the SD-WAN market (from the vendor Palo Alto), mainly because it uses AI/ML to make intelligent and improved decisions on network operations and provides enhanced security and flexibility.

- **Aviatrix**: The Aviatrix multi-cloud network solution delivers a redundant and secure multi-cloud network. The Aviatrix network solution integrates with most cloud providers, making it possible to deploy its components (controllers, transit gateways, etc.) inside the cloud and hence seamlessly connect multiple clouds and on-premises networks.

Network costs

Architects not only need to design the solutions but should also be aware of the costs associated with their solutions. The preceding sections have seen many cloud networking features, services, and concepts. It is time now to understand the cost of cloud networks and how they play an essential role in the overall application hosting cost. We are not going to discuss cloud provider-specific pricing for every feature or pricing for external tools, as that is out of the scope of this discussion. However, it is essential to understand some critical cost considerations for cloud networking when designing application architecture on cloud.

- **Understanding what is free:**

  o **Virtual networks**: In a previous section, we discussed virtual networks (like AWS VPC) and many of their components, like security features (like AWS security groups and network access control lists), subnets, etc. There are no charges for creating and using virtual networks and their components. However, as we see next, any optional resources you create inside your virtual networks (like the virtual servers) are chargeable.

- **Understanding what is not free:**

  o **Data transfer**: First and foremost, any data transfer, i.e., data ingress from external sources to the cloud, is free. However, if the source and destination are within the cloud, transferring data from the cloud is not free because any data transfer out, i.e., data egress from the cloud, is charged to the customer. Hence, data transfer from a location in the cloud to the internet, to other locations within the cloud (across zones or regions), or to an on-premises network is charged. Note that the data transfer within a zone is not charged.

  o **Resources inside virtual networks**: Any resources you provide inside your virtual networks in the cloud will cost money. For example, virtual servers, load balancers, gateways, etc. Each of them has a different price tag depending on various factors, like the region in which they are provisioned and the specs used.

Optimizing network costs

Optimizing costs on the cloud is always a skillful activity, and network costs are no exception. Let us look at some common cost optimization strategies:

- Use a **content delivery network** (**CDN**) like AWS CloudFront to cache static data at the edge and avoid data transfer costs.

- Use peering connections between VPCs/VNets within the region.

- Right-size the virtual machines to avoid excessive network bandwidth usage.

- Using tagging strategies to track and analyze network costs and take actions if required.

Common cloud network topologies

In large-scale cloud architectures, multiple virtual networks (i.e., isolated sections in the cloud with a defined range of IP addresses), on-premises data centres, and offices need to be connected. The networking between these nodes can be done using one or more of the solutions mentioned in the previous section, depending on the type of topology you intend to create. We will discuss the following network topologies in this section.

Hub and spoke

This is a popular network topology in which a centralized hub connects many other networks instead of one-to-one connectivity between each network. This simplifies the network, especially when there are many network nodes. There are a few different options to create such a topology. Let us look at them in detail:

- A hub can be a virtual network with many spoke virtual networks connected to it via a peering connection. Usually, the hub virtual network is used to host all the shared services (like a network firewall) that can be used by other spoke virtual networks. The following figure is an example on Azure (the same can be done with other clouds as well):

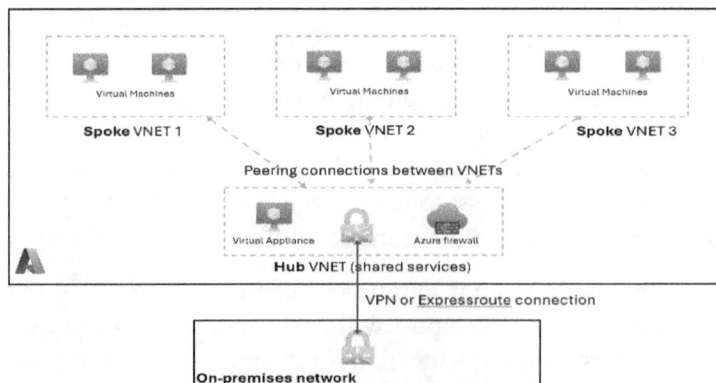

Figure 7.4: Hub and spoke network on Azure using VNet hub

- A cloud-native WAN offering can also act as a hub that can have many different networks as spokes (not only virtual networks), as shown in the following figure with Azure's virtual WAN as an example (similar can be done on other clouds with a corresponding offering like the AWS Transit Gateway). The WAN offerings are cloud-managed hubs, whereas, in the previous scenario, you have to manage the resource (virtual appliances) deployed inside the virtual network used as the hub.

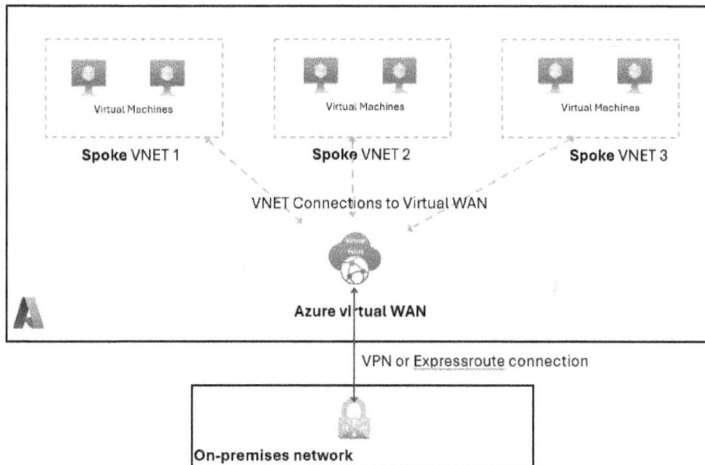

Figure 7.5: Hub and spoke network on Azure using virtual WAN as hub

Full mesh

In a full mesh type of network topology, every node in the network is connected to every other node, creating a mesh-like appearance. This type of topology is suitable for smaller setups but is not highly scalable because the mesh becomes increasingly complicated as the number of nodes increases. The main feature of this type of full mesh architecture is the peering connection used to connect virtual networks (all cloud providers offer a network peering feature). For reference, the following figure is a typical full mesh architecture in AWS with every VPC connected to another VPC, creating the full mesh type of architecture:

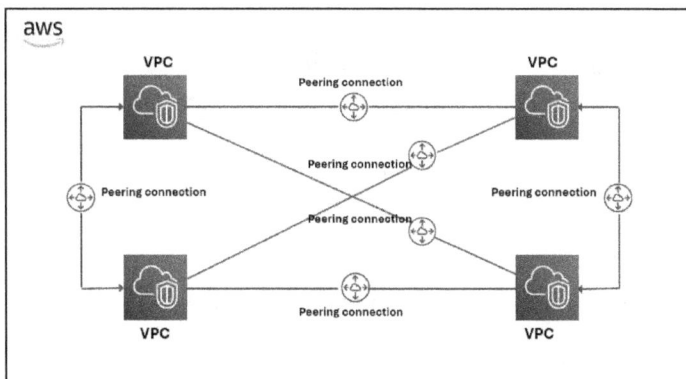

Figure 7.6: Full mesh network on AWS

Full mesh versus hub and spoke

The following table is a comparison between Full mesh and hub and spoke topologies:

	Full mesh	Hub and spoke
Scalability	Less scalable, as more nodes are added, the mesh becomes more complicated	Highly scalable, spokes can be added to the central hub without disturbing the whole architecture
Resiliency	More fault tolerant because there are multiple points of failure, i.e., failure of a single node will not impact the entire setup	It could be less resilient because the failure of the central hub can cause the downfall of the entire setup. Hence, it is important to have high availability for the central hub.
Management	Management tasks like policy deployments are tedious and complex, as the same task needs to be done for every node in the network.	Most management tasks can be done centrally on the hub, and hence are much easier.
Transitive behaviour	Peering connections are non-transitive, and hence the need for point-to-point connectivity	The transitive network can be built using a central hub solution, using solutions like Azure Virtual WAN and AWS Transit Gateway.

Table 7.2: Comparison between full mesh and hub and spoke

Conclusion

In this chapter, we start out the technical foray for our cloud adoption journey, looking at an essential aspect of cloud architecture, i.e., cloud networking. Though we did not intend to go into the deep technical nuts and bolts of networking, there is enough food for thought for you to assess and plan as part of the cloud adoption journey. It is imperative to consider things like hybrid network connectivity and financial aspects of cloud networking, as these can become a headache later.In the next chapter, we will continue the technical discussion of cloud strategy by focusing on another crucial topic—cloud security. No cloud discussion is complete without a mention of security, so that is what we delve into next.

Points to remember

Here are some key takeaways from this chapter:

- There are various building blocks of cloud networking
    - Zones
    - Regions

- o Virtual networks:
    - ▪ Subnets
    - ▪ Route tables
    - ▪ IP addresses
- o Hybrid networking
- o VPN
- o Dedicated private connections
- o Gateways:
    - ▪ NAT gateway
    - ▪ VPN gateway
- o Load balancing:
    - ▪ Layer four
    - ▪ Layer seven
- o DNS

- Intra-cloud networking is the architecture connecting components within the same cloud platform. It primarily consists of the following types of setups:
    - o Single zone architecture
    - o Multi zone architecture
    - o Multi-region architecture

- Inter-cloud networking is the architecture that connects multiple cloud platforms and, in some cases, also the on-premises data centers and offices:
    - o SD-WAN is a virtualized WAN architecture usually adopted for such use cases.
    - o There are various cloud-native and external SD-WAN solutions available.

- In the context of cloud networking, there are primarily two types of network topologies usually adopted:
    - o **Hub and spoke**: In this architecture, a central hub is connected to multiple spoke networks (virtual networks) in the cloud.
    - o **Full mesh**: A complete mesh network has every virtual network connected to every other virtual network.

      The main benefit of hub and spoke is that it is more scalable, whereas the full mesh network is more suitable for smaller networks.

Join our book's Discord space

Join the book's Discord Workspace for Latest updates, Offers, Tech happenings around the world, New Release and Sessions with the Authors:

https://discord.bpbonline.com

CHAPTER 8
Cloud Security

Introduction

In *Chapter 5, Designing for Cloud,* we looked at the design principles and best practices for designing workloads in the cloud across multiple architectural components, and security is one of them. Security is so integral to cloud computing that almost every chapter so far and probably after this will have some mention of it, because no discussion of cloud computing is complete without talking about security.

Cloud security is a broad discipline encompassing infrastructure, data, networks, and application security. When designing your workloads for the cloud, design principles and best practices for security covering all these security aspects must be considered to ensure the workloads are secure from internal and external threats. Ideally, cloud security should be proactive rather than reactive and of utmost priority for everyone involved.

This chapter aims to provide some insights into cloud security and what it entails. We will start with some key concepts of cloud security and then jump into the security domains of application and infrastructure security to understand some of the best practices and considerations that should help in decision-making when planning a cloud adoption. We will also look at the most common tools and platforms that should be part of your cloud architecture. Note that we are just scratching the surface when it comes to cloud security. It is such a sensitive, technical, and vast topic that a single chapter will never be sufficient. However, the idea is to instill the thought and lay the foundation for much detailed technical planning and assessment.

Structure

In this chapter, we will cover the following topics:

- Shared responsibility model
- Security in the cloud
- Zero Trust security architecture
- Cloud security posture management
- Application security
- Infrastructure security
- Identity and access management
- Logging and monitoring
- Tools for the trade

Objectives

By the end of this chapter, readers will be able to understand the core concepts of security in the cloud and how they relate to a cloud adoption strategy. The readers should be able to use the concepts discussed in this chapter as a reference in their planning and decision-making. Spread across the broader domains of infrastructure and application security in the cloud, and without going into architectural and engineering details, this chapter touches on every concept that can be used as guidance.

Shared responsibility model

Implementing security controls on the cloud mandates a clear understanding of the shared responsibility model. Every cloud provider advocates it and expects customers to understand the concept of sharing the responsibility when it comes to managing the security aspects of the cloud. The basic premise of a shared responsibility model is that the responsibility of securing the different layers of the end-to-end stack (from application to the underlying infrastructure) on the cloud is shared between the cloud provider and the customer, depending on the cloud deployment model infrastructure as a service, platform as a service or software as a service. Here is how we can differentiate between the responsibilities:

- Cloud providers are responsible for the security of the cloud, i.e., security of the infrastructure resources owned/provided by the cloud provider.

- Customers are responsible for security in the cloud, i.e., the security of their workloads in the cloud.

The boundaries of responsibility heavily depend on the cloud services you include in your architecture. Basically, the type of cloud deployment model you choose will dictate what the cloud provider is responsible for securing and what you, as a customer, are responsible for. Let us look at these boundaries in more detail in the upcoming sections.

Security of the cloud

Security of the cloud refers to the security of every infrastructure resource that the cloud provider owns and is responsible for. As mentioned, this varies based on the cloud deployment model. This could be the security of just the data center facilities, hardware, and networking, or might include OS and some software components as well. For example, for IaaS services like the virtual servers on the cloud (EC2 instances on AWS or Azure VMs), the cloud provider is responsible for managing the security of the underlying host and the virtualization layer. Since the customer owns and uses these servers, they are then responsible for managing everything above the virtualization layer, including the guest OS, software, and services installed on the servers, as well as the security of those servers. In contrast, for a PaaS service like RDS on AWS, the cloud provider is responsible for managing the database software (including patching, backups, etc.), and the customer is only responsible for securing the databases and data that they own.

Security in the cloud

Security in the cloud refers to the components that the customer must secure themselves, either using the controls provided by the cloud provider, external controls, or both. These are usually the things that sit on top of the cloud infrastructure that the cloud provider is responsible for securing. For example, all the application data, identities, or any application-specific software is the customer's responsibility.

The following table depicts the boundaries in a shared responsibility model:

	SaaS	PaaS	IaaS	On-Prem
Identities				
Application data				
Security controls (Encryption, etc.)				
Application software				
Application runtime				
Virtual machines/Operating system				
Hypervisor				
Physical networks				

Physical hosts				
Data centre				

CSP's responsibility	Shared responsibility	Customer responsibility

Table 8.1: Shared responsibility model

Multi-cloud environment

Shared responsibility model in a multi-cloud environment is not much different. A couple of important considerations worth noting are:

- Each CSP is responsible for its own security of the cloud because the cloud-specific details of each platform may vary.

- Due to a multi-cloud environment, there is an added complexity of the customer's responsibility across each platform.

Zero Trust security architecture

Before diving deep into cloud security, let us get introduced to a security framework called the Zero Trust security architecture (also known as ZTA). The main concept of a Zero Trust architecture is not to trust any component (person, device, or service) in the environment solely based on their network location or placement in the architecture or organization. All components are treated as untrusted from the outset, discarding an implied trust, and every instance of the communication between components must be verified as it could be a potential threat. Of course, the main objective of adopting a Zero Trust architecture is to enhance the security posture. When adopting a Zero Trust strategy, here are some of the design principles to be aware of:

- Always verify the access, regardless of where the request is coming from i.e. internal or external.

- As everything is untrusted, always design your architecture to protect each component from every other component of the architecture.

- Strictly adopt the principle of least privileges and **role-based access control (RBAC)**, i.e. grant only the permissions that are required to perform the job

- Limit the blast radius, i.e., the damage that a potential security attack can cause in your cloud environment. This is usually done by segmenting and isolating workloads and their components using virtual networks, subnets, etc. By including granular isolation, you are not putting all or many of your components in the same virtual network or subnet, as they do not necessarily need to talk to each other, and hence boundaries need to be created.

- As with any security practice, logging and monitoring are the critical components of a Zero Trust security strategy as well. The idea is to collect evidence to take action and improve your security posture.

A Zero Trust strategy is a deviation from traditional security practices where only the external communications are scrutinized, but internal ones enjoy an implied trust. Obviously, a Zero Trust strategy could be very restrictive, intrusive and exhaustive because you are enforcing strict controls and validations across your cloud environment which may not go very well with many key stakeholders.

Moreover, additional security controls can be deemed as impediment to productivity. For example, developers can complain about reduced permissions on certain components blocking them from testing code before releasing it for integration or acceptance testing. Hence, implementing it needs a lot of planning, collaboration, and buy-in from key stakeholders.

In a hybrid or multi-cloud setup, Zero Trust security architecture makes even more sense, even if the network connectivity is private and not over the internet. There are too many points of intrusion and hence potential security threats.

Let us take a simple example of zero trust architecture using a three-tier application:

- The web layer is protected by something like a **web application firewall (WAF)** layer as it is exposed to internet.

- The user attempting to access the application is authenticated by an identity provider like Azure AD.

- The communication between the web layer and app layer needs to be treated untrusted as well, even though it is internal to the application. This needs to be protected by controls like security groups and NACLs.

- Data is the critical asset and needs to be protected too using measures like key management system and data encryption.

- Lastly, sufficient logging and monitoring need to be in place.

This might sound tedious and complicated, but there are many benefits of adopting a Zero Trust strategy:

- Most obvious is an enhanced security posture, which directly helps in meeting certain compliance and regulatory requirements as well.

- Much less attack surface because we are not exposing everything to anyone implicitly, and network segmentation further helps the cause.

- Better visibility into the environment due to rigorous and real-time monitoring arrangements, which eventually leads to much more control of the environment.

- Improved visibility also means faster response time to security threats.

Cloud security posture management

Cloud security posture management (CSPM) is a security practice that aims to perform the following tasks across cloud environments (solo, multi, or hybrid):

- Provide granular visibility and ongoing monitoring

- Identify risks and misconfigurations

- Automate the checks and remediations

SIn simple terms, CSPM is a sophisticated tag for the centralized security management of an organisation's cloud setup. The main purpose is to do everything possible to give that centralized capability instead of adopting and managing multiple tools. There are various CSPM tools that customers should consider when adopting cloud (especially multi-cloud), which can make the cloud configuration much easier and centralized. Having said that, it is still possible that the adopted CSPM tool in turn employs and orchestrates a bunch of other tools to get the work done. Without a specialized tool, the complexity of cloud can be overwhelming and lead to misconfigurations.

Let us now discuss cloud security by looking at the key domains and sub-domains listed.

Application security

Application security involves security of the entire lifecycle—from designing to testing your applications on the cloud, i.e., the security measures injected into the entire SDLC process. Application security includes various components like secure development and deployment practices, secure application runtime, data security, etc. We will look into the details of these components in the upcoming sub-sections.

Application development and deployment

Security should be the top priority right from writing the code by adopting proper development hygiene and secure coding standards. Some of the security best practices for application developers include the following:

- **Securing the application code**: This includes proper authentication and authorization controls (like securing access to source code repositories), validating inputs to the code, and following secure session management practices (like handling cookies, session timeouts, etc.) to ensure only genuine users are allowed access to the application.

- **Checking for vulnerabilities in the code**: This includes testing the application statically (without executing the application) and dynamically (testing the running application) using specialised tools like SonarQube.

- **Implementing error handling**: This includes secure error handling (like avoiding generic error messages), handling exceptions, logging information related to errors to help debugging efforts, and avoiding **denial of service (DoS)** attacks by including rate limiting, throttling, and caching.

- **Securing the application runtime**: These are the practices that ensure the safe running of applications, such as the security of containers, **intrusion detection and prevention (IDS/IPS)**, and monitoring the running application.

DevSecOps

While we are on security in application development, it makes sense to also discuss DevSecOps. It is an approach to software delivery that focuses on the collaboration of development, operations, and security teams to deliver software products quickly and safely. If you understand the DevOps methodology, DevSecOps takes it further by including security at every stage, from planning to operating the application. The core idea of DevSecOps is not to work on securing your application as an afterthought but rather to have security baked into the application from its inception.

An integral piece of the DevSecOps software delivery approach is the **continuous integration and deployment (CI/CD)** development framework. While DevSecOps has a broader scope, CI/CD aims to make the build and release processes much more automated, eventually helping the cause of delivering the software delivery process much more efficiently and agile. DevSecOps is a conceptual practice that requires a cultural and mindset change throughout the organization. In contrast, CI/CD is a much more practical thing that helps adopt such practices using specialized tools and techniques.

All the best practices discussed in the previous section are directly attached to the DevSecOps school of thought. Where CI/CD adds value is the automation of the security checks and tests during the development and deployment phases. For example:

- Automating the repetitive tasks, hence ensuring consistency and avoiding manual errors.

- Accelerating the development processes, resulting in quicker time to market.

- Enabling continuous and early feedback, allowing the security issues to be fixed sooner rather than later.

Data security

The most important asset of every company is its data; hence, it deserves a thoroughly planned security strategy and a stringent set of security controls. In the upcoming sub sections, we will look at some common and essential strategies to protect data in the cloud:

Data encryption

Data is everywhere, it is stored on disks attached to your cloud servers, and it flows in and out of them all the time. Encrypting data at rest on the disks and in transit when it travels into and out of the cloud is an essential data security measure. The idea of encrypting sensitive data is to make the plain text data unreadable to unauthorized users by using encryption keys that are also safeguarded. There are two types of encryption algorithms:

- **Symmetric encryption**: This type of encryption uses the same key for encryption and decryption.

- **Asymmetric encryption**: This type of encryption uses a key pair, i.e., separate keys for encryption and decryption. A public key is used for encryption, and a private key is used for decryption.

Nowadays, most cloud-native services offer built-in encryption using cloud provider-owned keys or the flexibility of using customer-owned keys.

Key management

Key management is another critical aspect of data encryption that deserves much attention. The efficacy of any encryption algorithm depends on the security of the keys used for encryption. Every cloud provider offers a **key management service** (**KMS**) that lets customers securely manage the encryption keys by providing some or all of the following features:

- Generation or creation of new keys.

- Rotation of keys to reduce the risk of compromise.

- Deletion of keys that you no longer need.

- Safely use access policies to ensure safe storage of keys.

Most cloud providers also provide flexibility by letting the customers manage the end-to-end lifecycle of encryption keys, especially for businesses concerned about the security and control of their encryption keys. However, there is a trade-off—with more control comes more responsibility, i.e., safeguarding the keys, including ensuring the keys are rotated regularly to minimize the risk of a compromise. To manage the lifecycle of keys, customers can use **hardware security modules** (**HSMs**) provided by the cloud providers or from other third-party HSM providers, like *Thales*. HSMs usually cost more than using the default key stores supplied by the cloud's key management service. Still, they are apt for those customers who want to control the lifecycle and have mature key management processes in place.

Data backups

A very old-school but highly effective approach to secure your data against accidental loss, disasters, and cyberattacks is ensuring timely data backups. Some of the main benefits of an exemplary data backup policy are listed here:

- Protection of your business-critical data against accidents and disasters

- Ensure business continuity by minimizing data loss

- Adherence to specific regulatory and compliance requirements

Hence, ensure you have a robust data backup strategy to prepare for mistakes and eventualities beyond your control. An ideal backup strategy should consider the following factors:

- Thoughtfully planned full and incremental/differential backups based on your target **recovery point objective (RPO)** values. RPO is the data loss that can be tolerated in a disaster.

- Storing multiple copies of backups across multiple locations, i.e., data centres, availability zones, or regions, to prepare you for the worst. This can even include storing copies on various clouds and/or on-premises.

- Encrypting and controlling access to the backups is as important as doing the same for the live data.

- Designing the backup strategy with local and industry-specific regulatory and compliance requirements is essential.

- Testing the backup and recovery procedures before implementing them in your production environment.

Data access

Controlling access to the data in the cloud must be carefully planned and designed. Who has access to your data, and what is the level of access directly related to data safety against unauthorized access? Controlling access to data also depends on where the data has been stored and in what form. The default position for every access request to data in the cloud is deny, and that is why you need to carefully plan who needs to access and what level of access they would need. Here are some approaches to control access:

- First and foremost, regardless of the storage type, you need a very robust **identity and access management (IAM)** strategy to control access to your data and everything in the cloud. We will have a more focused discussion on IAM later in the chapter.

- Depending on the storage service in the cloud, access policies play an essential role in controlling access to stored data. Policies define the rules to grant or restrict access, i.e., which users can access, what action they can perform (insert, retrieve, delete, etc.), and what the effect is (deny, allow, etc.). Note that not every service in the cloud has the provision of attaching policies.

- Monitor, track, audit, and alert every access to your cloud environment. Sometimes, only external access is sufficient, but some organizations might also want to monitor internal access patterns. The more access data you collect, the better preventive actions you can plan.

Infrastructure security

The other domain of cloud security is infrastructure security, which encompasses the measures taken to secure the underlying cloud infrastructure used to host applications.

Network security

Cloud network security is about securing all communications to and from the cloud. The network traffic in the cloud is classified into two broad categories:

- **North-south traffic**: All network traffic between your cloud environment and internet or on-premises data centres is referred to as the north-south traffic. It can be in either direction (to or from). For example, external users accessing your web applications hosted on the cloud or your administrators accessing cloud infrastructure resources are classified as north-south traffic. This type of network traffic is the most susceptible to attacks as the connection involves an external entity on the other side.

- **East-west traffic**: This type of traffic flow refers to the communication within the cloud environment between resources. It is also termed as the horizontal traffic that stays within the cloud. It is less prone to attacks and, hence, less demanding in terms of security controls. Usually, the inbuilt security controls like security groups and **access control lists** (**ACLs**) in AWS or **network security groups** (**NSG**) in Azure are sufficient to control and secure the flows. However, many cloud customers need stringent security in their cloud environment, including inspecting and filtering all the east-west traffic.

Some of the common approaches used for network security are:

- **Web application firewall (WAF)**: A WAF is a solution to protect your web applications from common layer 7 attacks like SQL injection, cross-site scripting, etc. All popular cloud providers have a native WAF service, or you can opt for your favourite third-party WAF provider like Palo Alto, Imperva, etc. A WAF in front of the application hosted on the cloud serves multiple functions, like inspecting the traffic, filtering the traffic, blocking the bad traffic, and logging everything for future reference and analysis. All this is done based on the rules you define.

- **Network firewall**: You can inspect and filter (depending on the tool you are using) all east-west or north-south network traffic using some sort of network firewall inside the cloud environment. Similar to WAF, you can use the built-in cloud solutions or a third-party solution from popular vendors. The main difference between a network firewall and a WAF is that WAF is used for protection against layer 7 web attacks whereas network firewall works at layer 3 (network layer) and is used to inspect and filter the network traffic based on IP addresses, ports and protocols that is trying to reach the infrastructure resources inside your cloud environment.

- **Network segmentation**: By creating virtual networks and subnets, you can create granular segments inside your cloud environment. This has benefits like isolating the traffic by routing it to only the segments that are required in the communication, and you can easily control the traffic using built-in controls at the subnet level. The segmentation approach is used to protect east-west traffic within the cloud environment.

- **Encryption**: Encrypting the data that flows through the network to and from the cloud or inside the cloud is always a recommended approach. We have discussed data encryption separately in this chapter in detail.

- **Logging and monitoring**: Anomalous activities in your network could be a potential threat. Hence, tracking what is going on inside your network is important for multiple reasons. We have a dedicated section for logging and monitoring later in the chapter, as it is an integral part of end-to-end security on the cloud and spans applications as well as infrastructure.

Identity and access management

One of the most critical (yet basic) strategies for including the required authentication and authorization capabilities in your cloud environment is **identity and access management (IAM)**. It is one of the fundamental services that underpins every security architecture in the cloud.

The key components of a good IAM strategy are:

- **Identities**: Every entity that needs access to any resource in your cloud environment is classified as an identity and needs to be appropriately managed. It can be a human (like internal employees or external contractors) or a non-human entity (like applications or virtual machines). The key here is how and when you provision and remove the identities in your cloud environment.

- **Authentication**: Authentication is the verification of the identities of who they claim to be, i.e., ensuring that a user has the account they use to access the resources in the cloud. Some of the ways this process is done effectively are listed here:

- o **Password policies**: Enforce strong passwords that are hard to guess or hack. Simple passwords like your name or date of birth should not be permitted.

- o **Multi-factor authentication**: Enforcing MFA so that there are more than just passwords to verify the users. For example, mobile phones can be used for one-time codes along with initial passwords.

- o **Single sign-on (SSO)**: Providing an SSO capability so that users can use their pre-authenticated credentials to access services in the cloud.

- o **Temporary access:** Try to use temporary credentials for guests who do not need ongoing access to your cloud environment. If they have accounts with another identity provider, try using Identity Federation to allow temporary access instead of providing permanent credentials.

- **Authorization**: Authorization is the process of granting the required level of access to the identities that have been authenticated. Some of the best practices to control authorization to access cloud resources are:

  - o **Use RBAC policy:** This means granting permissions to identities based on their role in the environment. RBAC works on the concept of permissions and roles. Permissions are the actions the user can perform on a resource, and roles are collections of such permissions. A good example of RBAC is a tester role that has necessary read-only permissions to test applications but should not be able to make changes to the application.

  - o **Principle of least privileges:** The principle of least privileges is another practice that goes hand in hand with RBAC. This principle suggests that users be granted only the permissions required to perform the action they need to. For example, a finance user might only need to view the cloud bills and usage reports but not log in or access the cloud resources.

  - o **Access policies:** Use resource-level access policies wherever possible to limit access to those resources. Usually defined in terms of allowed actions the users can perform, these policies are a great tool to control granular level access for added security.

Logging and monitoring

Detection and investigation are key tenets of any company's security posture. Even when you have enough preventive controls, unwanted intrusions and exposures still happen. That is why you need logs to analyse further what, who, and when of each action performed in your cloud environment, and then be able to plan accordingly to respond to events promptly.

Monitoring and logging are more of the reactive approaches to security, but nonetheless, an effective strategy is one that allows the security and operations teams to react fast and minimize the damage, if any. Each component of your architecture on the cloud deserves a focused monitoring and logging strategy and equally appropriate tooling. Most importantly, the following areas of the architecture should be considered for monitoring and logging:

- Infrastructure components like computing, storage, network connections, etc.

- Application components like the web layer, application layer, databases, etc.

- Security components like firewalls, internal and external access, etc.

Monitoring and logging in the cloud can be complicated, with many pertinent questions to be answered, such as:

- What to monitor?

- What tools to use?

- Where and how to collect the logs?

- Who needs to be altered?

- How to report?

This goes a step further in a multi-cloud scenario with a need for integrated solutions. That is why we have a dedicated chapter on this, *Chapter 9, Cloud Observability,* where we will answer all the above questions.

Tools for the trade

Let us now look at some of the standard tools used to implement security at different layers of a cloud architecture based on the functions they perform.

- **Firewalls:**
  o Layer 7 solutions—Fortinet's FortiWeb, Cloudflare, Imperva WAF, AWS/ Azure native WAF solution, and many more
  o Layer 3 firewall solutions—AWS Network Firewall

- **DDoS protection:**
  o Cloud-native—AWS Shield, Azure DDoS protection, GCP Armor

- **Logging and monitoring:**
  o Cloud-native: AWS CloudWatch, AWS CloudTrail, Azure Monitor, Google Cloud Monitoring, etc.
  o Third-party tools: New Relic, Splunk, Datadog, etc.

Chapter 9: Cloud Observability covers logging and monitoring in depth. We will also discuss many of the popular tools in detail.

- **Identity and access management:**
    - Cloud-native tools: AWS IAM, MS Entra ID***, etc.
    - Third-party tools: Okta, Ping Identity, ForgeRock

Though Entra ID (formerly known as Azure AD) is a native solution from Microsoft, it is widely used as an IAM solution for various hosting providers, such as AWS or even on-premises systems.

- **Encryption**:
    - Cloud-native **key management solutions (KMS)**
    - External key stores, like Thales, HashiCorp, etc.

- **Data backups:**
    - Cloud-native backup tools—AWS Backup, Azure Backup, etc.
    - External backup tools—Commvault, Veeam, etc.

- **CSPM: Some of the popular CSPM tools used by customers are:**
    - AWS Security Hub
    - Microsoft's Defender for Cloud
    - Prisma Cloud by Palo Alto
    - CloudGuard by Check Point

Conclusion

When it comes to security on the cloud, there are no compromises. Security is paramount not only for customers but also for every cloud provider. In this chapter, we learned about the basics of cloud security and what the key considerations should be for anyone planning a cloud adoption. The two broad scopes of security on the cloud are application security and infrastructure security, further encompassing all the other security domains like data security, network security, identities, etc.

We also touched on the investigative side of cloud security (i.e., logging and monitoring), but the details are for the upcoming chapter, where we try to make sense of cloud observability. Before starting your cloud journey, thoroughly examine each of these domains and ascertain your current cloud maturity and security awareness. Identify the gaps and then make informed decisions about investments.

In the next chapter, we will expand on our logging and monitoring discussion by exploring the observability aspect of the cloud operations domain, which is critical to run your workloads as per the expected SLAs

Points to remember

Here are some key takeaways from this chapter:

- The shared responsibility model is the most fundamental concept of security on the cloud. You need to understand what level of security the cloud provider undertakes and what components you, as a customer, are responsible for securing.

- Zero Trust architecture is a do not trust anyone model in security, which is being adopted increasingly by customers moving to the cloud.

- The key security domains and sub-domains are:

  o Application security:

    ▪ Application development and deployment—secure coding practices, Devsecops approach, security for CI/CD pipelines, etc.

    ▪ Data security—Data encryption, backups, secure access, etc.

  o Infrastructure security:

    ▪ Network security

    ▪ IAM

  o Various cloud-native and external tools are available for every aspect of security in the cloud. The right tool is the one that ticks most of the boxes for you.

Join our book's Discord space

Join the book's Discord Workspace for Latest updates, Offers, Tech happenings around the world, New Release and Sessions with the Authors:

https://discord.bpbonline.com

CHAPTER 9

Cloud Observability

Introduction

In the last few chapters, we have looked at the technical aspects of a cloud journey that should be considered when formulating a cloud strategy. The next in line is a critical capability for operating any cloud environment called **observability**. Observability is the term used to get insights into your IT infrastructure and applications using specialized tools and technologies. Those insights can be used to gain visibility into their current state and also predict future behavior. The importance of observability is usually underestimated, resulting in less attention and investment than it deserves. There are plenty of issues with a poor observability setup on the cloud, for example, underperforming applications, unacceptable downtimes, unidentified security vulnerabilities, etc. In this chapter, we will highlight some key concepts and the importance of observability in a successful cloud implementation.

We started discussing observability in *Chapter 8: Cloud Security,* when we touched on the investigative side of security. This chapter further explores the observability aspect of operating your workloads in more depth.

Structure

In this chapter, we will cover the following topics:

- Observability in the cloud

- Multi-cloud monitoring
- SIEM
- Tools for the trade
- Recap of important strategies

Objectives

By the end of this chapter, readers should understand what observability is all about and why it is critical to the success of your workloads on the cloud and the overall business. Understanding and implementing observability is as crucial as all other aspects when planning a cloud adoption and developing a strategy. We will also discuss the most popular tools available in the market and their strengths to help you, as the strategy maker, make some informed decisions as part of your larger cloud strategy.

Observability in the cloud

Observability is an integral part of the IT operations discipline on any platform, whether on-premises or on the cloud. We are focusing on the cloud and its operations, but those with a data-centric background can easily relate to most of the concepts discussed in this chapter. Suppose you remember the four phases of a cloud adoption journey discussed in *Chapter 4, The Journey*. In that case, observability is part of the last phase, i.e., the operation of this journey that aims to provide visibility into your cloud workloads.

The key tenets of observability are monitoring the system's state, logging or recording the information about the system state, alerting the relevant stakeholders about anything that deserves immediate attention or remediation, and finally, analyzing the data observed and recorded to make sense of trends and draw some meaningful inferences using visualizations. The observability of an application should be a line item in your list right from the planning stage of the application. Let us have a look at all the components of an observability strategy.

Monitoring

Once an application has been deployed on the cloud, you must ensure it runs as expected. There are targets or objectives, called service level agreements (SLAs), that your application should strive to achieve. SLAs should be quantifiable, realistic, and achievable rather than overly optimistic and set unachievable targets that can lead to failure. If an organization's applications serve external customers, it is common to associate financial compensation with them to accentuate the customer's confidence. Some of the common SLAs that monitoring can ensure compliance with are:

- System availability and uptime guarantee SLAs

- Acceptable response time SLAs

- Security-related SLAs

An example of an industry-standard SLA is the uptime SLA of EC2 instances in AWS. At a regional level, they have a commitment of 99.99% uptime over a month for their EC2 instances. However, if the uptime falls below 99.99% and is above 99%, the financial compensation is 10% service credits.

As part of planning and designing the application, you also develop **non-functional requirements** (**NFRs**) that your monitoring strategy should align with. NFRs are the application characteristics used to define the scope of your monitoring strategy. For example, some common NFRs are:

- **Performance**: Response time, latency, etc.

- **Reliability**: Failover, availability, etc.

- **Security**: Data protection, privacy, etc.

- **User experience:** Response time, look and feel of application, etc.

You need to adhere to these SLAs and NFRs for various reasons, such as:

- Meeting your customer requirements and expectations.

- Make the service providers accountable.

- Compliance and regulatory reasons.

- Improving the reliability of the services.

- Providing a competitive advantage resulting in the success of the business.

Apparently, you cannot do this without a robust and thought-through monitoring strategy. Monitoring ensures visibility into the system and, hence, timely actions and issue resolution.

Application performance monitoring

Another critical concept to be aware of as part of observability, specifically the monitoring aspect, is **application performance monitoring** (**APM**). APM is the process of monitoring and tracking application performance. While monitoring on the cloud has a much broader scope, including infrastructure, APM is a branch of monitoring that focuses on the application performance and is used to track metrics such as:

- Latency

- Response time

- Memory

- CPU

Logging

The next part of an observability strategy is the logging of information (logs) captured from monitoring the applications and infrastructure using your chosen tools. It refers to collecting and storing data regarding the various aspects of your cloud environment. For troubleshooting the issues in your cloud environment, logging is probably the most important part of the overall observability strategy. The key benefits of having a comprehensive logging approach are:

- Logs aid in troubleshooting issues in your cloud environment, as they are critical for debugging and root-cause analysis.

- Logging is critical for identifying and fixing performance-related problems as well.

- For regulatory and compliance purposes, you might be required to capture and retain logs for a specific duration.

- Logging is a critical element of the cloud security posture, as you can use logs to detect potential breaches and anomalies.

- Logging is also good for the system's overall availability, as it can help administrators be more proactive based on trends before a real issue is encountered.

- A study of logs should also give crucial hints on capacity optimization.

Some of the key considerations when planning your logging strategy are listed here:

- Plan what you want to log across your environment. Some events and information could be deemed mandatory, but a lot of it is optional as well. It depends on what your organization thinks is necessary to take timely actions and make informed decisions.

- Consider log aggregation i.e. centralizing and analyzing logs from various sources across your cloud infrastructure. It provides central visibility to the team and the ability to do a faster RCA, along with resolutions. There are multiple tools that can be used for log aggregation, like AWS CloudWatch, Splunk, etc.

- Logging directly affects storage in terms of what you want to log and how long you want to retain the logs. The storage of log data, in turn, corresponds to the ongoing costs in the cloud.

- Data in the logs can be sensitive in nature and hence require security measures like encryption, access control, etc.

- Make sure you have an analysis and visualization step in your observability strategy because making sense of the log data (sometimes very technical) for wider organizations and many non-IT stakeholders goes a long way toward sending the right message. We will discuss the analysis in the section to come, *Analysis*.

Alerting

Moving on, the next component of the observability strategy is being able to trigger notifications at the right time to the right people for the right action to be taken based on the severity of the issue. Let us break the statement down:

- **Trigger notifications**: Alerts should be triggered based on certain events and conditions being met. For example, a security alert or disk storage filling up to 80% could trigger notifications in the form of text messages, email messages, or even phone calls.

- **Right time**: The timing of notification is critical for any intended action. Of course, the intention is to trigger real-time or near-real-time notifications. Delayed notifications and hence the actions would not make sense regarding customer experience and system availability. The timing of alerts is also linked to the metrics and thresholds that you agree with your management.

- **Right people**: People who receive these notifications could be the developers, the operation teams, architects, or even the managers. Deciding who the right people to receive is a very subjective consideration, but it is an important one.

- **Right action**: The intended actions can be automated or manual. Most tools and technologies provide capabilities for automated error rectification and system recoveries based on the alerts triggered. However, sometimes, old-fashioned manual actions are still required based on the complexity of the issue.

- **Severity**: Usually, you will assign a severity level to issues based on their impact on your system's availability and end-user experience. The higher the impact, the higher the severity, and hence, the appropriate action needs to be mapped to it.

Having a robust alerting system in the cloud observability solution significantly impacts how efficiently you respond to situations and enhances the availability of your workloads in the cloud.

Analysis

Finally, let us discuss the analysis part of the observability. Once you have collected all the logs and monitoring data, you and your management would like to make sense of it. Most of the logs are raw, making them hard for most non-technical stakeholders to decipher.

Moreover, the volume of collected logs is so massive that you need a way to summarize and visualize them to understand the system's performance and health. Analysing collected data is intended to draw meaningful insights about your cloud environment.

Data analysis is a hot topic these days. There has been so much innovation, particularly with **artificial intelligence** (**AI**) becoming a key enabler. There are obvious reasons why the data analysis discipline has gained so much attention and popularity lately in terms of a robust observability strategy. Some of them are as follows:

- You can be more proactive and predictive in detecting issues. By analysing the historical data, you can identify patterns and trends.

- Efficient analysis powers data-driven decision-making.

- Use the historical data to forecast future capacity requirements and performance efficiencies.

- Not only performance optimization, but you can also identify opportunities for cost optimization. For example, oversized or unutilized resources.

An integral part of the analysis is data visualization, which essentially presents data comprehensibly for a person of any technical background and skill set. This can be done in many ways, and the best one is the one that makes the most sense for the team. Some of the popular ones are:

- There are various chart and graph types—bar charts, pie charts, line graphs, etc.

- Heatmaps are used to identify areas of peaks and troughs.

- There are various custom dashboards that can be created to provide a holistic view for decision making.

Visualization can be made more interactive and user-friendly by letting the end users customize the dashboards according to their requirements. Most tools can filter the input data and customize the outputs.

Multi-cloud monitoring

Coming to a multi-cloud setup, planning and implementing an integrated observability strategy has different challenges and complexities. With a multi-cloud strategy, the focus is on getting a consolidated and consistent view of workloads across multiple cloud environments and responding promptly to issues. However, some of the challenges that an observability strategy in multi-cloud environments must address are listed here:

- Observability data is spread and siloed across multiple clouds.

- Dispersed data may not be relatable, and hence, it is challenging to paint a consolidated picture.

- Troubleshooting any issues in the multi-cloud environment is complicated, as finding the root cause could be cumbersome.

- All CSPs offer their native observability solutions, which makes it difficult to centralize the collection and analysis of data

There are several solutions (or a combination of them) you should consider for addressing these challenges, such as:

- **Tools**: Look at specialized tools that can provide an integrated and centralized view. These are mostly third-party tools, but some cloud-native tools also support monitoring and logging for multiple clouds. You need tools for everything—monitoring, logging, analysis, visualization, and troubleshooting, emphasizing the fact that tools are the most important aspect of the observability strategy.

- **Skills**: Consider reskilling, training, hiring, and other means of imparting the required skills to the team regarding multiple cloud platforms and specialized observability tools.

- **Efficiency**: Automate repeatable processes and tasks as much as possible to make them more efficient. Automation not only removes the scope of human error but also frees people for much more productive tasks.

- **Consistency**: Multiple clouds also mean different metrics, formats, and standards. When planning for a multi-cloud environment, you must establish consistent and common metrics, standards, and even terminologies that everyone can understand.

SIEM

Security information and event management (SIEM) is a branch of cloud observability with a security-specific focus on threat detection and incident management. SIEM tools are specifically designed to collect, aggregate, and analyse security-related information in your cloud environment and then respond to incidents using inbuilt alerting mechanisms or automated responses. SIEM tools usually collect data from almost every possible source in your cloud environment, like firewalls, routers, switches, servers, IDS/IPS devices, etc.

SIEM deserves special mention in this chapter because, lately, it has become an essential part of most organizations' overall observability strategy. Due to the sheer volume and variety of cybersecurity threats, adopting an SIEM tool makes sense as it can expedite and automate the detection and response for most security breaches. Of course, what you can achieve by having SIEM technology in your organization also depends on the choice of tools and skills.

Some key benefits of SIEM are as follows:

- Centralised management and view of the security data from across the cloud and hybrid environments.

- Real-time detection and response to security events. With advanced AI capabilities these days, detection and response have been even further improved.

- Enhanced reporting and auditing capabilities that align with the compliance requirements.

Tools for the trade

As mentioned, a few times already, the importance of tools in an observability strategy cannot be stressed enough. Let us list some standard observability tools, both cloud-native and third-party.

Cloud-native tools

Let us look at the native tools from the three major cloud providers:

- **AWS:**
  - **Amazon CloudWatch**: CloudWatch is a comprehensive service that is used to monitor cloud infrastructure and deployed applications, collect and store logs, and integrate with other services like *Amazon SNS* for sending alerts and notifications. Since it is a cloud-native service, it is deeply integrated with most AWS services and can provide useful insights into their performance and health. Furthermore, it gives APM capabilities using features such as CloudWatch Application Signals.
  - **AWS X-Ray**: X-Ray is another useful monitoring tool, but it is for distributed applications deployed on AWS. For example, you can track the entire route of user requests through your microservices-based applications as they travel across various components and hence map performance issues to specific components. Like *CloudWatch*, it also has integration with many AWS services used for application deployments.

- **Azure:**
  - **Azure Monitor**: Similar to AWS' CloudWatch, Azure Monitor is a comprehensive monitoring tool that provides monitoring, logging, and alerting features. It also provides features and capabilities, like the *Log Analytics Workspace*, which allows it to work with on-premises and other cloud platforms. Of course, the monitoring capabilities for non-Azure platforms will be limited and need to be evaluated on a case-by-case basis.

- **Google Cloud Platform:**
  - **Google Cloud Monitoring**: The corresponding observability tool in Google's armoury is its native Google Cloud monitoring solution, which also provides a comprehensive range of observability services. However, unlike Azure Monitor, its focus is on GCP resources and hence may not be suitable for a multi-cloud scenario.

Third-party tools

There are plenty of third-party tools available in the market that are specialized in the observability space, but we will look at a few of the most popular ones here:

- **Splunk**: Arguably, it is the most popular SIEM tool in the market right now. Splunk, as a platform, offers two versions:

  o **Enterprise**: A version that can be deployed on-premises or on any cloud.

  o **Cloud**: A subscription-based SaaS version that needs no infrastructure.

  Splunk offers several products in the observability category, such as Splunk APM (AppDynamics provided Splunk's APM capabilities after they were merged by Cisco), Splunk IT Service Intelligence, and Splunk infrastructure monitoring. Apart from its known SIEM capabilities, Splunk's main strength is its ability to handle large volumes of log data.

- **Dynatrace**: Dynatrace's most unique value proposition as an observability platform is its AI-powered approach to monitoring, detection, and root cause analysis. Though it is considered costly and complex compared to many other tools in the market, its strong support makes it a very viable cloud solution.

- **New Relic**: New Relic excels in application performance monitoring. It can be an excellent tool for application insights, backed by many user-friendly features like rich dashboards.

- **Datadog**: Datadog's most appealing aspect as an observability tool is its suite of comprehensive features, including APM, Infrastructure monitoring, SIEM capabilities, log collection and management, and many more. However, unlike many of its competitors, it might not be a good tool for managing large volumes of logs.

- **Prometheus**: Most popular for handling time series data, Prometheus has gained popularity as a cloud observability tool of choice because of its suitability for containerized systems and, most importantly, its open-source monitoring system.

Cloud-native tools are always a good and cheaper option, and most features are available out of the box. However, they might lack certain advanced capabilities, making the third-party specialized tools a better choice. Here is a quick comparison:

	Strengths	**Weaknesses**
Cloud-native tools	Strong integration with cloud services and features Most native services and features are very cost-effective	May not be suitable for multi-cloud use cases Vendor lock-in May lack advanced features
Third-party tools	Usually compatible with most cloud platforms Support for multi-cloud and hybrid cloud Much more mature than native services and offers a lot of innovative and advanced features.	Usually costlier than the cloud-native services May not integrate seamlessly with underlying cloud platform's every service and feature

Table 9.1: Comparison of cloud-native and third-party tools

Recap of important strategies

Having looked at the various aspects of an observability strategy, it is apt to summarize some of the proven and effective observability strategies:

- Define precise requirements of what events to log, how long to retain logs, and the level of detail required. This can impact the complexity and cost of your observability solution(s).

- Implement robust logging to ensure critical events, including system errors, security events, and user activity, can be logged. Of course, it again boils down to what is relevant for your particular use case(s).

- Use a centralized log management solution to collect, store, and analyse logs from various sources. Collecting logs separately and then merging them could be very cumbersome.

- Setting up real-time monitoring tools to detect anomalies and security threats is always handy in these times when immediate results are needed, and customer satisfaction hinges heavily on the overall experience.

- Use advanced analytics and predictive techniques to correlate events and identify patterns that can help you create future-proofed and proactive solutions.

- Configure alerts based on the criticality and severity of issues to ensure a timely response.

Last but not least, continuously review and tune your logging, monitoring, and alerting requirements and configurations to optimize performance and security. What is relevant today may not be important in the future.

Conclusion

Observability in the cloud is about keeping the lights on like traditional IT operations, but it is also about being proactive and ensuring the workloads perform at or above par in the future using analytical and visualization techniques. Observability can broadly be divided into four phases: monitoring, logging, alerting, and analytics. Each phase plays a significant role in forming an observability strategy on the cloud and leverages specialized tools—cloud-native, third-party, or a combination of both. SIEM deserves special mention as part of observability because of its impact on a cloud environment's security posture and customer experience.

As we conclude, it is also important to mention the impact of AI on observability strategies. With AI becoming a hot trend, observability in the cloud is also going through innovation. AI promises to enhance the experience and add value to the processes. For example, faster and automated anomaly detection, predictive analysis for future issues based on available data, automated remediation of several issues etc.

In the next chapter, we will examine the resiliency in cloud environments, which is critical for ensuring workload availability and business continuity.

Points to remember

Here are the key takeaways from this chapter:

- Observability has four important tenets:
  o **Monitoring**: It is about gaining visibility into workloads deployed in the cloud
  o **Logging**: Logging is about collecting and storing data from monitoring tools
  o **Alerting**: Alerting is about sending notifications and triggering responses based on collected logs and events
  o **Analysis**: It is about analysing and visualizing the data collected from the workloads
- **Application performance monitoring (APM)** is a specialized monitoring area that needs extra consideration and tools because most monitoring tools might only cover the infrastructure part of the environment.
- Key benefits of the right observability strategy on the cloud are listed here:
  o Make data-driven and informed decisions
  o Be more proactive in handling issues
  o Meeting customer expectations
  o Improving business to drive success
  o Enhanced security
- A multi-cloud observability strategy requires more planning and tools that can reduce the complexity and present an integrated view of the environment instead of having to separately manage every cloud platform in the mix.
- SIEM is an important branch of observability focused on collecting and analysing security-related information and events from across your IT environment, whether hybrid or multi-cloud.
- There are cloud-native and third-party tools available for observability in the cloud. What works best for you depends on your requirements.
  o Cloud-native tools are usually cost-effective and seamlessly integrated with the underlying cloud services.
  o Third-party tools are usually much more mature than cloud-native tools, but might be costlier and not completely integrated with every cloud service.

Join our book's Discord space

Join the book's Discord Workspace for Latest updates, Offers, Tech happenings around the world, New Release and Sessions with the Authors:

https://discord.bpbonline.com

CHAPTER 10
Cloud Resiliency

Introduction

By way of definition, resiliency refers to a system's ability to withstand and recover from disruptions (like a failure of a component), ensuring availability. The system's availability is directly proportional to happy customers and, hence, the success of your business. To increase availability, you obviously need to make the systems resilient. Resiliency should be considered one of the top priorities, regardless of the hosting platform. However, resiliency in the cloud is much different from what it is on-premises in terms of architecture, implementation, and management.

Cloud makes creating resilient systems much easier and quicker due to its inherent nature and all the great features available natively on most cloud platforms. Many proven design patterns can achieve the desired level of resiliency on the cloud within or across regions. Again, the best architecture depends on your specific resiliency requirements.

Resiliency is an integral part of the architecture theme called reliability, which we discussed in *Chapter 5: Designing for Cloud*. The main objective of this chapter is to focus on resiliency and highlight its importance for the reliability of cloud architectures. We will start this chapter with a definition of resiliency and some other concepts that are part of it. The idea is to familiarize readers with each of these concepts and be able to differentiate between them. This should help in planning the resiliency approach and the solutions underneath. We will also cover some architecture patterns that can be adopted for various resiliency requirements.

Structure

In this chapter, we will cover the following topics:

- Resiliency
- Plan for failure
- Business continuity planning
- High availability
- Disaster recovery
- Design patterns for resiliency
- Resiliency use cases
- Examples from the real world

Objectives

This chapter will strengthen readers' overall understanding of resiliency in the cloud. They can use it as a reference for any future cloud designs. By the end of this chapter, readers should be able to learn resiliency strategies and considerations in the cloud.

Resiliency

Resiliency in the cloud means the ability of your workloads to withstand excess stress, security attacks, bugs, or even the failure of component(s) and quickly restore and recover as much as possible to resume business operations. Some critical aspects of resiliency are:

- **High availability (HA)**
- **Disaster recovery (DR)**
- **Business continuity planning (BCP)**

They all sound very similar and are often used interchangeably. We will delve deeper into each of them and try to explain what each means and the strategies and solutions that can be used to ensure your cloud architecture is resilient, as per your requirements.

Since we are discussing cloud strategy in this book, it is crucial to understand that achieving resiliency in the cloud differs from achieving it in an on-premises setup. Most of these differences are attributed to the cloud's fundamental nature.

Here are some of the key differences between a cloud and an on-premises setup that can influence your resiliency architectures:

- **Cloud-native features**: All cloud platforms offer native and built-in resiliency features. Managed services, like the AWS **Relational Database Service (RDS)**, have built-in resiliency, so users do not have to worry about or design for it.

- **Agility**: Unlike traditional on-premises environments, where you manually rack and stack servers and other infrastructure elements, the cloud does not require users to worry about the physical infrastructure. Basic operations like infrastructure provisioning are minutes or seconds now and can even be automated. Resiliency planning is the biggest beneficiary of cloud agility because recovery strategies take this into account.

- **Cloud innovation**: It is a well-known fact that cloud technologies innovate very fast. Because of their agility, they also allow users to experiment and innovate. Hence, with evolving requirements, new solutions can be developed and adopted much quicker than in the on-premises world.

- **Financial considerations**: Any infrastructure provisioning in an on-premises setup requires significant planning and investment (till the decommissioning stage). However, due to the cloud payment models (like pay-as-you-go), cost is not a blocker anymore (if managed smartly).

Here is a quick summary of the differences:

	Cloud	**On-premises**
Platform native features	Cloud platforms offer various native features that have resiliency built-in	In an on-premises setup, the users have to build the required resiliency
Agility	Since the CSP takes care of all infrastructure resources, including data centre, application resiliency can be provisioned much faster	The users have to take care of underlying infrastructure resources, and hence, there is a lot of manual and long processes involved
Innovation	Cloud technologies keep innovating regularly with new features and services. Resiliency solutions can also evolve with these innovations	There is a lot of cost and effort involved in implementing and managing any groundbreaking solutions
Cost	Due to quick infrastructure provisioning and pay-as-you-go billing model, cost of resiliency solutions can be optimized	Since everything from planning to deployment is manual and requires huge upfront investments, on-premises solutions are hard to be cost-efficient

Table 10.1: Resiliency in cloud vs. on-premises

Understanding resiliency requirements

Your resiliency plans, strategies, and solutions depend heavily on your application requirements. Every application is different, so solutions are planned accordingly. This is because of the following reasons:

- Every application in your landscape can have separate requirements based in their criticality and hence the resiliency plans and architectures should be tailored accordingly.

- You can prioritize the resiliency efforts only if you understand application-specific requirements, i.e., some applications might be more business-critical than others and hence need much more attention.

- Understand that making applications resilient to failures comes at a financial cost because you will need extra resources and skills to make them happen.

- Sometimes applications have constraints that might not allow a specific resiliency plan. For example, some **commercial off-the-shelf** (**COTS**) products do not allow access to the underlying components of the code or any custom data replication setup, making it difficult to implement your desired resiliency strategy.

Hence, the resiliency requirements can vary based on the type of business (for example, banking, e-commerce, etc.) and application behaviour and criticality. However, to generalise, some of the most common resiliency requirements are listed here:

- System availability or uptime for end users in terms of hours or percentage. For example, near-zero downtime or 24/7 availability of a net banking platform.

- Amount of data loss that you can afford for your application in case of a disaster (also called **recovery point objective** and is discussed later under the section *Disaster recovery*). For example, new zero data loss for a healthcare system, as data integrity is paramount to such platforms.

- Time required to bring the application back up and running in case of a disaster (also called **recovery time objective** as is discussed later under the section *Disaster recovery*).

- The system should be able to handle high volumes of traffic during peak times of the day without failing or slowing down. For example, e-commerce sites during special shopping events.

- System should be able to respond to a request within a certain time for it to be deemed healthy.

Plan for failure

Everything fails, all the time is a famous quote from Amazon's Chief Technology Officer, *Werner Vogels*. This means that you should always plan for failures, as every component of your architecture is susceptible to them. There are specific resiliency strategies and techniques you should consider when architecting in the cloud, for example:

- Avoid single points of failure throughout the application. We mentioned earlier that every component of the application should be made redundant, i.e., a copy of every component, at least in production.

- Test your resiliency plans periodically and make changes as required. Cloud is ever evolving, and business requirements also change over time. Hence, make sure the DR and business continuity drills are conducted regularly (the frequency depends on the business criticality of the application).

- Automate the infrastructure provisioning because backing up data and keeping it in sync at multiple locations is sufficient for recovery. You also need the underlying infrastructure to be available as soon as possible. Automation would ensure that you do not have to perform manual remediations and do not lose valuable time during a disaster. Automation of infrastructure provisioning also aligns with the well-known concept of immutable infrastructure using mechanisms like IaC. Multiple tools in the market can help you do this, for example—HashiCorp's Terraform, AWS CloudFormation, Azure **Resource Access Manager** (**RAM**), etc. The major benefits of an immutable infrastructure using IaC are that the infrastructure provisioning is automated, consistent, and easily scalable. Of course, since everything is coded, you can also do version control and auditing.

- Have continuous monitoring measures in place. Enough has been said about observability (refer to *Chapter 9*). However, it is still important to emphasise that with appropriate monitoring and altering mechanisms, you can often avoid certain failures and ensure response/remediations.

In the following sections, we will examine all the resiliency aspects listed earlier and the specific considerations for each.

Business continuity planning

First up, let us discuss an important concept called **business continuity planning** (**BCP**). Actually, it is very easy to confuse BCP with resiliency as both are very related, but there are some differences between them that are important to understand. In fact, BCP should be considered a part or subset of your resiliency plan on the cloud.

Business continuity refers to the assurance that when a disruption occurs to your business, recovery will be done immediately or as soon as possible within an acceptable time. Hence, BCP involves end-to-end planning for that recovery, including runbooks with instructions, step-by-step procedures for recovery, communication plans, and staff training to execute such procedures when a disruption occurs. Quite apparently, BCP is more reactive, i.e., recovery action is taken in response to a disruption.

Next, we will discuss two more important concepts that are often confused as similar but are not – **High availability (HA) and Disaster recovery (DR).** There is a clear difference between them. It is essential to understand what to use when so that you can make the appropriate architectural decisions and design your solutions accordingly. We will come back to BCP after this discussion, as there is an important linkage that you should be aware of.

High availability

A HA solution aims to minimize the application downtime in case of disruption (like a component failure) by keeping the lights on and handling the user requests, even if it means running a subset of the applications or a scaled-down version. High availability in the cloud is mainly achieved by spreading the application across multiple nodes, racks, data centres, or zones.

Some strategies for achieving high availability in your cloud architecture are listed here:

- **Make the application fault-tolerant**: Introduce redundancy for every layer and component of the application. This can be done by distributing the application to multiple nodes. Strategies like clustering can significantly increase an application's availability.

- **Adopt auto-scaling measures**: Auto-scaling ensures there are enough servers/ nodes for an application to handle user requests in case of partial failures or an increase in load. To make auto-scaling successful, consider including load-balancing mechanisms to distribute load equally among the available nodes.

- **Include failover mechanisms**: Include backups for all architecture components so that you can automatically fail over to ensure application continues to run.

A classic and pervasive example of an HA solution that introduces redundancy in your architecture is the use of clustered servers like an Oracle **Real Application Cluster** (**RAC**). Simply speaking, a RAC consists of two or more physical nodes with shared storage underneath so that even if a node fails, the Oracle database continues handling requests. Clustering can be applied (out of the box or manually built) at any solution layer to enhance availability. RAC is a vendor solution for the database layer, but you can build clusters manually for other layers or products.

Before closing the topic of high availability, let us also understand two strategies that are instrumental in creating highly available applications.

Fault tolerant architecture

As mentioned above in the HA strategies, a fault-tolerant application continues to work even if one or more components fail. To achieve fault tolerance, you would typically adopt measures like redundancy, rigorous health checks, and building immutable infrastructure.

Self-healing architecture

The core of self-healing architecture on the cloud is automation and scalability. Self-healing refers to the application's ability to detect failures and recover automatically in response to them. This means that if one node of the application layer fails, another node spins up automatically in response. This is called an auto-scaling process in the cloud. It relies heavily on monitoring to detect failures and trigger the auto-scaling policies in response.

Fault tolerant and self-healing architectures are closely related concepts. However, there are some important distinctions as well, refer to the following table for a better understanding:

	Fault-tolerant architectures	**Self-healing architectures**
What?	Preventing failures from causing systems to go down	Automatically detecting and fixing the faults
How?	Techniques like redundant hardware and clustering	Uses monitoring, diagnostics, and automated remediation

Table 10.2: Fault tolerant vs. self-healing architectures

Disaster recovery

Disaster recovery (DR) is the application's ability to recover from a failure and start servicing the end users as quickly as possible. DR solutions are associated with catastrophic disasters like earthquakes or power failures that can cause an entire site or data centre to fail. Sometimes, it may not be possible to recover the application completely due to irreparable damage. However, the idea of DR is to restore the critical services, components, or applications at least and reduce the impact on business. Before we go any further, with disaster recovery and its strategies, let us understand two important terms without which the strategy would not make much sense.

RPO and RTO

A disaster recovery plan should have specific objectives associated to it. The two universal objectives every DR plan works toward are as follows:

- **Recovery point objective (RPO)**: RPO is the maximum acceptable data loss for your application, i.e., what is the maximum data loss you can afford?

- **Recovery time objective (RTO)**: RTO is the maximum acceptable delay in recovering the services in case of an interruption, i.e., What is the maximum acceptable downtime when a disaster occurs?

With these objectives in mind, let us look at some disaster recovery strategies in the cloud.

DR strategies

We know cloud computing has the concept of zones and regions. This means your applications on the cloud can be confined within a zone, within a region (multi-zonal), or can span across multiple regions. Another flavour of cloud architecture uses various cloud platforms, which we have already discussed in *Chapter 6: Multi-cloud Adoption*.

Single-zone cloud architecture is the most basic one, with minimal ability for disaster recovery, because there is no alternate site that can be used to restore the application in case the primary site fails. Such architectures are suitable for non-production workloads or non-mission-critical ones. However, if your workloads are mission-critical and DR is your priority, design your workloads to span across multiple zones or, if possible, various regions (if there are no constraints).

There are two types of architecture patterns commonly deployed for achieving disaster recovery on the cloud:

- **Active/Passive**: Active/Passive means only one site** is active at a time, and the other site** in the architecture is not serving any traffic.

- **Active/Active**: In this type of architecture, two active sites** serve traffic at any given time.

Note: Site in the context of DR strategy could be a zone inside a region or a separate region altogether.

We have discussed the above design patterns in *Chapter 5: Designing for Cloud* (in the context of cloud architecture themes) and *Chapter 6* (in the context of multi-cloud environments). As mentioned, you can have DR-enabled architecture across multiple zones as well as regions in a cloud environment.

With all the above foundational knowledge, let us now understand the various DR strategies on the cloud. There are primarily three DR strategies you should consider when designing your application architecture on the cloud:

- **Backup and restore**: This is the most basic and cost-effective DR strategy you can implement. This is how it works:

    o   Backups of all cloud resources are stored at the primary and standby sites. Your RPO requirements determine the frequency of backups.

    o   Application is restored at the standby site using the latest backups in case of an event.

    o   Suitable for non-critical workloads with a high tolerance of RPO/RTO values i.e. in hours.

    o   Falls into the active/passive type of DR design pattern, as only one site is active.

- **Hot standby**: This is the other end of the spectrum regarding a DR strategy and is the costliest. This is how it works:

    o   At least two sites are fully provisioned, synced, active, and serving user traffic. This means there is a standby site that has an exact replica of the application and is always in sync with the primary in terms of data at any given time. The data replication is usually asynchronous.

    o   Suitable for the most mission-critical production workloads with the lowest RPO/RTO values tolerance, i.e., in seconds.

- o Falls into the Active/Active type of DR pattern as both sites are active and serving end users.

- o Cost must be given consideration as it comes with the extra cost of a fully provisioned second site.

- **Warm standby**: This could be a middle ground between a backup/restore strategy and the hot standby. This is how it works:

  - o The standby site is partially provisioned and up, but not taking any traffic. Mostly, the databases at the primary are replicated to the standby and are always in sync. Some other critical components can also be pre-created and synced in advance.

  - o In case of a disaster event, a failover to the secondary site happens, and the remaining components of the application are provisioned and restored at the standby site. The speed of failover depends on the readiness of the secondary site regarding application resources.

  - o Suitable for workloads with RPO/RTO values in minutes or less than an hour. Since the environment is partially in sync, the time to recovery is much less than the backup/restore pattern. Plus, if data is already in sync with the primary, lower RPOs can be met.

  - o Falls into the Active/Passive type of DR pattern as only one site is active and service user traffic.

  - o The cost of this design pattern can vary depending on what components of the architecture you want to pre-create and keep in sync at both sites. Basically, the more the readiness of the standby at the other site, the higher the cost and the quicker the failover.

We will have architecture diagrams depicting these DR strategies later in the chapter. Note that all these DR strategies can be implemented across multiple zones, regions, or even cloud platforms (as seen in *Chapter 6*). All cloud providers fundamentally recommend similar DR strategies, though names and implementations may vary due to their native services.

As mentioned earlier, HA and DR might sound similar as both offer resiliency in some form. To make things clear, here is a comparison of HA and DR concepts:

	High availability	**Disaster recovery**
What is the intention?	Minimize the downtime in case of partial failures of the system	Restore the system after a disaster causes complete failure
What is the scope?	Usually, localised failures (like a failure of a node or a component)	Usually, failure of an entire site (like a data centre, zone, region, or even a cloud platform)

	High availability	Disaster recovery
When is the solution required?	When the system is running, and you need to keep it running	When the system fails, and you need to restore it
What is the solution cost?	HA solutions are usually costlier as more resources are required to keep the system running, like more nodes in the cluster	Cost of a DR solution depends on various factors, like how quickly you want the system to be restored

Table 10.3: Comparison of HA and DR

Wrapping up this discussion on the various aspects of resiliency, let us return to BCP again. As apparent from the above discussion, BCP and disaster recovery focus on ensuring that businesses continue running when a disruption happens. However, BCP has a much larger scope than DR because BCP focuses on the entire business, whereas DR is more specific to IT workloads (data, infrastructure, etc.). To make it clear, a DR strategy should be part of the larger BCP plan that includes elements other than your workloads as well.

Here is a quick comparison to summarise this discussion:

	BCP	DR
Scope	Scope of BCP is much broader as it covers the organization's entire business functions	DR has a much narrower scope as it focuses on restoring IT systems
Objective	To ensure that critical business operations can continue, i.e., keeping the business running	To recover data, systems, and infrastructure to a functional state as quickly as possible
Timing	Concerned with ongoing operations during and after a disruptive event	Concerned with the post-disaster recovery process

Table 10.4: Comparison of BCP and DR

Design patterns for resiliency

Though the best resiliency architecture depends on your application's requirements, there are some common generic patterns that we can use as a reference and tweak as necessary. Let us look at them in this section in detail. Note that these patterns have been depicted with AWS as the cloud provider, for example, but the same can be achieved on any other cloud platform (of course, the corresponding services of the cloud must be used).

Active/Passive

Active/Passive is the design pattern in which only one site is active at a given time. Another site can be used as a standby for failovers in case of an event. In the following subsections, we will understand in detail two types of patterns in this category:

Backup and restore

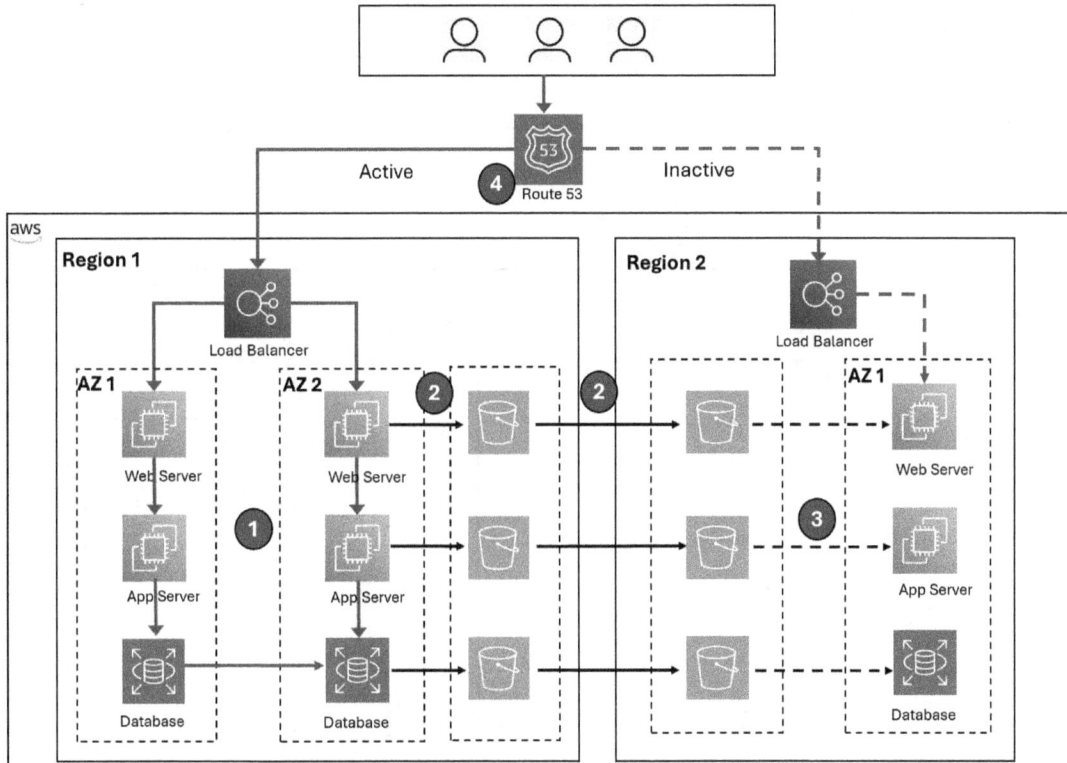

Figure 10.1: Backup and restore resiliency pattern

Here is a description of the architecture pattern:

- A primary region serves all the user traffic. Within the primary region, the resources can be deployed across multiple zones (called availability zones in AWS) behind a load balancer to distribute the load appropriately. This is optional but recommended.

- The resources in the primary region are being backed up locally (for local failures like accidental data corruption) as well as remotely to another area to protect against disaster events causing failure of the primary region.

- In a disaster event, the latest backups in the secondary region will be used to restore the application resources and bring up the standby environment.

- AWS DNS service called Route53 is being used to manage traffic routing between the regions. In the event of the primary region or connectivity failing, the traffic is failed over to the secondary area, built from the backups.

Warm standby

Refer to the following figure for the Warm standby resiliency pattern:

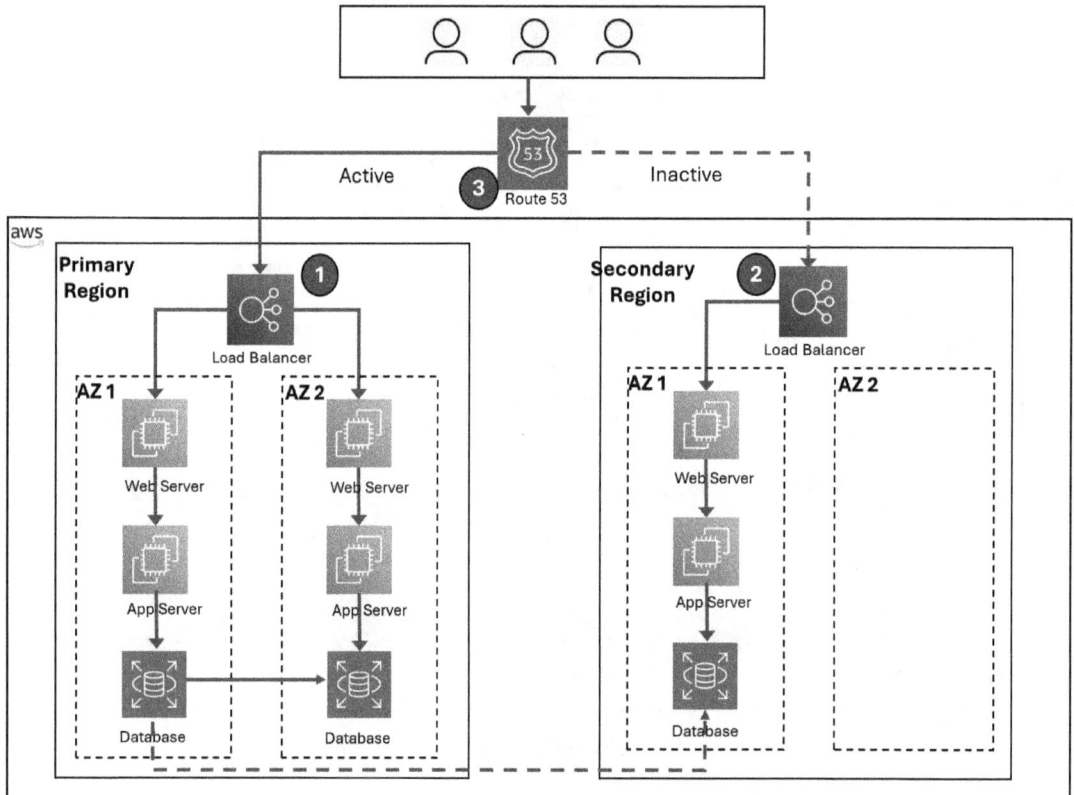

Figure 10.2: Warm standby resiliency pattern

Here is a description of the architecture pattern:

- There is a primary region that is serving all the user traffic. Within the primary region, the resources can be deployed across multiple zones (called availability zones in AWS) behind a load balancer so that the load can be distributed appropriately. This is optional but recommended.

- There is a secondary region that does not serve any user traffic under normal circumstances. Not all application resources have been deployed in this region. The database is mainly replicated and synced from the primary area. Apart from that, pre-creating other resources like app servers and web servers is completely optional and depends on your resiliency requirements, as the cost of architecture is the trade-off that you should be aware of, i.e., you can pre-create as many or as few resources as required and scale later. The diagram shows servers being available in a single availability zone behind a load balancer, which can be scaled to multiple zones if the secondary is promoted to a primary role.

- An AWS DNS service called Route53 manages traffic routing between the regions. In the event of the primary region or connectivity failing, the traffic is passed over to the secondary region, which is partially pre-built and synchronized to start serving the user traffic.

Active/Active

The other category of resiliency pattern is the Active/Active pattern, in which all sites (zones or regions) are active at a given time. Usually, it is implemented across two sites, but more can be used to provide higher resiliency.

Hot standby

Let us look at the Hot standby:

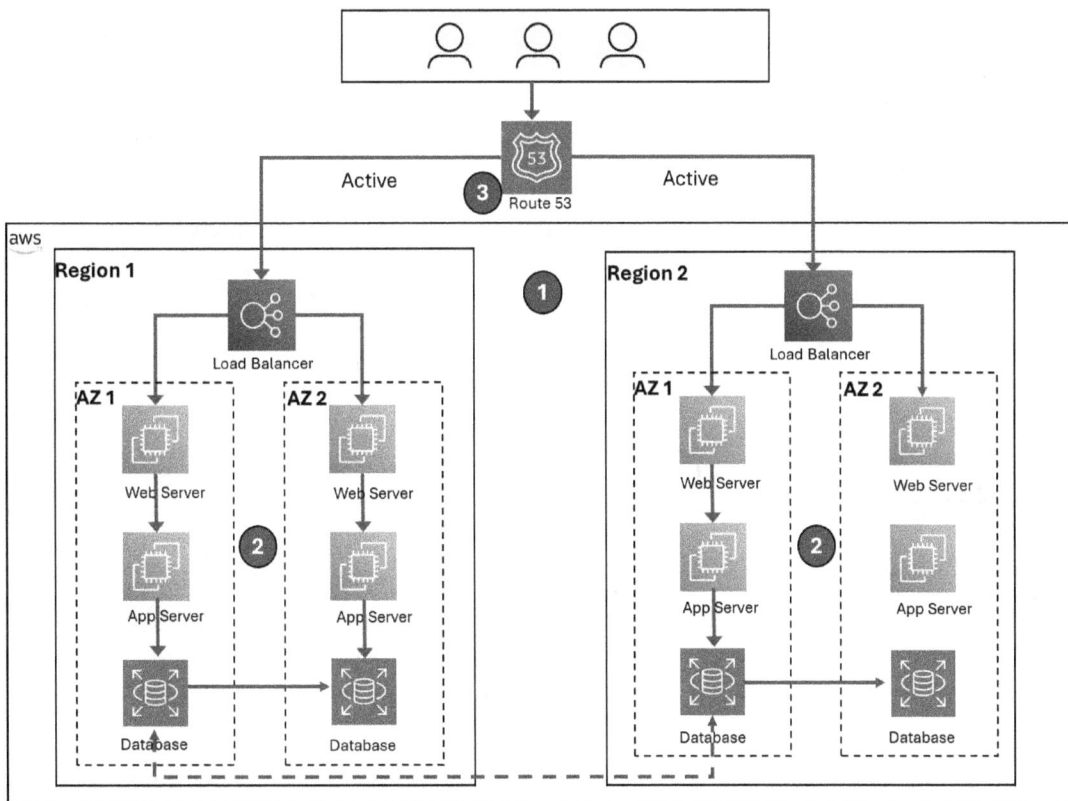

Figure 10.3: Hot standby resiliency pattern

Here is a description of the architecture pattern:

- This architecture has minimum two active regions (hence the name Active/Active) that serve all user traffic simultaneously. Within both regions, the resources can be deployed across multiple zones (called availability zones in AWS) behind a load balancer so that the load can be distributed appropriately. This is optional but recommended.

- Both regions are fully equipped to serve the user requests with all application resources deployed in both regions. The databases are synced at both sites. Data replication should be configured depending on which regions are serving the write requests.

- An AWS DNS service called Route53 manages traffic routing between the regions. Since both regions are active, requests arerouted to the region based on the appropriate routing policy.

Here are some important considerations for this pattern:

- The pattern can be combined with other resiliency strategies like local backups or backups to different zones/regions to provide a quick restoration option in case of accidental data corruption.

- Read requests can be served from all active regions, and ideally, users are routed to the closest area for better performance using the geolocation or latency-based DNS policies

- Writes can happen in both active regions, which adds to the complexity of the architecture by introducing bidirectional replication to keep both databases in sync. To avoid this complexity, you can keep write requests confined to a single region and replicate them to the other region for synchronization.

- The high cost of this design pattern should be given consideration when making architectural decisions.

Resiliency use cases

In this section, we will look at some everyday and practical use cases of resiliency in the cloud:

- Failure of an entire data centre or a zone in the case of cloud computing. This could be due to natural phenomena like earthquakes or floods. Let us understand this in more detail:

  o For critical applications that cannot tolerate data loss and downtime, the most pertinent resiliency pattern is the multi-zone Active/Active deployment of the application.

  o Depending on the RPO and RTO requirements, non-critical applications or non-production environments can survive with an Active/Passive deployment using a backup/restore or warm standby pattern.

o If your workloads are confined to a single zone in the cloud, you must rely on the last available backups, assuming they have been stored in an alternate location.

- On-premises data centre is used as the primary hosting location for all workloads, but a cost-effective DR solution is required. The primary considerations are:

  o Using another on-premises data center for DR may not be cost-effective, as it requires a lot of investment.

  o Cloud can be used as a DR location for the primary on-premises data center.

  o Depending on the RPO and RTO requirements, the hybrid pattern can be deployed in an Active/Active or Active/Passive manner.

  o The primary considerations for a hybrid pattern are network connectivity, cost, and complexity of the architecture.

- Data safety is paramount, and you cannot afford to lose data in case of a disaster. RPO is near zero in this case. This is discussed in further detail:

  o Use a multi-region approach to replicate and store data backups.

  o If there are strict data residency requirements (like data must stay within the country), consider using multiple cloud regions within a country. Remember, a region in the cloud does not mean a different country. The same country can have multiple cloud regions that you can use to replicate and store data.

  o If the data residency requirements are not strict, consider storing data in regions outside the primary country of business, as it protects against events that can impact the entire country (for example, war situations).

Examples from the real world

Let us look at some real-life examples where resiliency architecture on the cloud has been truly embraced:

- Netflix (a well-known OTT platform) leverages a multi-region architecture on AWS to achieve high availability.

- Intuit (a financial technology firm) uses multi-cloud architecture (AWS and Azure) to achieve HA.

Numerous such examples can be quoted to demonstrate resiliency in the cloud. However, the point to note here is that all such examples and case studies will use one of the use cases or design patterns we have already explained in this chapter.

Conclusion

Resiliency is an essential aspect of your cloud architecture. Regardless of the criticality of the application, you must include resiliency in some form to ensure business continuity. In this chapter, we looked at various aspects of resiliency, such as high availability, BCP, and disaster recovery, along with standard and recommended strategies to achieve the desired aspect of resiliency.

Understanding the differences and overlaps between these resiliency components is essential when planning your overall cloud adoption strategy. Some common design patterns have also been included for readers to reference. In the next chapter, we will look at a reasonably recent but logical objective of multi-cloud environments called Interoperability. This fascinating area provides a new way of thinking for people involved in cloud strategy.

Points to remember

Here are the key takeaways from this chapter:

- There are a few terms that are used very often in the context of resiliency. It is essential to know the differences and mapping between them to be able to plan resiliency for your cloud architecture:
  - **BCP**: Business continuity planning refers to an assurance that recovery will be made immediately or as soon as possible within an acceptable time when a disruption occurs to your business. It has a broader organization-wide scope.
  - **High availability**: A HA aims at minimizing the application downtime in case of disruption (like a component failure) by keeping the lights on.
  - DR is the application's ability to recover from a failure and start servicing the end users as quickly as possible. It is usually part of the BCP and is targeted at IT workloads.
- Resiliency requirements are centred around two important concepts:
  - **RPO**: Maximum affordable data loss in case of a failure.
  - **RTO**: Maximum affordable downtime in case of a failure.
- Always plan for failure and have resiliency in the checklist of your applications on the cloud, even if the application is non-critical.
- Some key resiliency strategies are:
  - Make application components redundant.
  - Make your architecture fault-tolerant and self-healing.
  - Test your resiliency strategies regularly.

- o Include observability to detect failures fast.

  - o Bring automation into play to be more efficient during recovery.

- As a best practice, redundancy can be included by using multiple sites to deploy architectures on the cloud. A site could be a zone or a region in the context of a cloud platform.

- There are two categories of design patterns on the cloud:

  - o **Active/Active**: More than one active site handling user traffic at a time.

  - o **Active/Passive**: Only one active site handles user traffic at a time.

- A hot standby is an example of an Active/Active design pattern:

  - o At least two sites fully provisioned.

  - o High in cost.

  - o All sites can be designed to handle reads and writes.

- A warm standby is an example of an Active/Passive design pattern:

  - o Only one site is active and fully provisioned.

  - o An alternate site is partially provisioned (depending on your RPO/RTO requirements).

  - o Less costly as not all components have been provisioned at the alternate site.

- Another example of an Active/Passive design pattern is the backup and recovery pattern:

  - o Only one site is active and fully provisioned.

  - o Backups are taken and stored locally and at a remote site.

  - o Backups at the remote site are used for restoring the application in case of an event.

Join our book's Discord space

Join the book's Discord Workspace for Latest updates, Offers, Tech happenings around the world, New Release and Sessions with the Authors:

https://discord.bpbonline.com

CHAPTER 11
Interoperability

Introduction

The practical reality of cloud adoption is hybrid cloud and multi-cloud nowadays. We hardly see enterprises that rely on a solo cloud platform. Hence, with the growth of multiple hosting platforms in an organization, the need for seamless communication between these platforms is also growing because there is a lot of data flowing between these hosting platforms.

This is where the concept of interoperability fits in. Different hosting platforms in the ecosystem can communicate with each other. However, contrary to a general belief, interoperability is not just about data exchange, and that is what we will understand in this chapter when we delve into more details of this concept. The key objective of this chapter is to explain interoperability in cloud computing and the various aspects of interoperability that extend beyond the seamless data exchange between hosting platforms.

Structure

In this chapter, we will cover the following topics:

- Interoperability
- Interoperability use cases
- Interoperability challenges

- Interoperability design strategies
- Open-source technologies

Objectives

By the end of this chapter, readers will understand the concept of interoperability, related architecture strategies, and considerations when planning a cloud adoption and developing a cloud strategy. They should also be able to relate much of the information in this chapter to *Chapter 6: Multi-cloud Adoption,* where we discussed multi-cloud environments in detail, because interoperability is a key ingredient for the success of multi-cloud strategies.

Interoperability

As you plan your cloud adoption and new workloads in the cloud, interoperability is a topic that is bound to generate more and more interest among the key stakeholders and decision-makers. Organizations are wary of the ongoing co-existence of multiple hosting platforms, which gives precedence to the design that allows easy flow of information between those platforms, or sometimes needs to move components between the platforms, and still be able to run them properly. This is what interoperability is all about.

Interoperability is the feature of cloud computing that focuses on an integrated view of a multi-cloud or hybrid cloud environment powered by a seamless flow of data between different cloud or on-premises platforms. It is a broader architectural capability where different hosting platforms can work together seamlessly.

In fact, there are some other concepts that come under the umbrella of interoperability, such as the following:

- **Data interoperability**: One of the central themes of interoperability is the smooth communication between platforms, also called data interoperability. Data exchange is the key to moving applications between clouds or hosting interdependent applications on multiple clouds. Suppose you are a data-driven company and operate data-heavy workloads across various cloud platforms. Data interoperability is even more critical because a central data lake requires data flow across boundaries.

- **Orchestration**: With multiple clouds in operation simultaneously, a service orchestration platform plays an essential role by managing the entire landscape. *Chapter 6* discusses this as applicable to a multi-cloud environment and adoption strategy. The same fundamentals apply when discussing the interoperability of applications in a multi-cloud environment.

- **Portability**: Applications and/or data can quickly move between and work on different hosting platforms without significantly changing their architecture or components. Looking closely, portability is one of the ways to achieve interoperability. Though not a mandatory requirement, portability can substantially enhance the interoperability of your IT environment. In many places, portability and interoperability are used interchangeably, but portability is another feature that promotes interoperability.

It is also important to understand that interoperability is different from integration. While integration involves connecting different systems into a cohesive unit so that they can address a particular requirement, interoperability emphasizes the ability of different systems to communicate and exchange data, even if they are fundamentally different

Relevance to multi-cloud environments

We have discussed multi-cloud architectures in the previous chapters, including the challenges and benefits. Interoperability and related concepts are important in a multi-cloud setup because they help you realize the benefits, unlock the full potential, and mitigate the challenges of a multi-cloud environment that we previously learned about. Some of the reasons that interoperability resonates so closely with a multi-cloud environment are:

- **Multi-cloud adoption avoids vendor lock-in:** This is probably the number one reason for organizations to adopt more than one cloud in their landscape. The essence of interoperability is also to allow multiple hosting platforms to work together seamlessly by applying one or more of its core principles discussed earlier. There are numerous benefits to avoiding a vendor lock-in:

  o Flexibility to choose the best platform per your workload's technical requirements.

  o Flexibility also allows us to optimize the costs by leveraging and negotiating the best prices.

  o Flexibility also fuels innovation as you can adopt new technologies and services from multiple cloud providers.

- **Enhanced DR capabilities**: We discussed resiliency in *Chapter 10: Cloud Resiliency,* where a multi-site design pattern was also mentioned. By distributing workloads across multiple clouds, you can greatly enhance your DR capabilities. Such design patterns also require inter-cloud communication, data interoperability, and application portability, which are the key tenants of an interoperable multi-cloud environment.

- **Managing the complexity of multi-cloud**: Interoperability helps immensely in managing and reducing the complexity of adopting multiple cloud platforms. Basically, interoperability promotes commonality and standardisation, i.e., a common management interface, a standard set of APIs for interactions, and a standard set of tools.

Benefits of interoperability

Let us summarize the benefits of interoperability:

- **Flexibility to use multiple cloud platforms**: This one reason has numerous embedded benefits. For example, the opportunity to leverage the best technologies, negotiate cloud costs, and many more.

- **Collaboration**: Since the essence of interoperability is the data exchange, communication, and portability between diverse applications hosted on varied platforms, there is much better collaboration between teams that own and manage those applications.

- **Better application scalability**: Since there is active and smooth communication between hosting platforms, applications, data, and services can be scaled easily across multiple platforms.

- **Data centre footprint**: When you have designed your services for interoperability and portability, adopting the cloud is easy, resulting in a reduction of your data centre footprint and expenditures. Cloud adoption also goes hand in hand with legacy data centre-based services in a hybrid environment.

Interoperability use cases

The healthcare industry is probably the most pertinent and popular real-world example of interoperability in the cloud. This industry relies on sharing data, which is too large and primarily very sensitive. Data exchange is critical to provide a collaborative solution. For example, there are multiple systems in a healthcare network that a patient interacts with directly or indirectly: pathology labs, imaging devices, doctors, hospitals, insurance companies, etc. A patient's records need to be shared across the whole network consistently to allow associated professionals to access the data and make meaningful and timely decisions for the patient. These systems could be hosted on different clouds or on-premises data centers, making data interoperability one of the key requirements for this industry.

Another typical example could be various government departments in a state or country. A citizen's data could be saved in one department's database, but to ensure the entire ecosystem is efficient, other departments that need the same data about the citizens might need to share the data to avoid collecting everything again. This also means trusting the data sources in the ecosystem.

Similar to healthcare, many more industry domains where data sharing across entities is a key requirement, can benefit from interoperability.

Interoperability challenges

In all the above use cases, some obvious challenges must be addressed for interoperability to be implemented and work efficiently. They are essentially similar to what you have to deal with when setting up a multi-cloud environment. For example:

- **Security and compliance**: Ensuring data security and consistent policies across different hosting platforms can be daunting, especially when the controls, services, and support for external tools vary.

- **Standardization issues**: Standardization enables interoperability so that all platforms can talk and understand the common language. This includes standard set of APIs to interact with, supported data formats, supported programming languages etc. However, this could be a considerable challenge with varied platforms that support incompatible formats, versions, programming languages, etc.

- **Technical complexities**: Similar to the lack of standardisation, using cloud proprietary technologies does not help as they could follow different standards and formats. For example, AWS CloudFormation or any other native offerings are not interoperable, and hence, the workloads designed with such services cannot be interoperable between cloud platforms.

- **Lack of multi-cloud skills**: Interoperability means multiple cloud platforms, and hence, you need skills to work with and manage those platforms, workloads, and communication between them. Finding or training resources to work on more than one cloud platform could be challenging.

Interoperability design strategies

Notwithstanding the challenges, there are also numerous benefits of an interoperable architecture. Overall, interoperability makes it much easier to adopt multiple cloud platforms if that is the intended cloud strategy. However, this is all possible if you use the appropriate design strategies. Let us now look at some of the design strategies that should be considered to implement interoperability:

- **Reduce or eliminate dependency on cloud-native technologies**: Cloud-native technologies are suitable if you plan to stick to a cloud platform for the long term and have no plans for application interoperability and portability. Using cloud-native technologies like AWS CloudFormation for automation ties you to a particular cloud platform like AWS. Inter-cloud communication and an exit become extremely challenging and costly. However, using third-party tools like *Terraform* makes implementing interoperability and portability between different clouds easy.

- **Adopt open-source technologies**: To avoid dependency on cloud-native technologies, it is recommended to use platform-independent open-source tools and technologies. Open-source tools are recommended for the following reasons:

  o Use of open-source technologies promotes standardization because they can run on any underlying hosting platform.

- o Open-source technologies and platforms are community-driven. Due to the collaboration of experts from around the world, solving interoperability challenges is much easier.

- o Open-source technologies are known for the rapid pace of innovation and development.

- **Use containerization for applications**: If possible, modernize and re-architect your applications to use containers. Containerizing applications is a great way to make them portable. Standard container technologies like *Docker* and *Kubernetes* can be used to package and isolate applications, making them easier to deploy on any hosting platform and hence helping with the portability aspect of applications.

- **Use IaC to automate the infrastructure build**: Instead of using manual or console-based processes, use IaC to automate your entire infrastructure on the cloud. Be careful to use external tools like Terraform that work on every cloud platform and use variables only for platform-specific inputs. The importance of IaC is elaborated on later in the chapter when we discuss the popular open-source technologies.

- **Create abstraction layers**: You can hide the underlying complexities of multiple application layers or hosting platforms by creating abstraction layers. Hence, external communication does not need to be aware of every cloud platform, as it just talks to a single intermediary. There are various third-party orchestration services that can provide such an abstraction. API gateways are an excellent example in this category. API gateways receive requests, route them to the appropriate backend services, and transform data between different formats. For the backend, there could be multiple microservices, each fronted with its own API. An API gateway can be used to provide a unified API to external clients.

- **Implement centralised and robust security**: Security is obviously a precursor in any cloud environment, and more so when you want to have interoperability and portability of applications and data across the environment. For example, data flowing in all directions needs to be secured via measures like encryption and masking. Strong authentication and authorization for access to applications and data are some of the key security measures. A Zero Trust network should be implemented across the platforms so that every user and device is verified before granting access to network resources.

- **Implement centralized operations**: Centralized operations are another consideration in a multi-cloud and interoperable environment. Even if the applications and infrastructure have been designed to be interoperable, disparate management and operation processes can be a real challenge. Interoperability also demands a common approach to operating the applications and data that communicate across the cloud boundaries.

- **Implement data interoperability**: Moving and sharing data between platforms could be the first step in achieving interoperability at a larger scale in your cloud environment. Start with creating a centralized data lake and warehouse that integrates data from all sources. This would obviously need some **extract, transform, load** (**ETL**) tools that can work across the whole environment and enable the flow of data across boundaries. An essential requirement for data interoperability is also to deal with some common standard data formats that can work on multiple platforms, like *JSON*, *XML*, and many others.

- **Loosely coupled architecture**: Adopt a loosely coupled architecture for your applications, such as microservices and event-driven architectures. With a microservices architecture, you can modularise the application into more minor services that can operate independently and, hence, can be moved and deployed on separate cloud platforms as required. Event-driven architecture is another great approach to creating decoupled services, making it easier to integrate disparate platforms.

- **Integration mechanisms**: Communication between diverse systems spread across varied platforms needs some integration mechanism to bridge the gaps. Integration services act like an abstraction layer to provide a seamless communication route. Ensure you include an integration platform that can support multiple cloud and on-premises platforms to offer an interoperable environment.

Open-source technologies

We have discussed using open-source technologies and platforms to foster an interoperability environment. Let us look at some of the popular open-source products that you should consider:

- **Containerization**: Containerized applications are good for interoperability because they promote both standardization and portability. Every cloud provider is big on containerization and related services these days. However, as the theme is interoperability, the most common open-source technologies to look for are:

  o **Docker**: This is probably the industry's most widely accepted and implemented containerization technology. It is used to package applications and their dependencies into images that can be shared and deployed on any platform quickly. Hence, they are platform agnostic and can run on any cloud as a packaged image.

  o **Kubernetes**: Container orchestration is synonymous with Kubernetes. It provides standard APIs to manage containers and the applications built on containers across any cloud environment. Note that most cloud providers offer their managed Kubernetes services, but to avoid that, you can also use your own Kubernetes deployment.

- **API gateways**: They can be used as a consistent, centralized, and standardized access point for traffic trying to reach the APIs exposed by your applications across the board. They are good for interoperability because they act as an abstraction layer on top of your API-driven application and provide features like protocol translation and security. Most cloud providers offer their own API gateways, but various open-source and external providers exist. For example:

o **Kong**: One of the most popular open-source API gateways boasting of a huge community of developers, with a plethora of plugins to offer features like security, traffic management etc.

o **Traefik**: Another great example of open-source API gateways that is gaining popularity for simple and smaller deployments. As a gateway, it fits well into the container ecosystem of docker and Kubernetes.

- **IaC**: Automation is one of the most sought-after goals for every cloud deployment, including provisioning and managing the cloud infrastructure. This is where a capability like 'infrastructure as code' is instrumental. They are good for interoperable cloud applications because of features like repeatable deployments in a consistent manner and portability, which allow easy migration of applications across cloud providers and collaborative development environments. Similar to others, every cloud provider has their offering in this space as well, but to ensure interoperability, use a service such as Terraform

o **Terraform**: This is an open-source tool used to define your cloud infrastructure as code. The key advantage of Terraform is that it is platform agnostic and can work on any platform by just using platform-specific values as variables, hence keeping the code base unchanged. This feature enables easy migration and portability of applications between cloud platforms.

- **Service mesh**: A service mesh is vital to support interoperability in a multi-cloud environment. The primary function of a service mesh is to manage communication between multiple underlying services deployed on varied platforms. However, they perform other functions along with it, like enhancing performance, resiliency, and load balancing. A great example of a service mesh is Istio:

o **Istio**: an open-source service mesh that can be instrumental in managing a microservices-based architecture in a multi-cloud or hybrid cloud environment. Initially founded by Google, it has a very active open-source community that supports and contributes to development and enhancements.

- **Data streaming**: The importance of data in any IT setup is invaluable. Data streaming is an integral part of a data portfolio due to the numerous data sources available to ingest real-time data into your environment. Real-time data streaming services help build an interoperable multi-cloud environment by providing decoupling/ loose coupling of applications (i.e., no tight integration between applications on different platforms). The most pertinent example in this category is:

o **Apache Kafka**: Looking at data streaming, Apache Kafka is the go-to solution for most data professionals due to its mature community and numerous features. It can help quickly and efficiently build real-time data pipelines, along with decoupling applications spread across multiple hosting platforms.

- **Integration platforms**: Integration platforms are an integral part of the interoperable workflow as they provide a standard layer between disparate systems that might support different protocols, data formats, etc. In short, integration tools and platforms ensure seamless communication, collaboration, and data exchange when the systems do not speak a common language, much like creating an abstraction layer.

  There are many integration platforms, but not much in the open-source category. Apache offers some open-source platforms like *Camel* and *NiFi*, but they are not as popular or mature as some popular commercial tools. Realistically, you do not need an open-source tool for integration. Hence, we will mention a couple of popular commercial integration platforms:

  o **MuleSoft**: This is a very popular and scalable platform for complex hybrid environments that need API-driven integration workflows. The core strength of MuleSoft is its API-driven approach for connectivity.

  o **Boomi**: A very easy-to-use graphical UI-based platform that does not need a lot of coding experience to get started and is hence popular amongst the architecture community. It also has good support for all cloud platforms and on-premises deployments.

Open-source technologies play a pivotal role in fostering interoperability by providing standardization. Using these open standards and tools enables organizations to build robust, flexible, and scalable interoperability solutions, fostering a more connected and collaborative digital ecosystem. Since the open-source projects are community-driven, the development costs are much less, and security and transparency are much better.

Conclusion

Interoperability is aligned with a multi-cloud environment very closely. It is recommended to read this chapter in conjunction with *Chapter 6: Multi-cloud Adoption*, as the challenges, benefits, and design strategies are similar. The biggest hurdle in an interoperable environment would be disparate hosting platforms and varied support for tools and technologies. That calls for standardization and consistency, where open-source technologies play a crucial role instead of cloud-native services, which can make it challenging to interoperate and port the applications and data across cloud platforms. In addition, other considerations, like security, cannot be ignored in such an environment. Data interoperability is the foundation.

The next chapter will focus on data management in the cloud and look at some of the interoperability overlaps, such as data lakes and data streaming.

Points to remember

Here are the key takeaways from this chapter:

- Interoperability is the seamless integration and communication between multiple cloud or hybrid hosting platforms. Some closely associated concepts are listed here:
  - o Data exchange and sharing (Data interoperability)
  - o Application portability
  - o Orchestration service
- Interoperability is the essence of a successful multi-cloud setup. Data exchange and inter-application communication are unavoidable, and so is the need to make the systems interoperable. The benefits of multi-cloud adoption also apply to interoperability in the cloud. For example:
  - o Flexibility and avoiding vendor lock-in
  - o Fostering agility and innovations
  - o Enhanced DR capabilities
  - o Increased application scalability
- Interoperability has many practical use cases across varied industries. Wherever seamless data flow across systems or a multi-cloud setup is required, interoperability can be applied. Prominent domains are healthcare, the government sector, education, etc.
- Some key design strategies to achieve interoperability are listed here:
  - o Use of open-source tools and technologies in the architecture
  - o Less dependency on cloud-native technologies
  - o Containerize the applications
  - o Include an abstraction layer to hide the underlying complexity
  - o Implement centralized security and operations
  - o Use IaC for automatic infrastructure provisioning
- There are various tools and technologies that can be used for interoperable architectures; some common ones are:
  - o Containerization: Docker and Kubernetes
  - o API gateways: Kong
  - o IaC: Terraform
  - o Service mesh: Istio
  - o Data streaming: Apache Kafka
  - o Integration platforms: MuleSoft and Boomi

CHAPTER 12

Data Management

Introduction

This chapter aims to look into data management and related practices in the cloud. The idea is to highlight the importance of data management, particularly in the cloud, and how it plays a significant part in developing a cloud strategy. Data is the lifeblood and undoubtedly the most critical asset of an organization (also called the new currency nowadays). To make it interesting, data is ever-increasing and growing in complexity. Every organization and every person associated with that organization generates data every second. That is why data management and all the disciplines (like data governance, data storage, data security, etc.) are essential under its umbrella. Though the importance of data assets cannot be understated, be it in the cloud or in an on-premises setup, data management practices and approaches are very different in cloud.

Similarly, the risk profile and the benefits are also different compared to an on-premises environment. The need to collect and preserve data has never been felt more than it is now due to the growing trends around data analytics, ML, and AI.

Structure

In this chapter, we will cover the following topics:

- Business case for data management in the cloud

- Components of a data management framework
- Data lifecycle
- Data security
- Data governance
- Data trends
- Examples of data management in cloud

Objectives

By the end of this chapter, readers should be able to relate to the information provided. Readers who are new to the cloud should understand the data management requirements and associated challenges. Regardless of their experience level, they should be able to take away the elements of cloud data management and their relevance to a cloud strategy. Throughout this chapter, we will use an arbitrary retail company to explain the various components of the data management framework that should help solidify the learning further.

Business case for data management in the cloud

A good data management framework has technical benefits and a tremendous value proposition for business stakeholders. There are various business pain points that efficient data management can address; some of them are listed here:

- **Revenue**: Not enough data on customer segmentation, market analysis, and the competitive landscape will lead to missed opportunities and poor customer experience, which in turn will lead to business losses. A good data management strategy can drive revenue growth. For example, a personalized customer experience will lead to improved sales.

- **Reduced costs**: More and accurate data are key tenets of a data management strategy, which leads to optimized operational costs by streamlining the processes.

- **Improved decision-making**: Data management fuels informed data-driven decision-making.

Businesses need to consider data management as a strategic investment instead of a cost center. Having said that, companies should also identify key metrics that can be used to measure business success due to good data management initiatives.

Let us understand some of the key metrics that can be mapped to data management initiatives in the case of a retail company:

- **Revenue growth**: Consider the use of data analysis and AI to target customers with product promotions based on past purchase history. Measure the results in terms of the increase in sales after the new sales strategy has been implemented.

- **Cost reduction**: Consider automating inventory management using real-time data from the warehouses. Measure the success in terms of warehouse storage cost reduction due to optimized stock levels.

- **Profit margin:** This one is aligned with the above two metrics, i.e., increased sales and reduced costs.

- **Customer satisfaction (CSAT)**: After optimizing the online e-commerce platform with things like targeted promotions, real-time inventory availability, and personalized recommendations, conduct a CSAT survey and use that to measure the success of various initiatives.

- **Market share**: Consider using market and competition data to understand new growth areas, untapped markets, and product segments. Measure success by regularly analyzing market share compared to competitors.

Note: It is essential to define realistic and measurable goals. Unless data management initiatives are converted into tangible business initiatives, it is hard to get buy-in and funding from businesses for new initiatives and investments.

Components of a data management framework

Apart from direct business advantages, an efficient data management strategy is also crucial to successful cloud adoption. Let us understand this with the components that make up a data management framework:

- **Data lifecycle**: The end-to-end journey of your data has a massive impact on the success of a cloud strategy. Adopting the cloud requires considering the entire data lifecycle and how it is going to change with the cloud. Remember, with cloud, there are many more and better opportunities to consume (additional data sources), process, analyze, and visualize data.

- **Data analysis**: A cloud adoption strategy must consider data as the foundation. When an organization plans to adopt the cloud, it needs clarity on how it can efficiently use all available data to make data-driven decisions in the cloud. This is where data analysis plays a significant role; hence, the related approaches and tools must be considered.

- **Data inventory**: Cloud adoption will essentially involve migrating data (sometimes huge volumes and a variety of data) to the cloud along with applications. Hence, an up-to-date inventory of data (type, sources, classification, size, etc.) provides critical inputs to the decision-makers for formulating a data migration approach that eventually feeds into a cloud strategy.

- **Data security**: Cloud strategy includes a mandatory security stream, and data security in the cloud is another big-ticket item that cannot be ignored, i.e., access to data, data encryption, etc.

- **Data governance**: Once data is in the cloud, data governance should become a priority. Activities like making policies to govern data, ensuring compliance with data privacy regulations, and maintaining good data quality should be part of the cloud adoption roadmap.

Managing data in the cloud has various facets. If you look at the data lifecycle, right from acquiring the data to making sense of it, there are tasks and offshoots of the data management stream that require special skills and attention.

Since data is an organization's most critical asset, it is important to understand the various aspects of data management in the cloud and develop a strategy accordingly when planning to adopt the cloud. In the following few sub-sections, we will explain each of these components in more detail, emphasizing their relevance in the context of cloud adoption.

Data lifecycle

Data analytics uses data from varied sources and examines it to generate meaningful conclusions. This practice involves an end-to-end data lifecycle, which will be covered in this section. In general, the data lifecycle consists of a few stages, as listed in the upcoming subsections, and we will look at them from a cloud perspective.

Data capture or ingestion

This is the first step in the data lifecycle, focusing on data acquisition. During this stage, data sources are identified per business needs, data formats are identified, and data is ingested using the identified methods. Data could come from sources like external websites, social media, clickstreams, etc., in structured or unstructured form. This is where data architects will confirm the data sources used (based on business requirements), how the data will be collected (method), and in what format. For example, if using the APIs provided by social media platforms, you call those APIs to capture the data.

In the on-premises world, though it is possible to acquire data from varied sources, integrating the workflows into the hosted infrastructure (even if virtualized) could be complex. With the cloud, not only are the support for sources and formats of data virtually unlimited (It could come from SaaS platforms, external websites, social media, sensors, or anything else you could imagine), but integrating those sources with the cloud platform is much simpler. Though the concepts remain technically the same, the implementation on the cloud is more straightforward due to the native and external cloud-based tools available.

toOur arbitrary retail company has identified the following key sources of data that they want to use for further analysis and reporting: **point of sale** (**POS**) at physical stores, an e-commerce website, and various social media platforms. The intent is to get data from these sources into central storage, which will be further processed and analyzed.

The most prominent difference between cloud-hosted and on-premises environments in capturing data from these sources would be how these sources integrate with the environment. Theoretically, the capture and ingestion methods could be the same in both cases, but due to the tools and services provided by the cloud, the process becomes much more efficient. For instance, the POS system can send data in a real-time streaming manner to the cloud as well as an on-premises environment for storage, but to do it in an on-premises environment, there are a lot of challenges, such as:

- Significant infrastructure and effort investment to build a real-time streaming system.

- Making the system scalable to handle varying traffic in real time is virtually impossible. Instead, you would need to forecast and plan capacity.

- Finally, specialized skills are required to build and customize such a system.

On the contrary, many native cloud services can handle such streaming data. AWS offers managed services like Amazon Kinesis for streaming data and Amazon SQS for queuing messages. These services require much less management and development effort to build a streaming data flow. Even if third-party tools can be used, deploying them on-premises is much more complex than in the cloud.

In terms of tools, most commonly used during this phase of the data lifecycle, we have the following:

- **Cloud-native**: AWS Kinesis, AWS Glue, Azure Event Hub, Google Cloud Pub/Sub, etc.

- **External**: API gateways, Apache Kafka, Informatica, etc.

Data storage

After the data has been captured and ingested into your target environment, it is temporarily stored in its raw form. This is also called temporary storage or data staging because the data needs to be further processed/cleansed to analyze and make sense of it. The following sections elaborate on a few terms and concepts to be aware of in terms of data storage.

Types of data

In the legacy world of on-premises data centers, data resides inside databases or digital versions of paper documents stored on tapes, hard disk drives, or solid-state disks. Few options existed to handle and store the different types and large volumes of data. However, with the advent of cloud computing, many more avenues of data storage have popped up.

Before knowing the storage options on the cloud, let us understand the different types of data:

- **Structured**: This is data that can be fit and organized into a well-defined schema and data model. It is easily searchable and usually categorized by rows and columns, like in a relational database or an Excel spreadsheet.

- **Unstructured**: This data cannot be incorporated into a row-and-column data model and is usually free form. It could be a PDF document or anything that can be considered data but cannot be stored in a table.

- **Semi-structured**: Semi-structured data is a middle ground between structured and unstructured data. It also does not have a pre-defined schema, but still has some level of organization. The best examples are JSON and XML documents.

Physical storage

Based on the above context of different types of data and storage, let us now discuss physical storage on the cloud. As is obvious, some of the major advantages of the cloud are its almost unlimited storage, infinite scalability, and unprecedented flexibility. These characteristics make storage on the cloud ideal for modern data analytics solutions requiring tons of data that is growing every minute.

The type of physical storage in the cloud depends on the type of data that was mentioned earlier. Hence, it makes sense to map the two in the following table:

Type of data	Type of storage	Storage example
Structured	Relational databases backed by block storage	In AWS, an Oracle database hosted on an EC2 instance backed by **Elastic Block Storage (EBS)** volumes
Unstructured	Object storage or file storage	In AWS, digital documents are stored in S3 buckets or **Elastic File System (EFS)** shares
Semi-structured	Non-relational databases backed by block storage	In AWS—a MongoDB NoSQL database hosted on an EC2 instance backed by EBS volumes

Table 12.1: Cloud storage mapped to type of data

To provide more clarity on the physical storage types, let us look at each type of storage across the three most common cloud providers:

	AWS	Azure	GCP
Block storage	**Elastic Block Storage (EBS)** volumes	Azure Disks	Persistent Disks
File storage	**Elastic File Storage (EFS)**	Azure Files	Filestore
Object storage	S3	Azure Blob Storage	Cloud Storage

Table 12.2: Type of storage across multiple clouds

This was a general overview of all the cloud data storage options. When ingesting raw data into the cloud, the first stop to dump every type of data is usually object storage, which can handle thousands of terabytes of raw data in every form and shape.

Internal data sources like relational databases backed by EBS volumes sometimes feed into this central dumping ground as well. This centralized repository of the ingested raw data is called a data lake, and that is what we look at next.

Data lake

All raw data in its native form (structured, unstructured, or semi-structured) is stored in a central repository called a data lake before further processing and analysis. Due to the data type and size requirements, the data lake is most often backed by object storage. The data lake can scale massively to handle multitudes of data cost-effectively.

The reasons for dumping all raw data into a data lake backed by object storage are given here:

- The variety of data available nowadays is not limited to data that can be fit into a relational database. Data in every form and shape is useful, and hence, a storage medium capable of storing every data type is required.

- The availability of different types of data gives data scientists free rein to apply algorithms and analyze data that was not possible on a relational database.

- Object storage is much more cost-effective than block storage, making it ideal for storing massive amounts of raw data.

- Examples of object storage are Amazon S3, Azure blob storage, and Google Cloud storage. Their indefinite scalability and cost-effectiveness make this storage the best fit for a data lake. Once the data is in a data lake, data engineers can apply required data transformations to prepare it for data analysis.

Let us look at the tools and technologies commonly used for data storage and staging in the cloud:

- **Cloud-native**: Amazon S3, Azure Blob Storage, Google Cloud Storage, etc.

- **External**: Snowflake, Teradata, etc.

Data processing

This is the step where collected and stored data is cleaned and curated to bring it into a form that can be used by the further steps of the lifecycle. This step is probably the most time-consuming and resource-intensive of the whole data lifecycle for analytics. There are various ways in which data can be prepared and made usable. Either of these or a combination should be used, depending on the requirements:

- **Data cleaning**: This is the part where you would like to remove aberrations, errors, etc. In our retail company example, it could be handling missing values from POS data or removing garbage data from the e-commerce website-generated data.

- **Data transformation**: This is the part that involves calculations like data aggregations, grouping, etc. In our example, this could be calculating monthly sales for different product types or grouping customers based on their demographics or purchasing history etc.

- **Data enrichment**: In this type of processing, you are allowed to enrich and enhance the existing data by combining data elements or even adding data from external sources like market surveys, etc.

The intended output of this phase of the lifecycle is data that is ready, as per business requirements, to be loaded into a data warehouse for further analysis and visualization phases. Various cloud-native and external tools are available to perform data processing.

Some of the standard tools used for data processing and preparation are:

- **Cloud-native**: AWS Glue, AWS Lambda, **Amazon Elastic Map Reduce** (**EMR**), Azure data factory, Azure Databricks, Google Cloud dataflow, Google Cloud function, etc.

- **External**: Apache Spark, Apache Hadoop, etc.

Data analysis

Data analysis is a massive component of data analytics and overall data management on cloud. This step examines the processed data to conclude, find insights, and answer business questions.

Various data analysis techniques can be used once the data has been cleaned and curated, for example, let us look at some of them:

- **Descriptive analysis**: This type of analysis refers to examining and summarizing data to understand what is happening with the business, trends, etc. In our retail company example, descriptive analysis will show sales trends based on time, seasons, etc., good and poorly performing products, customers' purchase histories, and similar business trends.

- **Diagnostic analysis**: This type of analysis refers to answering *why* something happened that was uncovered during the descriptive analysis phase. It answers questions like why there was a sales drop. Continuing with our retail company example, you would perform a diagnostic analysis to determine things like why sales drop in a particular region, why certain customer demographics are not purchasing certain products, and why website traffic is dropping at certain times of the day.

- **Predictive analysis**: As the name suggests, this analysis refers to future forecasting, i.e., sales forecasting, etc. For the retail company, this would mean things like our sales in every region for the next quarter, which customer category is not purchasing certain products, and what products should be stocked more, considering performance and demand.

- **Prescriptive analysis**: This analysis suggests measures to optimize the business or operations of concern. In the case of our sample retail company, this would mean telling the best marketing strategies, product performance optimization techniques, cost optimization strategies, etc.

The growing field of AI makes data analysis even more powerful and worthy by revolutionizing how data can be used. We will not discuss AI as that is outside the scope of this book, but we will take a brief look later in this chapter.

Here are some of the popular data analysis tools:

- **Cloud-native**: AWS Athena, Amazon Redshift, Google BigQuery, etc.

- **External**: Tableau, Qlik Sense, etc.

Data visualization

After all the data preparation and analysis, it is time to present the findings and insights to the stakeholders. The output of the data analysis phase is known as data visualization.

The output of the data analysis can take many forms, like detailed reports with dashboards, graphs, charts, numbers, and actionable suggestions that businesses, especially non-IT stakeholders, can make sense of and take necessary action.

Taking our retail company example into the data visualization stage, let us look at some of the important insights:

- A line chart can be drawn showing sales trends over time.

- A bar chart can be drawn to show the regional sales trends

- A scatter plot showing customer segmentation based on demographics or purchase behavior can be drawn.

- A pie chart showing the e-commerce website usage and traffic patterns can be presented.

There can be many more based on what reports and dashboards you want to see, as long as the data is available. This is arguably the last but most crucial stage of the data lifecycle because, without a perceivable output that makes sense for every stakeholder, the entire lifecycle is not of much value. This is what the stakeholders will use to make important decisions.

Here are some of the popular data visualization tools:

- **Cloud-native**: AWS QuickSight, Azure Power BI, GCP Looker, etc.

- **External:** Tableau, Qlik Sense, etc.

The following figure shows a summary of the end-to-end data lifecycle:

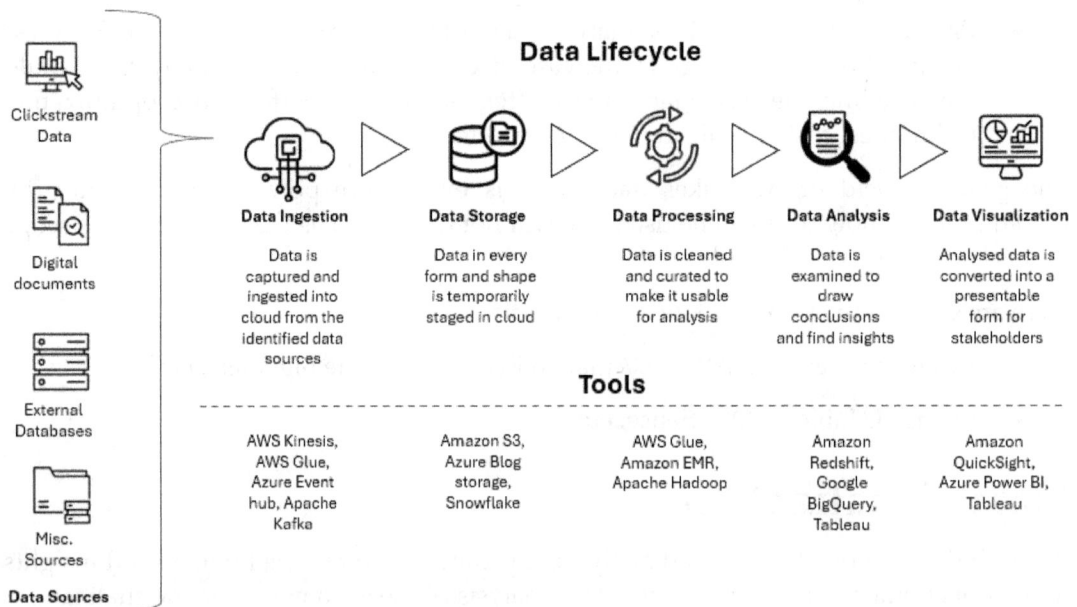

Figure 12.1: *Data lifecycle on the cloud*

Data inventory

As the name suggests, the up-to-date record of all the data assets in your organization is called the data inventory. Also referred to as a data catalog, the key attributes that a data inventory should record are listed here:

- Physical location where data is stored (cloud, on-premises, etc.).

- **Type of data**: Structured, unstructured, or semi-structured.

- Where the data belongs in the system, i.e., application, database, file server, etc.

- Data sensitivity classification per the company's standards, such as public, restricted, confidential, etc.

- Data retention and archival requirements are based on the type and classification of data.

- The type of content the data represents based on the business function, i.e., customer data, sales data, etc.

It might seem trivial, but having a detailed and recent data inventory in a data management strategy cannot be underestimated. In fact, for the overall cloud adoption strategy, it is pretty apparent that a good data inventory is needed as a reference. There are various benefits, such as:

- A good data inventory leads to good data discovery across all the distributed assets in the cloud or on-premises. This might even uncover certain areas (like legacy data) that might be unknown otherwise.

- A good data inventory is vital for drafting and implementing effective data governance policies. For example, applying controls to comply with regulations like **Health Insurance Portability and Accountability Act (HIPAA)**, **General Data Protection Regulation (GDPR)** etc. requires a good understanding of data classification. Security efforts can be planned accordingly.

- When migrating to the cloud, a good data inventory is essential for all the migration planning and design efforts. A well-laid-out data inventory determines what needs to be migrated, when, and how.

- Based on a good data inventory, you can optimize specific business areas. For example, knowing the data types and their retention/archival requirements can help you flush out old data that is not required anymore.

Various cloud-native and third-party tools can help create and maintain a data inventory. For example, here are a few of them:

- The 'AWS Glue data catalog' can create a repository of data stored in various AWS services, such as Amazon S3, DynamoDB, RDS, etc.

- 'Azure data purview' is another cloud-native service that is used for creating and managing data catalogs. It uses scanners to crawl various data sources and providers with various features like metadata discovery, extraction, and data classification.

- 'Apache Atlas' is a popular open-source tool used for metadata management for various data sources.

Data security

Cloud security is a dedicated chapter in this book (*Chapter 8*), which indicates the kind of attention and consideration that security deserves, including data security, when it comes to cloud adoption. Data security is critical to the data management framework and the overall cloud adoption strategy. Neither can be successful if data security has not been well planned and executed. Data security solutions and approaches have been discussed in *Chapter 8: Cloud Security,* but it is appropriate to highlight the importance of a robust data security posture before moving on.

Let us understand the significance in detail:

- You must handle data security accordingly based on various local and global regulatory requirements posed by frameworks like HIPAA and **Payment Card Industry Data Security Standard** (**PCI DSS**). Adherence to these requirements also demonstrates an organization's commitment to its customers and to the government.

- As is apparent, commitment to security is paramount to gaining customer trust, attracting more customers, and retaining existing ones.

- Business reputation is closely related to customer trust. A data breach can severely damage the organization's reputation and brand value, leading to business loss.

- Due to the cloud's shared responsibility model, securing application data is the customer's responsibility. This must be considered when formulating a cloud strategy.

- A multi-cloud environment adds the complexity of implementing a robust data security framework. Things like scattered data, decentralized controls, and unsupported services make implementing a strong data security posture difficult. Hence, planning the approach and tools properly is essential.

  In summary, data security cannot be an afterthought. Rather, it has to be treated as a core component of the cloud strategy and the cloud data management framework.

Encryption is a key component of data security. This includes encryption of data in transit, i.e., when data is moving between components or tiers, and encryption of data at rest, i.e., encrypting the storage devices/disks that hold the data. *Chapter 8: Cloud Security* includes more discussion on data encryption.

Data governance

A data governance stream involves rules and policies that make sure that the following are adhered to:

- The data is accessible to the right people at the right time

- Accurate auditing mechanisms are in place

- The data complies with the country/region/industry regulations, such as data residency requirements

- Controls and standards around data encryption, storage, retention, etc., are in place

- The quality of data is never compromised

- Data decisions are centralized and controlled rather than multiple siloed shops within the organization making decisions

- Most importantly, well-governed data builds trust within the organization and with the customers. Trust has a couple of advantages, such as:

  o Decision makers can make better decisions and improve customer experience based on the trust that has been provided by a robust governance framework

  o Trust enhances the market reputation, leading to the business's success

Although suitable for technical reasons, all these characteristics make data governance a bit more challenging and complicated on the cloud. People responsible for data governance need to be cognizant of the challenges and benefits that the cloud offers to realize the full potential of their organization's data.

In our retail company's use case, they can implement data governance at multiple levels to account for different types of data they handle instead of a cookie cutter approach across the board. For example, customer data governance ideally needs policies different from transactional data governance. Customer data governance should mandate a consolidated view of every customer, regardless of interface (in-store or online). In addition, strict adherence to data privacy regulations for customer data is required. The data governance should be around secure and auditable transactions for transactional data. Similarly, there should be customized data governance policies for product or marketing data.

Let us take another example from the healthcare industry to better understand data governance. Healthcare has stringent rules around handling patient data. That is where a solid governance policy comes into play. A data governance policy for a healthcare customer would include standards around access control, data privacy, and compliance with US regulations like the **Health Insurance Portability and Accountability Act (HIPAA)**. A governance policy for healthcare would also define acceptable data quality standards for patient data.

Though the fundamental principles of data governance remain the same, there are some important differences when it comes to data governance on the cloud, primarily due to the cloud's inherent qualities. Some of the key differences are:

- Cloud offers almost infinite scalability for most of its storage solutions, which is impossible with on-premises solutions.

- You have complete control in an on-premises setup, whereas with cloud, some access and activities might be restricted.

- When using the cloud, you are venturing into the cloud provider's network. Though fully controllable, this requires stringent authentication and authorization mechanisms.

- There are many more automation opportunities for data governance tasks on the cloud. For example, you previously employed specialized monitoring tools, whereas essential monitoring tools are available natively on the cloud.

Data trends

The increasing availability of data from sources unfathomable a few years ago and in forms unknown until recently has triggered a wave of data trends changing how we understand and interact with the world around us.

Lately, a new multidisciplinary field called data science has emerged. This vast field comprises game-changing trends like ML and AI, among others.

Artificial intelligence

AI is the ability of machines to mimic human intelligence and perform real-world functions like learning and solving problems that a human brain could solve. It is a broad field that aims to create intelligent machines, and there is more than one way to achieve this.

Machine learning

ML is a subset of AI that uses algorithms to learn patterns from data that can be used for improved decision-making. ML should be considered one of the techniques for achieving AI by learning from data instead of specific programming or hard-coded values.

The process of creating an ML model typically consists of the following phases:

- Collecting and preparing the data that will be used for training the ML model

- Choosing the right ML algorithm, which could be one of the following:

  o Supervised learning

  o Unsupervised learning

  o Reinforcement learning

- Now, train the model using the data and algorithms you finalized in the previous steps

- Test the model using new data that the model has not seen so far

- Finally, if everything is good, start using the model for your actual use cases

Generative AI

Another interesting and most recent trend fueled by data is the rise of **generative AI (GenAI)**. This type of AI focuses on creating new content based on the prompts and inputs provided by users. The content can be in any form, such as text, images, videos, etc. Lately, out-of-the-box applications like ChatGPT have gained popularity because of the revolutionary use cases to which they have been applied.

There are many more such applications earmarked for specific use cases, and this is not it; you can build your own GenAI applications using custom or pre-trained foundation models. While GenAI is revolutionary, there are some risks that, as a user or practitioner, one needs to be aware of, such as:

- **Data privacy**: As is apparent, GenAI models are trained on huge datasets that might include some confidential or sensitive data as well. Hence, if you are using such data to train your models, be aware of data leakage risks.

- **Bias and discrimination**: Data used for training the models could be biased, and hence, the GenAI models can amplify such biases, which could lead to unfair outcomes.

- **Ethical issues**: Use of GenAI can lead to various ethical issues, like using copyrighted data for training, legal and intellectual property rights, and misuse of trained models.

- **Responsible use**: To avoid misuse of GenAI, there needs to be governance and regulatory frameworks.

- **Deepfakes**: A new threat associated with GenAI doing the rounds is deepfake, which is the ability to create realistic fake images and videos.

The technical details of GenAI are out of scope, but for now, it is sufficient to understand that GenAI is a disruptive trend poised to change the world in the coming years.

Examples of data management in cloud

It is hard to name any specific companies that leverage cloud to store, use, and analyze data because almost every company using the cloud leverages native cloud data services in some form or another. To name a few prominent examples of organizations that store massive amounts of data in the cloud, leveraging the scalability and flexibility of cloud storage services to manage their vast data needs:

- **Google**: Relies heavily on **Google Cloud Platform** (**GCP**) to store data from services like Gmail, YouTube, Google Search, and Google Drive.

- **Amazon (AWS)**: Their cloud service, **Amazon Web Services** (**AWS**), is widely used by businesses across industries to store and process large datasets.

- **Microsoft (Azure)**: Microsoft offers cloud storage solutions through Azure, which is particularly beneficial for companies using Microsoft Office products and enterprise software.

- **Facebook**: Stores user data, photos, videos, and social interactions on cloud infrastructure to manage the immense volume of content generated on their platform.

- **Netflix**: Utilizes AWS cloud services to store and manage massive amounts of streaming video content, enabling efficient delivery to users globally. They also use data analytics to personalize content recommendations based on user behavior and watch history.

- Uber Leverages Google Cloud storage to manage ride requests, driver locations, and user data in real-time. They built a data lake to collect data from multiple sources. They actively use ML algorithms for things like estimated time of arrival, personalized recommendations, etc.

- Airbnb is known for using AWS for all hosting requirements. The data architecture consists of a data lake that is used to analyze booking data, usage data, etc. They then leverage this varied data to optimize prices using ML algorithms.

Apart from these big names, the healthcare industry uses the cloud to store sensitive patient medical records, imaging data, and clinical information on secure cloud platforms. Similarly, in the education domain, online education platforms use cloud storage at a large scale to store and stream their content to users.

Conclusion

We have just scratched the surface when it comes to data management in the cloud. The idea is to consider ways to handle data when planning or developing a cloud strategy, especially if you are a data-driven organization. In terms of tools and technologies, there is a rich ecosystem of cloud-native and external offerings for various types and aspects of data analysis, with new ones coming regularly.

Overall, the aforementioned aspects of data management can significantly impact your cloud strategy. Consider the challenges, tools, and skills critical for successful cloud adoption. Investing in the right tools, processes, and expertise will ensure a smooth cloud transition and unlock the cloud's full potential, driving business value, mitigating risks, and positioning the business for long-term success.

The landscape of cloud data management is constantly evolving, and hence, one must be mindful of future challenges as well. Data complexity and scale are ever-increasing, and hence there will be a need for more sophisticated data handling tools. Another prominent concern of hosting data on cloud is security and the threat landscape keeps evolving as well. Last but not least, the growth of AI could be a potential risk to data privacy.

In the next chapter, we will discuss the application development aspect of cloud adoption, looking at some modern application development frameworks, architectures, and approaches, such as DevOps, CI/CD, etc.

Points to remember

Here are the key takeaways from this chapter:

- Data should be the most critical component of your data strategy on the cloud and, in fact, the overall cloud adoption strategy. Successful cloud adoption is impossible without a plan to manage various aspects of data. Data management cannot be an afterthought.

- Data management aspects that need attention are:
  - Data analytics and data lifecycle
  - Data inventory
  - Data security
  - Data governance

- Data analytics is the process of drawing insights and conclusions from data and involves a lifecycle from ingestion into the environment to generating presentable outcomes. The various stages of the data lifecycle are:
  - Data capture/ingestion
  - Data storage/staging
  - Data processing/preparation
  - Data analysis
  - Data visualization

- Data governance is a framework that consists of policies, processes, and standards to perform key functions such as:
  - Control data access
  - Ensure compliance with regulations

- o   Maintain and improve data quality
- o   Mitigate any potential risks
- o   Tracking data usage and storage
- With the burst of data in recent years, new data trends have emerged, changing how we know the world. For example:
  - o   Artificial intelligence
  - o   Machine learning
  - o   Generative AI

Join our book's Discord space

Join the book's Discord Workspace for Latest updates, Offers, Tech happenings around the world, New Release and Sessions with the Authors:

https://discord.bpbonline.com

CHAPTER 13

Application Development

Introduction

The legacy approaches to application development focused on monolithic architectures where all application components were tightly coupled, making management aspects (upgrades, scalability, etc.) tedious and cumbersome. Modern application development in the cloud is a complete paradigm shift from the legacy approaches. It embraces cloud-native architectures like microservices, enabling a loosely coupled architecture that enables independent scaling and faster deployments. Considering the principles of modern application development on the cloud, strategists should make informed decisions about technology choices, resource allocation, and overall cloud adoption strategy.

This chapter aims to provide an overview of modern application development architectures and approaches to the cloud. We will examine various application development concepts, such as DevOps, CI/CD, microservices, etc., that have gained popularity over the years as more organizations adopt cloud computing.

Structure

In this chapter, we will cover the following topics:

- Modern application development approaches
- DevOps principles and practices

- CI/CD methodologies

- Cloud native architecture strategies

Objectives

By the end of this chapter, readers should be able to understand the popular application development approaches and architectures on the cloud. The information provided in this chapter is not a technical in-depth exploration into application development on the cloud, but rather an overview of the key concepts. The intent is to empower the readers to make informed decisions when developing a cloud adoption strategy for their organization.

Modern application development approaches

Though the traditional development practices that have been used for ages emphasized stability, they were known for tedious, inefficient, and lengthy development cycles because of various inherent characteristics, such as:

- **Waterfall delivery model**: The waterfall delivery model involves sequential execution of activities that lead to lengthy release cycles. Under this model, requirements are gathered upfront, followed by sequential design, build, testing, and deployment steps. Any fixes for bugs caught during testing or feedback post the final release have to wait until the next release cycle, which is inefficient.

- **Monolithic applications**: Historically, applications have been known to be significant in size using a tightly coupled architecture (i.e. all components of the application are dependent on each other). This means that any impact on one element of the application will impact the availability of the whole application.

- **Manual processes**: Traditionally, application development and deployment have involved manual processes, which are not only tedious but also time-consuming and error-prone.

- **Siloed and one-dimensional teams**: Traditionally, software development and deployment had one-dimensional teams for development, testing, operations, and other functions with clear boundaries of responsibilities. This environment is inefficient and lacks communication and collaboration between teams that should ideally work much more closely.

- **Underlying infrastructure**: Traditional application development is mainly associated with on-premises infrastructure, which lacks flexibility, scalability, and agility. Not that the cloud cannot be used for legacy ways of application development. Still, cloud-based infrastructure has features that are most suitable for new ways of application development, which we will touch upon in this chapter.

Over the last few years, businesses have changed how they operate historically. The competition is so cutthroat that long release cycles spanning months and poor customer experience are simply unaffordable. Hence, to keep pace with the rapidly changing business landscape, the focus shifted towards faster time to market, increasing agility, improving quality, and reducing overall costs.

Some of the aspects of modern application development practices that make this shift possible are listed here:

- **Modern frameworks**: Frameworks like Agile and DevOps have revolutionized the way traditional waterfall and siloed development happen.

  o   Agile development methodology divides the development and deployment into short perceivable sprints that make the whole process iterative, provide frequent feedback, and promote close integration between the development team.

  o   DevOps philosophy amalgamates software development processes and IT operations, i.e., a close collaboration between development and operations personnel. While the Agile framework emphasizes development, DevOps extends the same principles to include operations. We will explore DevOps and its key principles later in this chapter.

- **Automation**: Manual processes are slow, inefficient, and error prone. This is true for application development activities as well. Recently, automation has become central to application development, deployment, and operations. This is efficient from a process and usage point of view and also frees up resources to work on more productive tasks. CI/CD pipelines are great examples of how automation is baked into the complete development and deployment cycle.

- **Agility**: Organizations want to move fast due to changing market dynamics and increasing competition. Modern application development frameworks focus on agility, speed, and continuous improvement.

- **Cloud-based infrastructure**: Due to the cloud's fundamental nature and features like on-demand provisioning, flexibility, elasticity, and scalability, applications can leverage these attributes and provide features like auto-scaling and load balancing out of the box, thus reducing costs and simplifying management.

- **Cloud-native architectures**: Traditionally on-premises infrastructures were most suitable for large monolithic applications where components were tightly coupled with each other and sometimes with the underlying infrastructure.

- However, cloud-native architectures have changed how applications are designed and developed. Strategies like microservices, containers, serverless, and **application programming interface** (**API**) driven architectures are closely associated with these new ways of development on the cloud, providing the scalability, resilience, and flexibility that were lacking from legacy architectures.

In the upcoming sections, we will pick some of the critical concepts mentioned above and provide more clarity on application development in the cloud.

DevOps principles and practices

As the name suggests, DevOps is a collaboration of development and operations teams to develop, deliver, and manage applications using an approach fundamentally different from what it used to be. The core principles of a DevOps philosophy are collaboration, automation, continuous integration, and delivery and IaC.

It is worth going into more detail about these core principles that make DevOps practices and skills most sought-after. Let us look at them:

- **Collaboration**: The most unique aspect of DevOps is its ability to break the silos between teams to foster a culture of instant collaboration and communication, which in turn encourages shared responsibility of involved teams rather than a single team owning a particular phase of the whole process. For example, involving operations early in the development phase provides a more practical perspective because the application's people know the real-life challenges. Hence, their inputs will lead to a much more efficient product.

- **Continuous monitoring**: Continuous monitoring of the health of applications and infrastructure and providing regular feedback to development and operation teams are fundamental to DevOps implementation. This is important to ensure bugs are caught and fixed early, and areas of improvement are identified and iterated on faster.

- **Automation**: The engine that powers the implementation of DevOps principles is the automation of various systems and processes. DevOps strongly preaches the principle of automating all repetitive tasks to make the process efficient by reducing human errors and increasing speed using specialized tools. Many areas of DevOps automation are core to the implementation of DevOps philosophy, such as the following points:

  o **Continuous integration and continuous delivery (CI/CD)**: Another core principle of DevOps philosophy is CI/CD, which automates the software delivery pipeline. In CI/CD, CI advocates frequently merging the code into the code repository, followed by build and unit tests. Further, CD focuses on automating the release process.

  o **Infrastructure as code (IaC)**: Yet another principle under the automation category that refers to provisioning and managing infrastructure through code. This is a building block of every cloud deployment to ensure consistency and repeatability. Popular tools are Terraform, **Ansible, CloudFormation** (**AWS**), and **Azure Resource Access Manager** (**RAM**).

    o **Configuration management**: Configuration of servers and applications can also be automated to ensure consistency and avoid human errors. Specialized tools like Chef and Puppet are used for this.

DevSecOps

A nice and sought-after variation of the DevOps philosophy is DevSecOps, which integrates security practices within the DevOps ways of working. It ensures that the security team collaborates with the development and operations teams so that security is considered at every stage of a **software development lifecycle (SDLC)**.

Some of the key practices involved in the DevSecOps philosophy are listed here:

- **Security testing**: Continuous security testing throughout the SDLC.
- **Infrastructure security**: Ensuring infrastructure configurations are secure and compliant.
- **Threat modeling**: Identifying potential security threats and vulnerabilities.

There are various benefits of DevSecOps practices, such as DevOps. Here is a quick look at some of them:

- By integrating security throughout the SDLC, vulnerabilities can be identified early and manage the risks.
- Early detection of security issues can significantly lower the cost of fixing them later.
- DevSecOps helps organizations meet regulatory requirements and industry standards for security.

CI/CD methodologies

Now, let us dig deeper into the CI/CD concepts we discussed in the previous section as part of the DevOps discussion. CI/CD is such an integral part of a software development strategy that it is essential to go a bit deeper to understand what it is capable of and why it is the default methodology for every cloud development nowadays. A CI/CD methodology aims to build frequently and make smaller and more frequent application releases.

The pipeline's CI part involves developers committing and merging more minor code changes to a central repository frequently, sometimes multiple times a day, instead of making a big change after many days/weeks. The merging process triggers an automated build process and sometimes bundled unit tests as well to produce a final deployable build. Of course, some checks and hooks ensure concerned people are notified of any errors or if a manual intervention is required.

The CD part of the pipeline takes the build artifacts from CI. and automates the release process to get the error-free build into production or a lower production-like environment if desired before production. Suppose the release process has a final step to deploy in production manually. In that case, the CD is referred to as continuous delivery. If the end-to-end process, including deployment to production, is automated, then the CD is called continuous deployment.

The benefits of using CI/CD practices to optimize software development and delivery are numerous. Some obvious ones are listed here:

- Early feedback loops leading to early bug detection and better code quality and outputs.

- Improved time to market powered by automated delivery and deployments.

- Ability to respond to market changes quickly by building and releasing more frequently.

- Enhanced collaboration between development and operations teams.

- Not only has the efficiency of developers improved, but they are also freed up from doing tedious manual tasks and can focus on writing good quality code.

While this is not a discussion of the detailed technical aspects of software development using CI/CD methodology, it is important to understand the steps and key components to appreciate the efficiency it brings to software development in the cloud.

Here is a review of the flow and key elements of a CI/CD pipeline:

- **Commit**: The pipeline starts with a code commit to a version control system like Github. This commit step or a manual commit can be scheduled to trigger the automated pipeline.

- **Build**: Once triggered, the pipeline checks out the latest code from the repository, compiles it and packages it into an executable artifact, like a docker image or a **Java Archive (JAR)** file. If required, automated unit testing is also performed for individual package components. Optionally, a notification for the completion of the build can be sent to the developer/product owner.

- **Testing**: If no manual approval hook exists, automated tests should run after the build is complete. Depending on your requirements, various types of testing can be performed in this phase, such as integration testing, performance testing, etc. A notification can be sent to the required stakeholders once the testing is completed successfully or if there are any errors.

- **Staging deployment**: As a best practice, usually a production-like or production replica is used as a staging environment to deploy the built and tested artefact. After testing, the pipeline's continuous delivery part should deploy the artifact into this environment where a UAT can be performed.

- **Production deployment**: A manual approval step might be included before the final package can be deployed to production after staging deployment. However, manual approval can be omitted if an automated deployment is intended; hence, this part is called continuous deployment.

It definitely makes the software development process on cloud much more efficient, but building and deploying CI/CD pipelines is a complicated task and hence needs specialized tools, such as the following:

- **Version control**: Git, GitHub, Bitbucket etc.
- **Build**: Maven, Docker etc.
- **Testing**: JUnit, Selenium etc.
- **Deployment**: Ansible, Terraform, CloudFormation etc.
- **CI/CD orchestration**: Jenkins, Azure DevOps etc.
- **Monitoring**: Prometheus, Grafana etc.

To conclude and make the above concepts clear, here is a visual summary of an end-to-end CI/CD pipeline:

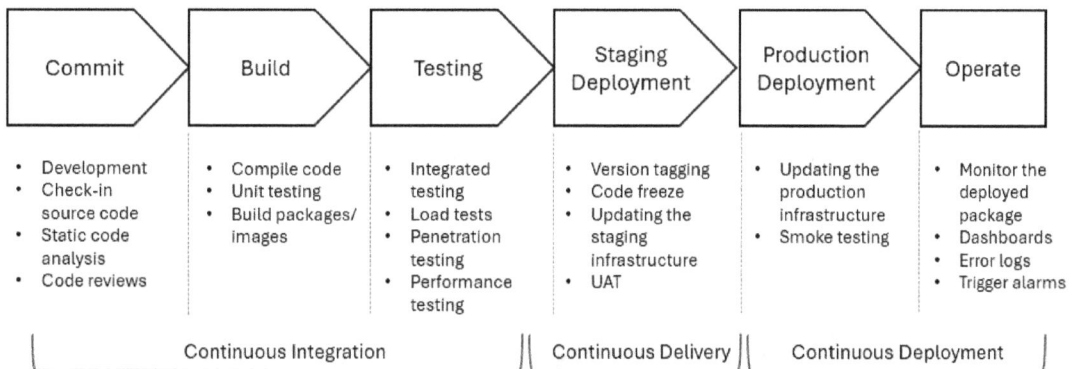

Figure 13.1: CI/CD pipeline

Cloud-native architecture strategies

A discussion on application development in cloud is incomplete without understanding some common cloud-native architecture approaches. These are the reasons why modern development frameworks are efficient and popular amongst the developer community.

Microservices

Before defining microservices, let us do some base setting. Before cloud computing came into prominence, organizations had been making large monolithic applications made of tightly coupled components deployed over large physical or virtual servers sitting in data centers and could not be scaled on demand. There are two terms from the above statement that need attention, let us look at them:

- **Monolithic**: A monolithic application is designed as a single unit, has the common codebase and a centralized data management.

- **Tightly coupled**: A tightly coupled architecture is closely related to a monolithic application in which all components are interconnected and depend on each other. Failure of one component impacts the whole application.

Some apparent problems with this type of legacy architecture are listed here:

- **Scalability**: Scaling a monolithic application can be cumbersome and costly because the entire application needs to be scaled which is not only inefficient but also needs lot of planning and possible downtime.

- **Technology lock-in**: Usually, with a monolithic application, you will adopt a technology stack for the entire application instead, even though some application components may not benefit from that. Also, migrating to better technology might require the entire application to be re-architected.

- **Management complexity**: Large monolithic applications require large teams to work in sync, which requires a lot of coordination. Any change or problem with one application component requires the entire team to work together.

- **Resilience**: If a component fails, the whole application is impacted.

- **Slow-release cycles**: Bug fixes or enhancements to a monolithic application will take a long release cycle, sometimes weeks or months.

The following table is a quick comparison of a monolithic application and a microservices-based application:

	Monolithic	Microservices
What?	An application that is built as a single unified unit with all components tightly coupled and a single codebase	An application that is broken down into a collection of small and independent services that can be deployed and scaled separately
Scalability	Limited capabilities because scaling requires scaling the entire application, even if only a specific component needs it	Individual services can be scaled independently, optimizing resource utilization
Maintenance	Cumbersome and time consuming, entire application is impacted	Much simpler as individual services can be managed separately, and the application can still serve the users
Deployment	Initial development and deployment could be a very lengthy process. Even any later releases, including bug fixes or minor enhancements require deploying the entire application	Deployment of every service can be done independently

Table 13.1: Monolithic vs. microservices

With this context setting, we can now understand microservices-based architecture. This architectural approach involves breaking down an application into a set of independent services, usually modeled around a business function. Each service communicates with other services through mechanisms like HTTP or API.

Here are some apparent advantages of this type of approach:

- They can be scaled and deployed independently of other services, improving the application's availability and performance.

- The services are loosely coupled, leading to independent operations without impacting other application parts.

- Small and autonomous teams can work on each service independently, reducing coordination effort.

- Every service can use a different technology stack instead of a one-size-fits-all strategy. For example, based on the service type, an appropriate programming language can be used.

Containers

In today's increasingly competitive landscape, application development and deployment practices have been transformed to keep pace with evolving market needs. Traditional methods have often been called out for being inconsistent because things might work on a developer machine. Still, the code might fail when built and deployed on test or production environments. This could be due to missing libraries or dependencies, different versions of external applications, or even operating systems.

Enter container-based architecture has revolutionized how applications are packaged, deployed, and managed. This approach offers significant advantages in modern software development and deployment. Containerized architecture is a way to package up an application code and all its dependencies (libraries, configuration files, etc.) into a single unit called a container.

Container-based architecture leverages containerization technologies. Here are some popular ones:

- **Docker**: The most popular containerization platform, providing tools for building, running, and managing containers.

- **Docker hub**: A public repository where developers can store and share container images.

- **Kubernetes**: A container orchestration platform that automates the deployment, scaling, and management of containerized applications.

All cloud providers offer native services built on top of these open-source technologies. For example, AWS offers **Elastic Container Service (ECS)** and **Elastic Kubernetes Service (EKS)**.

The benefits of a containerized approach are as follows:

- Since everything has been packaged as a single movable unit, the container can run consistently across different environments.

- Containers are portable; they can be shared and run on any server with a container runtime like Docker.

- Containers are lightweight. Unlike a virtual machine, containers share the host operating system's kernel and use fewer resources.

- Containers are a great fit for microservices-based architectures, as each microservice can be packaged and deployed independently, promoting agility and scalability.

- Containerized applications can be easily scaled up or down based on demand

Serverless computing

On the cloud, both IaaS and PaaS-based deployments include the task of server management. However, with the evolution of cloud computing, a revolutionary approach to building and running applications has gained popularity: serverless computing. The serverless approach abstracts away the traditional complexities of server management, allowing developers to focus solely on the code that drives their applications.

Even with a container-based architecture, there are servers to manage. Instead of worrying about the underlying servers to provision or configure, developers can just focus on developing quality code, and the cloud provider can take care of the infrastructure.

Some key characteristics of serverless computing are:

- As said earlier, there are no servers for users to manage. The cloud provider manages the underlying servers.

- Pricing is based on the code's run time and the resources used by the code. You do not pay for idle resources when the code is not running.

- The underlying resources scale automatically up or down based on the demand of the application.

- Serverless functions need a trigger to be executed. Events such as an HHTP request or a scaling operation can trigger the functions, which is why this is called event-driven architecture.

The choice between serverless architecture and containerized architecture is tricky. When designing and developing new applications on the cloud, architects and developers are often faced with choosing the best approach. Both these modern application architecture approaches have their pros and cons. However, there are significant differences in their underlying principles.

Let us compare them to get a better understanding of which approach is best suited for your use case:

	Serverless	Containers
Infrastructure management overhead	This is taken care of by the cloud provider	There are underlying servers to manage**
Scaling	Automated	Mostly manual
Billing/Pricing	Only pay for the time your code runs	Pay for provisioned resources
Deployment	Very simple, just write the code and submit	More complex and more skills are required
Control	Less the infrastructure is managed by the cloud provider	More
Portability	Very limited because mostly you are tied to an operating environment and a cloud provider	High because the containers act as an autonomous unit that can be shared and moved
Use cases	Even driven applications	Microservices are a common use case

Table 13.2: Serverless vs. containers

Note: Most cloud providers also offer native serverless container services.

In summary, choose serverless architecture for event-driven applications or background tasks and cases where you want to minimize operational overhead and cost. On the other hand, containers are best for microservices-based architectures where control, portability, and loosely coupled architecture are the key criteria.

API driven architecture

We have mentioned a few cloud-native architecture approaches in this chapter. However, there is a glue that makes these approaches work effectively and seamlessly: APIs. API-driven architecture is deeply intertwined with application architecture, such as microservices, containers, and serverless architecture.

An API-driven architecture is an approach where applications are designed and built around APIs, regardless of the application type you are building. Applications expose their functionalities through well-defined APIs, which act as the integrating entity, defining how internal system components or external systems can interact. Consider API as a messenger between systems that encapsulates the rules and configuration for systems to interact with each other.

- An API-driven architecture is essential for cloud-based application development, both from a technical and strategic perspective. When framing a cloud strategy, application development approaches and frameworks supporting business and technology objectives must be included as a key input. Strategy makers should involve stakeholders who can answer questions such as:

    o How to make the development teams productive?

    o How to integrate new services with existing ones or external platforms?

    o How to make our offerings scalable and secure?

Here is why an API-driven architecture should make its way into a cloud strategy:

- **Business agility**: APIs are typically used to decouple services, which is why they are associated with microservices-based architectures. Decoupling eventually leads to faster development cycles and simplified integration of services internally and externally. Hence, organizations can respond to new business opportunities and challenges much faster.

- **Cloud operations**: Fostering a loosely coupled architecture, APIs enable independent scaling of services based on demand.

- **Digital transformation**: Most digital transformations happen incrementally, i.e., in phases, as applications are migrated and modernized. Hence, APIs provide the glue that integrates legacy systems with modern cloud applications, eventually supporting the cause of digital transformation.

In an API-based application design, a key component to include is the API gateway. This is the central hub for the orchestration and management of all APIs you plan to have in your landscape.

Based on the product you choose, there are many critical functionalities that an API gateway can perform, such as:

- Centralized API management

- Request routing and traffic management

- Security of APIs through authentication and authorization measures

- Caching frequently accessed responses

Example of a cloud-native architecture

The aforementioned architecture approaches are synonymous with cloud-native applications. It is very common nowadays to leverage all these approaches together. Let us take a look at a real-life example that brings all of them together and is relatable. Consider an e-commerce application with multiple functions.

Here are the steps that we can use to design this application, in a cloud-native architecture using the approaches discussed in this chapter:

1. As the first step, let us break down the application's backend into essential functions and represent them as individual services. At this point, we are adopting a microservices architecture for our application.

2. Next, we will determine how each of these services will be built and deployed, i.e., containers or serverless (since we are discussing cloud-native, a.k.a modern application architectures here, we will stick to these).

3. Concluding our logical application design, all these services will be exposed via **Representational State Transfer (REST)** APIs.

Let us put this all together in the following table

Microservice	Technology	Container or Serverless
Product catalogue	Could be any of the following—Python, Java, Node.js, or Go—depending on the service and best fit	Packaged as docker containers and deployed using Kubernetes
Shopping cart		
Order processing		
Inventory		
Product image resizing	AWS lambda or Azure functions	Serverless

Table 13.3: Summary of the example cloud-native architecture

An important consideration is the use of technology to build all these microservices. Since it is a loosely coupled microservices architecture, all services are independent. Hence, there is flexibility in choosing the best technology for a service instead of adopting the same technology.

Here is a workflow that integrates these services:

- The customer visits the e-commerce website by opening the front end in a browser.

- Customer wants to browse the available products. The front end calls the API of the *Product catalog* service to retrieve and display the product information on the front end.

- The customer finalizes a product from the list and adds it to the cart. At this point, the front end calls the Shopping cart service API to add the product to the customer's cart.

- Now, the customer wants to place the order. To confirm the order, the front end sends the order details to the *Order processing* service via its API.

- At this point, the *Order processing* service calls the API of the *Inventory* service to check the availability of the product and to update the inventory.

- Finally, the *Order processing/* service processes the payment via a payment gateway.

Note: This is a high-level overview of an application built using a cloud-native architecture approach. We have not gone into many technical details, such as the front end, payment gateway, etc. Hopefully, this example will help to put things into perspective and make the concepts clear.

Conclusion

Application development on the cloud significantly differs from what it used to be in legacy environments. We have moved from the monolithic world of immense and tightly coupled deployment units to a much more granular microservices world of smaller and loosely coupled services that can be managed and operated by smaller independent teams without impacting surrounding services.

In this chapter, we have seen modern architecture and its benefits. We have also examined the relevance of contemporary development architecture to a cloud strategy. In the next chapter, we will discuss the new and emerging trends related to cloud computing.

Points to remember

Some key takeaways from this chapter are:

- The legacy application development process had various weaknesses that the modern cloud development frameworks can address, such as the following:
  - Lot of manual processes
  - Inflexible and unscalable legacy infrastructure
  - Large monolithic applications
  - Sequential waterfall development models that were inefficient
  - Longer and slower application release cycles
- Some of the modern approaches to application development on the cloud are listed here:
  - Agile and DevOps frameworks
  - CI/CD methodology
  - Microservices based architectures
  - Containerized applications
  - Serverless computing
  - API driven architecture

- DevOps is a collaboration of development and operations teams to develop, deliver, and manage applications. The core principles of a DevOps philosophy are collaboration, automation, continuous integration and delivery, and IaC.

- CI/CD stands for continuous integration and continuous delivery (or continuous deployment). It is a set of practices that automate and streamline the process of building, testing, and deploying software, enabling teams to release updates more frequently and reliably.

- Phases of a CI/CD pipeline are as follows:

  o Commit

  o Build

  o Test

  o Staging deployment

  o Production deployment

  o Monitoring

- Containerized architecture is a way to package up an application code and all its dependencies (libraries, configuration files, etc.) into a single unit that can be shared and moved easily between environments.

- An API-driven approach emphasizes creating a collection of interconnected services, each exposing its functionality through well-defined APIs.

Join our book's Discord space

Join the book's Discord Workspace for Latest updates, Offers, Tech happenings around the world, New Release and Sessions with the Authors:

https://discord.bpbonline.com

CHAPTER 14
Associated Trends

Introduction

Throughout this book, we have discussed various strategic and technical concepts related to cloud computing, cloud adoption, and multi-cloud environments. With so much happening in the field of cloud computing, many new trends and developments have emerged in the last few years. One of the big trends to keep an eye on is AI and its various branches. AI's unprecedented growth enables new levels of insight and decision-making, leading to a fundamental shift in how we interact with technology and the world around us.

The cloud is an essential enabler because it provides the scalable infrastructure, vast data storage, and accessible computing power necessary to train and deploy complex AI models. In addition, several *Ops* trends in cloud have emerged lately. More specialized approaches are required to bring more structure, automation, and intelligence to run and manage cloud-based systems and applications. Each of these trends may have a different type and range of impact on a cloud adoption strategy. For example, FinOps enables businesses to control cloud costs and maximize ROI, making cloud adoption more financially sustainable. AIOps makes cloud environments more manageable. Understanding these trends is a must for organizations planning to adopt and leverage cloud platforms.

Several key trends are converging to shape the revolutionary cloud landscape, which we will focus on in this chapter. We will cover the various *Ops* terms and trends that are gaining a lot of attention and becoming indispensable for the success of a cloud adoption.

Structure

In this chapter, we will cover the following topics:

- Future of cloud computing
- AIOps
- GitOps
- FinOps
- DataOps
- GreenOps
- CloudOps

Objectives

By the end of this chapter, readers should understand these trends and relate their cloud implementation to the practice examples provided alongside each trend. Even if you are new to these terms, reading this chapter should give you much-needed clarity, and the examples provided should resonate with your own situation.

Future of cloud computing

Cloud computing is necessary for modern IT setups instead of just a bandwagon. The adoption of cloud computing has shown significant shifts in how organizations build, deploy, and interact with technology. A key area of cloud computing evolution is multi-cloud, which we have touched on at various places in this book regarding benefits, challenges, and best practices. Understanding that multi-cloud is slowly becoming a norm and a standard practice is non-trivial.

Let us look at a quick stat to substantiate the increase in popularity of multi-cloud adoption. According to Flexera's state of cloud report for 2023, about 90% of organizations have a multi-cloud strategy (though not fully implemented). This is a clear indication of the upward trajectory. The reasons and benefits are obvious; we have discussed them in *Chapter 6: Multi-cloud Adoption)* in more detail.

In the future, for successful multi-cloud adoption, AI will be a strong driver and enabler. Let us look at the reasons behind this:

- With AI-powered tools, the complexity around managing workloads across multiple clouds can be handled at scale.

- Data is an organization's biggest asset from various internal and external sources and cloud platforms. AI projects will require ever-exploding volumes of data residing across multiple clouds.

- Using data from multiple cloud platforms, AI-powered tools can analyze and visualize system health and performance, eventually ensuring application reliability and availability.

- Multi-cloud needs a unified view of security posture to enforce consistent security policies. AI powered security tools that can manage security across multiple platforms will be valuable.

- AI can automate many routine IT tasks, such as provisioning resources, deploying applications, and responding to incidents. This simplifies multi-cloud operations.

Not forgetting the specialized AI/ML services provided by every cloud provider. We have discussed leveraging the best possible cloud services as a massive benefit of multi-cloud adoption. With a rush to jump onto the AI bandwagon, being able to choose and use the best available offering from all cloud providers is a practical use case of future multi-cloud adoption.

Adoption of cloud now is not only about migrating workloads to the cloud anymore. Focus is on optimizing, securing, and sustaining those cloud environments for long-term success. Specialized operational practices are becoming increasingly essential for navigating the complexities and realizing the benefits of modern cloud landscapes. In the next few sections, we will explore how these trends are shaping the future of cloud adoption.

AIOps

Artificial intelligence for operations (**AIOps**) is a process that uses AI techniques and practices (like NLP and ML) to manage IT infrastructure. It is about automating critical operational tasks, improving the overall efficiency of IT operations, and providing real-time insights into IT operations.

To gauge the importance of AIOps, here is a look at some of the distinct advantages of AIOps:

- **Managing cloud complexity**: Cloud environments generate a massive amount of data ingestion and storage in the form of logs, traces, and metrics. AIOps allows you to make sense of this data and tame the complexity of cloud environments.

- **Proactive operations**: AIOps can analyze historical data and real-time data to predict patterns, enabling IT operations teams to perform a **root cause analysis** (**RCA**) and resolve system errors quickly and proactively.

- **Application performance**: AIOps can analyze application performance data and traces to identify potential bottlenecks or performance issues. Based on the analysis, certain AI algorithms can also automatically optimize the application configuration.

- **Cost optimization**: AIOps can analyze usage patterns and identify cost optimization opportunities. Algorithms can identify unused capacities and predict future cloud spending based on existing expenditure data. As is obvious, cost optimization is one of the most common drivers of cloud adoption. Hence, AIOps also supports cloud adoption initiatives.

- **Support for DevOps**: AIOps can be used to perform quality checks on application code by using automated code reviews and detecting bugs early, rather than delaying them until the end of the testing cycle.

In contrast to AIOps, the traditional operations approach is more reactive and manual. There is a lot of manual effort required for tasks like patching and configuration management. Most often, the responses are post-incident rather than a proactive approach. Moreover, the automation is limited to basic scripting and task scheduling.

Use cases

Let us see the difference that AIOps can make with the help of some practical use cases:

Use case	Traditional operations	AIOps
Root cause analysis	Involves manually reviewing logs and traces, which can be slow and tedious, and there is scope for error.	AI algorithms are used to analyze data from all systems and identify dependencies, which quickly isolates the root cause along with insights.
Threat detection	Relies on manual monitoring, struggles to evolve to handle new threats	AI algorithms analyze network traffic, system logs etc. to detect and respond in real time. There is also an adaptive learning to improve continuously.
Incident management	Manual monitoring is mostly reactive. Troubleshooting is manual, which is time-consuming and error-prone.	AI algorithms analyze massive data in real time, take automated actions, and use patterns to identify and alert on potential threats.

Table 14.1: AIOps use cases

GitOps

We discussed DevOps and its usefulness in the previous chapter (*Chapter 13: Application Development*). An offshoot of DevOps that focuses on automating infrastructure provisioning is GitOps. It promotes the use of IaC and stores it in a Git repository, making it the single source of truth for your infrastructure. Like the application source code, operations teams that adopt GitOps use configuration files stored as code (IaC) to generate the same infrastructure repeatedly.

Some GitOps principles that should be understood are listed here:

- GitOps uses a declarative language to define and configure infrastructure, for example, YAML.

- Git is used as the central repository for all infrastructure and application code and configurations.

- Any changes to Git repositories trigger automated deployments.

- Changes to the configuration in Git are continuously monitored, and corrections are made automatically by an operator.

Let us look at some key benefits of GitOps:

- **Agility**: Git repositories trigger automated deployments, which results in faster release cycles and shorter time to market.

- **Security**: Git provides features like automated security checks and audit trails, which are beneficial for the security of your cloud deployments.

- **Operational overhead**: Overall infrastructure management is automated, which reduces the manual overhead of the operations teams.

- **Self-service**: Infrastructure changes are as easy as a Git pull request, enabling developers to handle the changes themselves.

- **Rollbacks**: The DevOps team can experiment with new features freely, as reverting changes is as easy as using a Git history command.

Use cases

By the name, it might look very similar to DevOps. In terms of automation and pipelines, there are similarities, but let us clarify GitOps with a couple of practical use cases:

- **Managing a Kubernetes cluster**: A Kubernetes cluster is defined using an IaC tool like Terraform and stored in a Git repository. Whenever a change is made to the cluster, the changes are made to the Terraform file and committed to the Git repository. Since the operator is continuously monitoring changes to Git, when there is a new commit, the changes are applied to the infrastructure automatically.

- **Load balancer configuration**: Imagine a load balancer configuration has been changed in the repository that holds the configuration file. A Git pull request is raised to change the configuration, which is then merged into the repository.

  This triggers the operator, who identifies the changed configuration and matches it with the current configuration of the load balancer. The operator then asks the orchestration system (like Kubernetes) to update the load balancer configuration. After monitoring the new configuration, if the team decides to undo the changes, they can easily revert them. All this is automatically handled by the GitOps pipeline.

FinOps

Financial operations (FinOps), or in the Cloud, is a discipline that helps organizations manage and optimize expenses in the cloud. It combines the organizational culture with engineering practices and operational procedures to attain the business value of cloud expenditures and preaches ways to control and optimize cloud spending. In short, it is a collaboration between finance, engineering, and operations teams.

One misconception is that FinOps aims to reduce cloud costs. While cost optimization is a goal, FinOps has a much broader scope: helping businesses realize the value of every dollar spent.

Some key principles of a FinOps discipline are listed here:

- **Collaboration**: As previously mentioned, a collaborative effort exists between finance, engineering, and operations teams.

- **Accountability**: Teams using the cloud should be held accountable for their spending. Everyone involved in cloud-related activities should understand the financial implications of their decisions. This might even require some training on cloud cost management.

- **Transparency**: Cloud costs should be easily understandable by all stakeholders, including the executives. FinOps should provide such transparent views.

- **Informed decision making**: One of the critical principles is that cloud spending decisions should be informed based on data. Historic data on cloud spending should be collected and analyzed to do forecasting and budgeting.

The pay-as-you-go model of cloud computing looks pretty lucrative and pocket-friendly. However, it can easily lead to bill shock if not appropriately managed.

That is where FinOps helps businesses. Let us look at some of the essential benefits of FinOps:

- **Cost optimization**: One of the most obvious ones is optimizing cloud spending. You can identify and eliminate cloud wastes, right-size the infrastructure resources, and even shop around for better pricing with the help of FinOps procedures.

- **Budgeting and forecasting**: FinOps processes provide visibility into cloud spending, making forecasting and budgeting effective based on actual data.

- **Agility**: Similar to other trends, FinOps also promotes agility by helping data-driven decision-making about cloud spending. Hence, organizations can respond to business needs much faster.

- **Transparency**: One of the principles of FinOps is providing transparency. Stakeholders can get a detailed view of where the money is being spent and why

- **Value for money**: In addition to the discussed benefits, an overarching benefit inherent to FinOps is the actual value for money spent.

Due to the required cultural change in terms of collaboration, accountability, and transparency, all teams using the cloud are obliged and empowered to plan their projects and investments wisely. This, in turn, leads to the organization creating better products and driving useful outcomes for customers, and hence, growth in business. This is the real value of FinOps.

Use cases

Let us see some applications of FinOps in the real world using an example of a media company that streams recorded and live events for viewers worldwide. This company's workloads fluctuate daily based on viewing times and new releases. Apparently, they also use massive cloud storage, some transcoding services, and probably delivery services like a **cloud delivery network (CDN)**.

Here are the possible use cases of FinOps for this company:

- Based on the usage analysis, they can automatically scale up their resources during peak hours and scale down later, thus minimizing resource wastage.

- For the workloads that have a long-term predictable usage, they can reserve the capacity and save significantly.

- They use tagging strategies to allocate costs as per teams and cost centers, thus making everyone accountable for what they spend.

- They have created dashboards for each team showing usage and spending. This transparency encourages cost optimization efforts.

There could be many more applications of FinOps, but this was just to give you an idea of how it can help your organization achieve its financial goals. Some of the common cloud-native tools used for FinOps practices are AWS Cost Explorer and Azure Cost Management. Apart from these, there are various third-party and open-source tools and platforms as well.

DataOps

DevOps principles are usually applied to a software development lifecycle to improve efficiency and productivity. It brings the development and operations teams together to deliver applications. Similar principles (such as agility, automation, and collaboration) can improve the quality and efficiency of data delivery and analytics significantly when applied to a data lifecycle, and the practice is called DataOps.

Here are some benefits of a DataOps philosophy:

- **Agility**: DataOps brings agility into the process by enabling organizations to adapt to business requirements much faster. Automated data pipelines also enable faster data delivery.

- **Data quality**: Automated checks and continuous monitoring ensure that data is accurate and reliable

- **Security**: Automated checks and access control measures improve data security in the cloud

- **Observability**: DataOps has a component of monitoring and tracking, which improves observability in data pipelines.

- **Data governance**: Similar to DevOps, version control and audit trails can be applied to a data pipeline to help establish data governance.

Use cases

DataOps could be a bit complicated to understand because it is hard to visualize DevOps principles for a data pipeline.

Let us understand DataOps with the help of some real-life use cases for an arbitrary online retailer:

- A large online retailer wants to update its inventory in real time and also create real-time insights to aid the sales and marketing teams. They need to build real-time data pipelines as a first step using streaming services like Amazon Kinesis or Azure Stream Analytics. Then, to ensure data accuracy and integrity, they should include automated data quality checks using services like AWS Glue DataBrew and Azure Data Factory.

  They can also use CI/CD principles to deploy and update data models in data warehouses using tools like GitHub Actions, AWS Redshift, etc. Finally, they should build real-time dashboards using tools like Amazon QuickSight, Azure Power BI, Tableau, etc.

- The same retailer also wants to predict their customer churn and implement targeted marketing campaigns to retain them. To do that, the first step is to collect data from various sources, for which they can use a cloud-based service like AWS Glue or Azure Data Factory to create ETL processes that load this data into a centralized cloud data lake. Then, they need to automate their data pipeline using orchestration tools like AWS Step Functions, which run steps to clean, process, and load the data into a central warehouse like AWS Redshift. Now, an ML model needs to be developed and deployed, and they can use a cloud-based service like Amazon SageMaker.

Note: This is just a high-level overview of how DataOps can benefit our superficial retailer using some real-life workflows. There can be many more areas where DataOps can benefit businesses.

GreenOps

Sustainability is a hot topic and a top priority for every organization these days. This is where GreenOps gained prominence. **Green operations** (**GreenOps**) is a discipline that aims to minimize the impact of IT operations on the environment. It considers every stage of an IT lifecycle and involves optimizing resource utilization, reducing energy consumption, and promoting environmentally friendly practices.

Here are some key principles of a GreenOps philosophy:

- Use energy efficiently by reducing the energy required to run the IT infrastructure.

- Reduce the carbon footprint by minimizing greenhouse gas emissions.

- Minimize the environmental impact of IT hardware and e-waste.

- Choose environmentally friendly IT resources.

- Continuously improve, monitor, and report on the sustainability of IT resources.

With the growing demands of preserving the environment and reducing the carbon footprint, sustainable IT operations have gained momentum worldwide, and cloud platforms are no exception. Customers who use various cloud platforms are also responsible for the environment, and hence their IT operations need to support the sustainability cause.

Sustainable IT operations have numerous benefits, such as the following:

- **Reduced environmental impact**: This is an expected outcome of a GreenOps initiative. By following the principles of GreenOps, organizations can minimize their greenhouse gas emissions, engage in responsible disposal of e-waste, and choose environmentally friendly hardware.

- **Cost reductions**: GreenOps promotes resource optimization, right-sizing of infrastructure, and serverless architectures. All these measures help with significant cost savings.

- **Compliance with regulations**: Stringent regulations are being imposed to promote sustainability and a green environment. By adopting GreenOps principles, organizations can comply with such regulations.

- **Brand reputation**: Sustainability is a big focus worldwide now, and organizations that are actively involved and contributing to the cause have an opportunity to enhance their brand reputation and get a competitive advantage.

Use cases

Let us understand GreenOps philosophy with some real-life use cases:

- A company has large workloads on the cloud, including some heavy batch jobs that execute for a few minutes daily and are triggered by an upstream notification event. This is a perfect use case for adopting serverless architecture (like AWS Lambda). By adopting serverless architecture, this company can significantly reduce energy consumption and costs associated with idle compute time.

- A company using AWS as their chosen cloud platform adopts various measures in line with GreenOps principles that reduce energy consumption by their workloads. This includes using monitoring tools to assess the resource usage and right-size their EC2 instances on AWS accordingly. Instead of employing large instances that consume more energy and power, they moved to smaller instances based on usage patterns. They also use AWS Graviton instances, which are designed to be more energy-efficient than traditional x86 instances.

- A company stores massive amounts of data in AWS and uses Amazon S3 as its storage. This data consists of frequently accessed data and a big chunk of archival data. To reduce energy consumption and storage costs, they use data lifecycle policies to move the storage to lower and cold storage tiers that consume less energy and are significantly cheaper.

CloudOps

CloudOps is not really a trend but more of a new term that has been coined to represent cloud operations. Any IT setup needs operations teams and procedures to manage the applications and infrastructure. When the setup is on the cloud, the associated operations are bucketed into the term called CloudOps. Another way of looking at it is that CloudOps is DevOps's *Ops* part. It covers the processes, tools, and best practices to manage and maintain cloud infrastructure and applications reliably, securely, and cost-effectively on the cloud.

The coverage includes the following:

- Infrastructure provisioning, configuration, and management

- Application deployment and management

- Implementing security controls

- Observability of workloads

- Responding to and resolving incidents

Apparently, CloudOps encompasses a broad range of activities, including infrastructure provisioning and automation using IaC, application deployment and scaling through CI/CD pipelines, security monitoring and compliance, performance optimization, and cost management.

Use cases

Let us understand CloudOps with a real-world use case of a company that wants to deploy and manage its applications on AWS and ensure all aspects of operations are handled efficiently. Some CloudOps aspects that they have adopted are:

- **Infrastructure management**: They use Terraform to define the AWS infrastructure resources. The code is stored and version-controlled in a Git repository.

- **Application deployment**: They use Docker and Kubernetes for applications, and hence the ECS and EKS services on AWS. They have also set up a CI/CD pipeline using Jenkins for orchestration.

- **Security**: They use AWS Security Hub for a centralized view of security findings, AWS CloudTrail for auditing all API calls, and AWS Config to ensure infrastructure compliance.

- **Monitoring**: They use AWS CloudWatch to monitor the resources and trigger alarms and notifications.

- **Cost management**: They use AWS Cost Explorer to analyze cloud spending and identify cost optimization opportunities.

Conclusion

In this chapter, we looked at the dynamic evolution of cloud from the lens of trends that are and will be shaping the cloud adoption. Cloud landscape is changing, and the adoption by customers is becoming more appealing than ever due to all these trends that are re-defining the meaning of cloud and the benefits that come along. Consider the strategic financial discipline of FinOps, the sustainable practices of GreenOps, the agility of GitOps, the data-driven approach of DataOps, and the operational backbone of CloudOps.

These are no longer buzzwords. The key takeaway is that the future of cloud computing lies in specialization and integration. Each Ops discipline addresses a critical aspect of cloud management, and their power is amplified when they work in harmony. Therefore, these trends should not be viewed as isolated concepts but as interconnected pieces of a larger puzzle. As more organizations move towards the cloud in the future, the evolution of such trends will be pivotal in unlocking the cloud's full potential. AI will be the backbone for most of these trends and even more impactful cloud adoption.

Points to remember

Some key takeaways from this chapter are:

- The future of cloud adoption is not just migrating workloads from on-premises to cloud and trying to cash in on the scalability, flexibility, and cost optimization aspects of cloud, as was the case a few years back. It is about embracing a fundamental shift in how we approach IT.

- Many Ops trends are shaping the future of cloud computing, and they are not just buzzwords. They are about making the erstwhile processes on the cloud more efficient and worthy.

- AIOps is a process that uses AI techniques and practices (like NLP and ML) to manage IT infrastructure.

- GitOps is about automating the provisioning of infrastructure using GitOps by the use of IaC and storing it in a Git repository, making it the single source of truth for your infrastructure.

- FinOps is a discipline that helps organizations manage and optimize expenses in the cloud. By combining the cultural aspects of the organization with engineering practices and operational procedures.

- DataOps is the application of DevOps principles (such as agility, automation, and collaboration) to a data lifecycle, significantly improving the quality and efficiency of data delivery and analytics.

- GreenOps is a discipline that aims to minimize the impact of IT operations on the environment at every stage of the IT lifecycle. It involves optimizing resource utilization, reducing energy consumption, and promoting environmentally friendly practices.

- CloudOps is the practice of managing and performing IT operations in the cloud. It covers the processes, tools, and best practices to run the workloads reliably, securely, and cost-effectively on the cloud.

Join our book's Discord space

Join the book's Discord Workspace for Latest updates, Offers, Tech happenings around the world, New Release and Sessions with the Authors:

https://discord.bpbonline.com

Index

www.ingramcontent.com/pod-product-compliance
Lightning Source LLC
Chambersburg PA
CBHW061809210326
41599CB00034B/6938